INTRODUCTION TO DATA COMMUNICATIONS:
A PRACTICAL APPROACH

INTRODUCTION TO DATA COMMUNICATIONS: A PRACTICAL APPROACH

Stan Gelber

Copyright © 1991 Professional Press Books

All rights reserved. No part of this publication may be reproduced, stored in a retrieval system, or transmitted in any form or by any means whatsoever, except in the case of brief quotations embodied in critical reviews and articles.

The information in this book is subject to change without notice and should not be construed as a commitment by the author or the publisher. Although every precaution has been taken in the preparation of this book, the publisher assumes no responsibility for errors or omissions.

Printed in the United States of America.

Cover design by Michael Cousart.

Trademark Acknowledgments

Amdahl is a registered trademark of Amdahl Corporation.
AT&T is a registered trademark and StarLAN is a trademark of American Telephone and Telegraph Company.
Codex is a registered trademark of Motorola Codex Corporation.
Compaq is a trademark of Compaq Computer Corporation.
IRMA is a trademark of Digital Communications Associates Inc.
DEC is a registered trademark and DECnet, VMS, and VT are trademarks of Digital Equipment Corporation.
Hayes is a registered trademark and Smartmodem is a trademark of Hayes Microcomputer Products Inc.
Kermit is a trademark of Henson Associates Inc.
Hewlett-Packard and HP are registered trademarks and MPE is a trademark of Hewlett-Packard Company.
IBM is a registered trademark and OS/2, SDLC, BSC, CICS, NCP, BTAM, VTAM, ACF, VM, RSCS, NetView, DCA, DIA, DISOSS, NJE, SNA, TSO, ISPF, MVS, and DOS are trademarks of International Business Machines Corporation.
MCI is a registered trademark of MCI Communications Corporation.
MNP is a registered trademark of Microcom Inc.
Microsoft is a registered trademark and Windows is a trademark of Microsoft Corporation.
StrataCom is a registered trademark of StrataCom Inc.
Sun Microsystems is a registered trademark of Sun Microsystems Inc.
NonStop and Guardian are trademarks of Tandem Computers Inc.
Unisys is a trademark of Unisys Corporation.
UNIX is a registered trademark of UNIX System Laboratories Inc.
XNS and Ethernet are trademarks of Xerox Corporation.
All other trademarks are the property of their respective owners.

Library of Congress Cataloging-in-Publication Data

Gelber, Stan.
   Introduction to data communications : a practical approach / Stan Gelber.
     p. cm.
   Includes bibliographical references and index.
   ISBN 1-878956-04-3
   1. Data transmission systems. 2. Computer networks. I. Title.
TK5105.G45 1991
004.6—dc20   91-25945
                                                    CIP

Please address comments and questions to the publisher:

Professional Press Books
101 Witmer Road
Horsham, PA 19044
(215) 957-1500 FAX (215) 957-1050
Internet: books@propress.com

Contents

CONTENTS	v
PREFACE	xv
ACKNOWLEDGMENTS	xvii
PART I. **INTRODUCTION, OVERVIEW AND** **HISTORY OF DATA COMMUNICATIONS**	**1**
CHAPTER 1. INTRODUCTION	**3**
A Brief History of Computers and Communications	3
Analog and Digital Communications	5
The Application of Data Communications	6
Network Implementation	9
Sharing Data Using Communications Resources	10
Analyzing Requirements	11
Case Study	13
Review Questions	14
CHAPTER 2. DATA COMMUNICATIONS AND **NETWORK PLANNING**	**15**
Evolution of Computerized Communications	15
Hardware Requirements	18
CPU Processing Capacity	21
Network Handling Capabilities	22
Communications Hardware Considerations	23
Transmission Links	24
Software Requirements	24
Application Control Software	24
Terminal Network Software	25
Network Control and Interface Software	25
Network- and Performance-Monitoring Software	25
Communications Services	25
Carrier Services	25
Specialized Carriers	25
Communications Service Providers	26
Case Study (Continued)	26
Review Questions	27

PART II.
SOFTWARE REQUIRED FOR DATA COMMUNICATIONS — 29

CHAPTER 3. COMMUNICATIONS SOFTWARE — 31

Introduction 31
Role of Software in Communications 31
    Network Configuration and Maintenance 32
    Network Control 32
    Application Management 32
System Software 33
    Operating System Software 35
    Communications System Software 36
    Network Support Software 38
Application Software 39
    Conversational Online Application Programs 42
    Transaction-Based Application Processing 42
Case Study (Continued) 43
Review Questions 44

CHAPTER 4. APPLICATION DEVELOPMENT — 45

Introduction 45
Modes of Communication Processing 46
Transaction-Based Communications 47
    Transaction-Based Communications Management Software 47
    Transaction-Based Application Program Activities 48
Conversational Communications 51
    Time-Sharing Communications 51
    Selected Communications Software 52
Case Study (Continued) 54
Review Questions 55

PART III.
DATA TRANSMISSION CONCEPTS
AND COMMUNICATIONS SERVICES — 57

CHAPTER 5. TRANSMISSION MODES AND METHODS — 59

Introduction 59
Bandwidth Concepts 59
    Broadband Transmission 61
    Baseband Transmission 61
Modes of Transmission 61
    Simplex Transmission 62
    Half-Duplex Transmission 62
    Full-Duplex Transmission 63
Grades of Services 64
Transmission Methods 65
    Asynchronous Transmission 65

Synchronous Transmission 66
 Case Study (Continued) 66
 Review Questions 67

CHAPTER 6. COMMUNICATIONS SERVICES   69

 Introduction 69
 Public and Private Carriers 69
  Common Carriers 70
  Other Carriers 70
  Satellite Services 70
  Value-Added Carriers 71
  International Record Carriers 71
  Public Data Network Services 72
  Time-Sharing Service Providers 72
  Packet-Switching System Services 72
 Transmission Services 73
  Datagram Packet Service 74
  Unreliable Datagrams 74
  Reliable Datagrams 74
  Virtual Circuit Service 74
  Switched Circuit Services 76
 Types of Communications Services 76
 Public Switched Telephone Network 77
 Dedicated Telephone Service 78
  Conditioning 79
 High-Speed Wideband Services 80
 Digital Services 81
  Dataphone Digital Service 81
  High-Speed Digital Service 82
 ISDN 84
  ISDN Specifications 86
  Standard Interface Connections 87
  Out-of-Band Signaling 87
 Case Study (Continued) 88
 Review Questions 91

CHAPTER 7. TRANSMISSION CONCEPTS   93

 Introduction 93
  Nyquist Theorem 94
  Shannon Theorem 94
 Modulation 96
 Basic Modulation Techniques 96
  Amplitude Modulation 97
  Frequency Modulation 97
  Phase Modulation 99
  Variations 100
 Digital Transmission 102
  Bipolar Current Loop 103

Return-to-Zero (RZ) 103
Non-Return-to-Zero (NRZ) 103
Case Study (Continued) 105
Review Questions 105

PART IV.
HARDWARE, MEDIA AND INTERFACES — 107

CHAPTER 8. HARDWARE LINKS — 109

Introduction 109
Communications Media 110
    Two- and Four-Wire Twisted Pairs 110
    Coaxial Cable 111
    Fiber-Optic Cable 111
    Fiber-Optic Technology 112
    Microwave Transmission 114
    Satellite Links 114
Data Transmission Errors and Impairments 116
    Wired Switched Networks 116
    Wired Dedicated-Line Networks 117
Case Study (Continued) 118
Review Questions 119

CHAPTER 9. DATA COMMUNICATIONS HARDWARE — 121

Introduction 121
Communications Processors 123
Multiplexers 125
    Operational Characteristics of Multiplexers 126
    Frequency-Division Multiplexers 127
    Time-Division Multiplexers 127
    Statistical Time-Division Multiplexers 129
    Wave-Division Multiplexers 130
    Multiplexer Framing 131
    Error Control 131
Packet Assembly and Disassembly Devices 132
Network Controllers 133
Terminal Controllers 134
Terminals and PCs 136
    Dumb Terminals 136
    Smart Terminals 136
    Terminal Emulation Using PCs 137
Remote and Network Job Entry Terminals 137
Multiuser Workstations 138
Gateways and Bridges 138
    Gateways 139
    Bridges 139
Case Study (Continued) 139
Review Questions 142

CHAPTER 10. COMMUNICATIONS USING MODEMS — 143

- Introduction 143
- Modem History and Development 144
- Modem Standards 144
    - Bell Standards 144
    - CCITT V Standards 144
- Modem Internals 146
- Transmission Methods 147
    - Asynchronous Modems 147
    - Synchronous Modems 148
- Operational Modes and Optional Features 148
- Types of Modems 149
    - Acoustical Couplers 150
    - Standalone Modems 150
    - Integrated Modems 150
    - Limited-Distance Modems 150
    - Line Drivers 151
    - Fiber-Optic Modems 151
    - Modem Eliminators 151
    - Modem Sharing or Pooling Devices 152
    - Split-Stream Modems 152
    - Extended Circuit/Tail Circuit Modems 152
- Digital Service Units and Channel Service Units 153
- Diagnostics and Testing 153
- Error Correction 154
- Interfaces 155
    - Permissive Connections 155
    - Programmable Connections 156
    - Private-Line Interfaces 156
- Case Study (Continued) 156
- Review Questions 157

CHAPTER 11. HARDWARE AND LOGICAL INTERFACES — 159

- Introduction 159
- Interface Responsibilities 160
- Types of Interfaces 160
    - EIA-232-D Interface 160
    - EIA-232-D Signal Sequence Phases 161
    - RS-449 Interface 162
    - CCITT X.21 Interface 164
    - CCITT V.35 Interface 165
    - Centronics Parallel Interface 166
    - Dataproducts Printer Interface 166
    - IEEE-488 Interface 166
    - Review Questions 169

PART V. STANDARDS, NETWORK ARCHITECTURES, TOPOLOGIES AND PROTOCOLS 171

CHAPTER 12. REGULATORY AGENCIES AND STANDARDS 173

The Need for Standards 173
    Software and Language Compatibility 173
    Hardware Electrical Interfaces 174
    Media Compatibility 174
    Communications Signal Compatibility 174
    Format Standards 174
International Standards Organizations 174
    International Telecommunications Union (ITU) 174
    International Standards Organization (ISO) 175
European Standards Organizations 175
    European Computer Machinery Association (ECMA) 175
    European Conference of Posts and
        Telecommunications Administrations (CEPT) 176
North American Standards Organizations 176
    American National Standards Institute (ANSI) 176
    Electronics Industries Association (EIA) 176
    Institute of Electrical and Electronics Engineers (IEEE) 176
    U.S. National Bureau of Standards (NBS) 176
    U.S. Federal Communications Commission (FCC) 176
    Corporation for Open Systems (COS) 176
De Facto Standard Setters 177
    IBM 177
    AT&T Bell Laboratories 178
    Digital Equipment 178
Case Study (Continued) 178
Review Questions 178

CHAPTER 13. NETWORK CONFIGURATIONS, NETWORK DESIGN AND SECURITY 179

Introduction 179
Centralized, Decentralized and Distributed Networks 180
    Centralized Networks 180
    Decentralized Networks 180
    Distributed Networks 180
Point-to-Point, Multipoint and Peer Configurations 180
Methods of Communicating 181
Types of Topologies 183
    Star Topology 183
    Ring Topology 184
    Bus Topology 185
    Multipoint Bus Topology 186

    Tree Topology 187
    Mesh Topology 188
    Mesh of Trees Topology 189
  Network Design and Selection 189
    Computer/Terminal System Resources 190
    Customer or User Base 190
    Economic Considerations 190
    Carrier Considerations 190
    Staffing for Maintenance and Administration 190
  Network Integrity 191
  Network Security 191
    Configuration and Control Software 191
    User Access 191
    Hardware Access 191
    Data Security 192
  Network Backup 192
    Communications Links 192
    Hardware 192
  Case Study (Continued) 193
  Review Questions 194

CHAPTER 14. NETWORK ARCHITECTURES   195

  Introduction 195
  Standard Architectures 196
  Elements of Layered Operations 196
    Data Transfer 196
    Flow Control 196
    Segmentation and Reassembly 197
    Sequencing 197
    Error Detection 197
    Notification 197
  IBM Systems Network Architecture 197
    Physical Units 198
    Logical Units 198
    Systems Services Control Points 198
    Domains 199
  The OSI Model 200
    Layer Seven: Application Control 201
    Layer Six: Presentation Control 201
    Layer Five: Session Control 201
    Layer Four: Transport Control 202
    Layer Three: Network Control 202
    Layer Two: Data Link Control 202
    Layer One: Physical Control 202
  CCITT X.25 Standard 203
  Manufacturing Automation Protocol 203
  Case Study (Continued) 204
  Review Questions 205

CHAPTER 15. PROTOCOLS 207

Introduction 207
Data Communications Protocol Concepts 208
   Bit- Versus Byte-Oriented Protocols 208
   Protocol Functions 209
   Data Link Communications Codes 209
   Error Detection 211
Layer-Two DLC Protocols 212
   Asynchronous DLC Protocols 212
   Binary Synchronous Protocol (BSC) 213
   Synchronous Data Link Control (SDLC) 214
   High-Level Data Link Control (HDLC) 215
Link Access Procedure-D (LAP-D) 218
Layer-Three (Network-Layer) Protocols 220
   Internet Protocol (IP) 221
   Error PDU Format 222
   Internet Control Message Protocol (ICMP) 223
Layer-Four (Transport-Layer) Protocols 224
   Transmission Control Protocol (TCP) 225
   OSI Transport Protocol (TP) 227
Upper-Layer Protocols 228
   TELNET Protocol 228
   File Transfer Protocol (FTP) 229
   Simple Network Management Protocol (SNMP) 231
Case Study (Continued) 231
Review Questions 233

PART VI. LANS, TROUBLESHOOTING, NETWORK MANAGEMENT AND FUTURE TRENDS 235

CHAPTER 16. LOCAL AREA NETWORKS 237

Introduction 237
IEEE Project 802 238
   Project 802 Activity Log 238
LAN Design 238
   Media Connectivity 238
   Internetwork Connectivity 239
   Network Management 239
   Cost Control 239
   Security 240
   Integration 240
Baseband and Broadband LANs 240
   Baseband Transmission 240
   Broadband Transmission 240
   Channel Bandwidth Allocation 241
LAN Control 243
Media Access Control 244
   Deterministic Access 244

    Nondeterministic Access 244
    Access Methods 244
  Noncontention-Based Access 245
    Token-Passing Ring 245
    Token-Passing Bus 246
    Token-Passing Fiber Ring 248
  Contention-Based Access 248
    CSMA 248
    CSMA/CD 249
    CSMA/CA 250
  LAN Performance 250
  Case Study (Continued) 250
  Review Questions 252

CHAPTER 17. NETWORK TROUBLESHOOTING   253

  Introduction 253
  Types of Errors 254
    Software Errors 254
    Hardware Errors 254
    Network Link Errors 254
  Problem Analysis Procedures 255
    Problem Determination 256
    Problem Resolution 256
  Software Diagnostic Tools 257
  Hardware Diagnostic Tools 257
    Hardware Monitors 257
    Modem Diagnostics 257
  Network Hardware Diagnostics 258
    Protocol Analyzers 258
    Breakout Boxes 259
    Status Activity Monitors 259
    Cable and Fiber Analyzers 259
    Network Control Monitors 259
  Levels of Monitoring and Control 260
  Case Study (Continued) 260
  Review Questions 261

CHAPTER 18. NETWORK MANAGEMENT AND CONTROL   263

  Introduction 263
  Network Control Centers 264
    Performance Monitoring 264
    Configuration Control 265
    Fault Isolation 265
    Access Security 265
  Network Control Center Advantages 266
  Network Control Center Equipment 266
    Network Control Center Console Monitor 266
    Artificial Traffic Generator 266
  Case Study (Continued) 267
  Review Questions 268

CHAPTER 19. FUTURE TRENDS — 269

- The Next Generation 269
  - Computers 270
  - Local Area Networks 271
  - Communications Processors 271
  - Multiplexers 272
  - Modems, CSUs and DSUs 272
  - Media and Cabling Systems 272
  - Application Development Software 272
  - Communications Control Software 273
- Standards 273
- Link Services 273
- Open Systems Architecture 274
- Case Study Conclusion 275

APPENDIX A. SELECTED STANDARDS — 277

APPENDIX B. ANSWERS TO REVIEW QUESTIONS — 285

GLOSSARY — 293

BIBLIOGRAPHY — 303

INDEX — 305

Preface

This text is the product of a course on data communications that I developed several years ago for training departments at organizations such as Xerox, MCI, AT&T, Versatec, Mitel and Fujitsu. When I started to develop the course, I reviewed almost every data communications book I could find. I was looking for an introductory book that I could recommend to my students for supplemental reading. My research uncovered a wealth of material, but in most of the books I reviewed, the basics were difficult to follow because superfluous technical information obscured the logical flow of the subject, whereas other books were overly technical.

This book is intended for anyone who desires a comprehensive, basic introduction to data communications. It explains concepts basic to all data communications and networking activities regardless of the equipment manufacturer, although most of the examples in the book are drawn from the IBM world. Although geared toward those who want a practical approach to planning, designing and implementing a corporate data communications network, the book is just as applicable to students, as well as to PC users who want to implement communications capabilities.

Data communications is a very technical topic, consisting of many interlocking pieces. This book provides a foundation for understanding the technology and for determining which areas are important in the data communications decision-making process and the implementation of data communications systems and networks.

This book is divided into six parts:

Part I covers the foundation for data communications and the evolution of communications into data communications.

Part II explains the role of system programs, communications programs and application programs in data communications. It describes how the various pieces of software interact to provide communications to the end user.

Part III presents information on how data is converted into analog and digital transmission signals and then transported via various types of communications facilities to its destination.

Part IV introduces the various types of communications hardware, transmission media and hardware and logical interfaces used in data communications networks.

Part V begins a discourse on the standards, methods and procedures for implementing a data communications network. It covers important standards, architectural approaches and the various protocols in use.

Part VI introduces local area networking and covers the ins and outs of managing a network and the diagnosis and repair of a problematic network. The book concludes with a forecast of future trends.

A case study is included at the end of most chapters as an ongoing example of the construction and implementation of an IBM-oriented data communications network. Although non-IBM manufacturers in some cases use different methods and equipment for data communications functions, basic data communications concepts do not vary from manufacturer to manufacturer.

Acknowledgments

For encouragement and help from Jean Pierog, who taught me grammar and how to spell, no words can express my appreciation.

Thanks to George Curach, a friend when I needed one, and to Dick Cowden, who has been my mentor, my teacher and my travel agent. Thanks also to the many friends who kept after me to convert my "Data Communications Concepts" course into a book.

Part I

Introduction, Overview and History of Data Communications

Chapter 1

Introduction

A BRIEF HISTORY OF COMPUTERS AND COMMUNICATIONS

Simply put, data communications is the movement of information from one point to another across a communications network. The function of data communications is to transfer data from location A to location N efficiently, reliably and as inexpensively as possible. This function requires software, hardware, transmission links and services.

The evolution of data communications technology is rapid and dynamic. Likewise, the ongoing development of the digital computer has enabled us to progress technologically at an accelerated rate. New discoveries, new technologies and the refinement of existing technologies create an incredibly exciting environment for rapid growth. It is sometimes easy to forget that 40 years ago, practical use of computers and data communications did not exist.

In the 18th century, a form of mechanical data processing existed for a number of activities, including cloth weaving and census taking. Today, while we view information processing as a computerized function using program logic, all of the necessary mechanical computer logic functions were present in those early hardware devices, except for the ability to communicate the data from one device to another.

We use the term "hardware" to describe the equipment required to process raw data into information or transfer the data across a communications link. (Figure 1.1 illustrates typical data processing hardware.) The term "software" refers to the processes and various logical instructions required to direct the hardware in specific tasks. (Figure 1.2 illustrates an example of support software.)

To better understand the development of data communications hardware and software, it is important to emphasize that the evolution of the computer, like the evolution of data communications, was not the result of work by a single person or organization. Many teams of scientists working in many locations explored different, or in some cases the same, ideas. Unfortunately, the development of the computer was not based on the concept that computers some day would be required to communicate with one another. This lack of foresight created a situation whereby computers and communications evolved in separate directions that were, for the most part, incompatible.

The start of modern day computing began in 1946 with the development of the ENIAC computer at the University of Pennsylvania. This development team was led by J. Presper Eckert and John Mauchley. The ENIAC was the first large-scale electronic computer and had the capability of performing 357 multiplications per second.

In 1949, the first computer to use all electronic diode-based logic and capable of executing a stored program was developed by the U.S. National Bureau of Standards (NBS). A number of organizations continued development and the Universal Automatic Computer (Univac 1) was completed in 1951 by the Remington Rand Corporation. Installed at the U.S. Census Bureau, this machine was considered the first commercially produced American computer.

By 1950, Remington Rand and IBM Corporation were the two major companies seriously developing commercial computers. One of the most important early developments for data communications was IBM's introduction of the 729 magnetic tape storage device in 1953. It represented a major advance in computer processing in that it could store 100 characters on an inch of tape and move at 75 inches per second. This capability increased considerably the speed of processing data into information using the digital computer.

By the late 1950s, the need to move data from one location to another was growing.

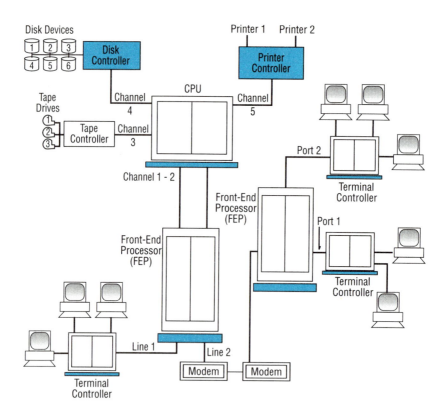

Figure 1.1 Typical Data Processing Hardware

Fireman's Fund Insurance Company, among many other companies, used a variation of the IBM 729 tape drive in combination with a Bell dataset (a device that connected to both the telephone network and the tape drive) to send computer data between the east and west coasts of the United States.

With the advent of this new technology, computer data was converted into a form suitable for transmission across the public telephone network. This information was received by a tape drive/dataset at the remote location using the same signaling principals as those employed in the telegraph system. While these early data communications activities were slow and analog in form, they created tremendous opportunities for business to expand outward to distant locations.

ANALOG AND DIGITAL COMMUNICATIONS

Communications can be classified into two distinct categories, *digital communications* and *analog communications*. Digital communications are generated by a microprocessor-controlled device or computer and consist of signals containing two different electrical voltages. Analog communications — such as voice, television and fax — use continuous variable electrical signals to transport the information. (Figure 1.3 illustrates an analog and digital waveform as seen on an oscilloscope.) With the introduction of new digital technologies as well as a worldwide Integrated Services Digital Network (ISDN), these two classifications are becoming less distinct.

Although we still use nondigital transmission methods extensively, indications are that in the not-too-distant future, all forms of electronic communications will be accomplished via the digital route. This is evidenced by the rapid introduction of digital telephone and digital television. In these cases, analog real-time communications sources are converted via digital (data) processing into a real-time digital signal (see Figure 1.4). This signal is

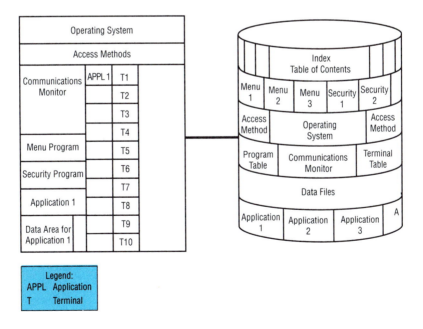

Figure 1.2   Typical Communications Support Software

then transmitted across a communications link and reconverted into an analog signal, once again, at the receiving side.

The benefits of digital communications, whether it is data generated by a computer, digitized voice or video, include accurate reproduction of the source material, elimination of noise that creates distortion, and rapid transmission of the signal. Figure 1.5 shows an example of digital transmission.

THE APPLICATION OF DATA COMMUNICATIONS

Data communications has become a vital function in today's world. A typical application of data communications can be demonstrated by illustrating a corporation with two distal computer centers (see Figure 1.6). These facilities are located 100 miles apart. One center functions as the corporate computer center and the other is a support computer center, located at a manufacturing facility.

At the corporate computer center, user terminals are directly connected (wired) to the computer and are used for a variety of activities that include data entry, sales and manufacturing inquiry and program development. Because terminals are directly connected by wire to the computer, they are limited to a distance of 5,000 feet, but they have very fast access times. These local or directly attached terminals allow user departments to input their own data directly into the computer system. The computer supports remote access (the ability to talk to another computer or terminal via telephone links) and may be used for backup and communications activities, except that these functions have not yet been implemented.

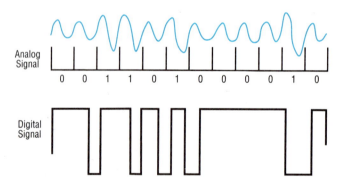

Figure 1.3   Analog and Digital Waveform Example

Figure 1.4   Real-Time Digital Signal

Input data and update information are assembled manually and entered for processing via an online terminal to tape or disk by each department's data entry section. Depending on the processing requirements, the computer will either store the data on disk or tape for future reference and processing, or process it immediately.

The remote computer center is configured similarly to the corporate center configuration; it also has user terminals that are attached via direct cabling throughout the factory. These terminals are used by manufacturing and factory support personnel to assemble, track, manage and ship products.

After analyzing the corporate computer environment and the organization's needs, the company determines its requirement for the electronic movement of data and information between the two data centers. In the past, this has been accomplished using courier services. However, the volume of data that must be shared and the necessity for each center to have it immediately available for user access mandate that a data communications network be implemented.

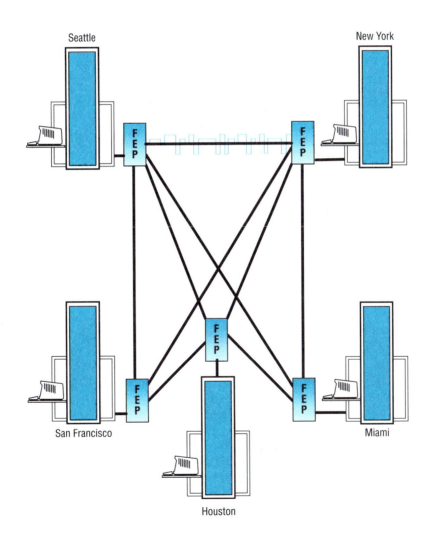

Figure 1.5 Example of a Digital Transmission Network

Introduction to Data Communications: A Practical Approach

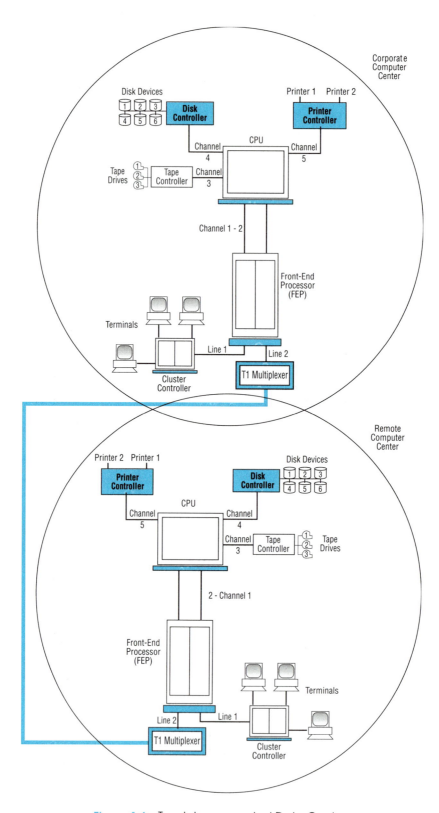

Figure 1.6   Two Interconnected Data Centers

NETWORK IMPLEMENTATION

To establish a data communications network between two or more computers or digital devices, you must implement several interrelated elements. Once you have justified the need for a connection between the two locations, you will need to establish a communications link between them. This data link will allow the two computer centers to share resources and data. Typically, the connection is accomplished using long-established telephone company or other carrier facilities.

The communications link not only provides data and voice communications between the two computer center locations, it also provides backup facilities for each of the computer centers should a disaster strike one of them. The implementation of this link alone does not accomplish the data communications task. The link itself is nothing more than the medium connecting the computers together.

Additional hardware may be required at both ends of the link to support the data communications activities. In some cases, computer manufacturers include communications facilities as part of their hardware and software. However, customers usually need to purchase the required hardware and software at extra cost. The required hardware may include the following components.

Communications Processors. Depending on the number of terminals requiring access to the processing power of the host computer and the types of applications required by users, a communications processor may be mandatory. The communications processor is designed to provide software and hardware management of the terminal and communications network for the host computer. Figure 1.7 shows a typical communications processor configuration.

Multiplexers and Concentrators. Multiplexers and concentrators are designed to take advantage of the capabilities of the media by allowing multiple devices to share the available capacity. Depending on the number of remotely located terminals, a multiplexer may provide cost benefits when used.

Modems, Digital Service Units and Channel Service Units. Modems, digital service units (DSUs) and channel service units (CSUs) convert digital signals used by the computer into signals that can be transported across communications links such as telephone lines. They are required for data communications between host computers and terminals in a remote environment.

Network Control Monitors. Network control monitors may be required in large networks to monitor and advise online, terminal and link conditions across the network.

After the required hardware is in place, software for both application processing and communications processing can be identified for specific hardware platforms. Many hardware manufacturers provide the necessary communications components in the basic computer hardware. Some also will provide the software, but this is the exception rather than the rule. As an example, IBM provides extensive communications capabilities, but they all cost extra and in many cases can only be leased rather than purchased. Figure 1.8 illustrates layered communications software resident in computer system memory.

Types of software required to support data communications functions are described in the following sections.

Communications Systems Software. This type of software may be required and is usually embedded in the operating system or becomes a systems task under control of the operating system. Its role is to assist the operating system in managing local and remote terminal and network access.

Communications Control Software. Communications control software manages the online application programs, resolves logical transmission errors and ensures that network access conflicts are resolved in an equitable manner. This type of software assists the application program in providing terminal processing.

Online Application Software. Online applications are required to perform the necessary data processing as well as provide the logical interaction between the terminal user and the data. A typical online application such as loan administration provides access, processing and display formatting of loan information.

Network Control Software. Network control software may be required for managing network and internetwork access and communications. This type of software is required to ensure compatibility and management of communications activities between devices within the network as well as outside the network.

SHARING DATA USING COMMUNICATIONS RESOURCES

The rationale for implementing computer communications is the ability to access vital information immediately at both ends of the link for decision-making activities. From a technological perspective, the ability to communicate information provides additional storage and access availability because important data can be distributed and quickly accessed

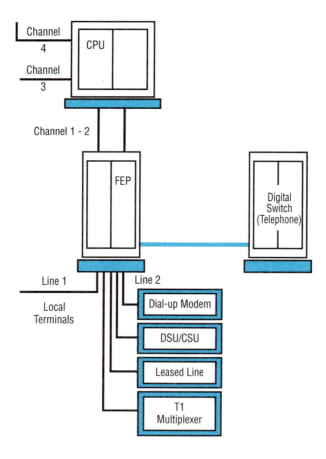

Figure 1.7 Communications Processor Configuration

Introduction

from remote points. Data communications also leads to significant cost and time reductions associated with shipping reports and data from one location to another. Finally, productivity is markedly enhanced.

The ability to collect and disseminate information across long distances and to provide users with immediate access to data opens up a world of opportunities. The sharing of data and resources across vast distances has allowed mankind to operate in outer space, map gene structures, access airline schedules, monitor electrical power generation and perform countless other activities.

The ability to distribute data across regional areas and make it instantly available allows timely decisions based on accurate information. Technological advances, however, are not without cost and short-term disadvantages. Before implementing a data communications network, be sure that long-term benefits will be realized and expenses can be controlled.

ANALYZING REQUIREMENTS

The first step in selecting and implementing a data communications network is to analyze the company's organizational and information environments. Careful analysis should determine needs, costs and resources required by the corporation. The following considerations are vital to the selection of an effective, efficient data communications system.

Data Traffic Requirements. An analysis of data traffic is required to justify the costs of implementing a data communications network.

Evaluation of Short- and Long-Term Goals. The team that is responsible for creating the data communications network should evaluate the organization's short- and long-term growth objectives as well as its financial status.

Cost Justification for Network Selection. Consider whether the expenses for the research necessary to determine the most appropriate data communications system are justified. Many covert expenses can drive up the cost of installing such a system. The major expenses

Figure 1.8 Layered Software in the CPU

involved in the selection, implementation and maintenance of a communications network are planning and ongoing costs for support and line charges.

Selection of Data Communications Equipment. Thousands of companies provide data communications equipment for the end user. The company planners must exercise care in the evaluation and selection of this equipment. Questions any planner should consider include:

- What are the life cycles of the equipment needed?
- Will requirements be met as they relate to capacity and reliability?
- Is the desired product (or products) available or will it be necessary to accept additional capabilities that are not needed?
- Will the equipment be upgradable or will we have to purchase new equipment as the company's needs expand?
- What are the odds that the vendor will continue to be in business and provide support for the equipment purchased?
- How reliable is the equipment itself and how reliable and efficient is the vendor in terms of repair turnaround time?

Technical Resources Needed to Support the Network. This is an area frequently overlooked by planners. As a planner, key questions you should ask include:

- Does the vendor have the technical expertise to support the installed equipment?
- What is the availability of expert support?
- Will the vendor supply or will we be able to hire technicians for on-site support of the vendor's products (because many products are complex and skilled technicians may be in short supply)?
- Does the vendor provide educational support for its products, and what are the costs for these services?

Selection of Application/System Software. A tremendous number of diverse online application programs for the user community exists, so how do you determine what is best for the company? Consider these questions:

- What have other companies experienced with a particular brand of program?
- Who supports the code and what happens if the vendor goes out of business?
- Does the organization create its own applications and will you be able to find programmers with the expertise to write and maintain the program code?
- What are the costs associated with purchasing the required code as opposed to developing the programs in-house?

System software can be difficult to install and maintain, and it can require specialized knowledge to keep in an operational state. Will the vendor provide technical support and education? Will it be responsible for providing corrections when problems occur? Since many computer companies lease their software rather than sell it, what are your recurring costs for its use? Are you able to acquire the expertise to develop the system software in-house using the programming staff? What will the net costs be to the company?

Technical Resources to Support Application/System Software. Most companies installing data communications products have technical resources already in place to support the computer environment, but will those resources be strained to support the new capabilities? Are technical resources available on the market or will you have to train additional employees to support the communications activities? What will the overall costs be for new hires, training and vendor support?

Types of Communications Links and Services. One of the most difficult decisions in data communications is the type of link and service required by the organization to link facilities together. Communications links can range from satellite services to private microwave to dial-up telephone links. The type of link needed is dictated primarily by distance, access right of way, speed required and the necessary capacity. It is also important to acquire additional capacity to enable the system to grow.

Overhead Associated with Link Charges. One of the most important considerations is the ongoing monthly expense for communications lines. This represents a large expense and enlightened planning is imperative. Suppliers of communications services typically insist on long-term leases, but rates constantly change and you should ensure that the organization is not locked into a contract that could be economically unfavorable in the future.

CASE STUDY

This case study is about a fictitious company, the Bank of Scotts Valley, but the solutions are applicable to similar real situations (see Figure 1.9).

A small, newly created local bank is in the process of defining the requirements necessary to upgrade from a manual processing environment to a data processing/data communications one. The bank wishes to computerize and have online access to checking

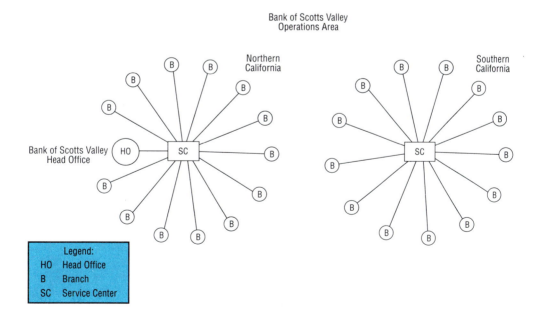

Figure 1.9 Bank of Scotts Valley

account information, savings account information, loan administration, stock transfers, mortgages and planning services. It also plans to offer Automatic Teller Machine (ATM) services to its customers and would be interested in participating in an international ATM network at some point in the future.

The bank's computer network will initially need to support a minimum of 30 branch offices and 10 business centers. Each of the branches will require eight to 15 teller workstations, two administrative workstations and up to three ATMs.

Careful planning of the network will be essential to ensure a stable, manageable and reliable environment for the development of informational services. Key requirements include:

- Backup capability should the primary sites or lines become inoperable
- Connection capabilities for communication with other networks for the exchange of information
- Efficiencies of the network that would ensure acceptable levels of performance
- Cost-effectiveness for both short- and long-term time frames

The bank's management has decided to implement a multiple-site computer environment. This will protect the bank's business activities should a physical disaster such as an earthquake occur. Throughout this book, I will describe the communications software required at the bank computer centers, along with the hardware needed to support the network. The types of communications services needed at both the branch level as well as the ATM level will be detailed, along with the method and facilities required to support them.

In addition, I will examine the required internal and vendor maintenance resources. The case study will conclude with a look at future services that might be implemented along with the type of organization needed to support those services.

REVIEW QUESTIONS

1. Why has the data communications industry grown at such an accelerated rate?
2. What does the term "data communications hardware" refer to?
3. What are the advantages of implementing a data communications network?
4. What is the predominant transmission method used today for data communications?
5. Are backup facilities a consideration in establishing communications links to other computers?
6. What are the disadvantages associated with data communications?
7. Is cost the only factor that needs to be considered in the implementation of a communications network?
8. What is the basic responsibility of a remote computer center?
9. What considerations should be evaluated when planning a data communications network?
10. What are the characteristics of digital communications?

CHAPTER 2

Data Communications and Network Planning

EVOLUTION OF COMPUTERIZED COMMUNICATIONS

Although we have a tendency to view communications today from an electronic digital perspective, communication was a necessity of life long before the introduction of data communications and computerized processing. Communication was accomplished using a multitude of methods, including the written word, smoke signals, sound, reflections of sun rays using a shiny object, and the spoken word.

As mankind evolved and entered the mechanical and electronic eras, the need for much faster and more reliable communications became apparent. This chapter discusses some of the methods that have been developed.

The beginning of modern day digital communications probably can be attributed to Samuel Morse who, on May 24, 1844, established the first digital communications link between Washington D.C. and Baltimore, MD. This communications link was what we commonly call the telegraph system using Morse's code set. This very simple system consisted of a pair of wires attached to a power source with contacts at both ends.

Morse devised a code that associated letters and numbers with audible clicks resulting from the opening and closing of electrical contact keys located at both ends of the link. This code consisted of a number of clicks sent in a specific period of time. As an example, the letter "A" was represented by a click referred to as a dot, a pause and another click, referred to as a dash. Morse's code set consisted of a unique combination of dots and dashes that represented the letters of the English language, special characters (?!,.&*) and numbers. Figure 2.1 is an example of Morse code.

The principle reason for the development of the telegraph system was the expansion of the railroads westward and the thought that this new telegraph system could play a vital role in this expansion. It is important to recognize that the growth of the telegraph system paralleled that of the railroad and that the development of commerce required rapid and reliable communications. Morse's telegraph system played an instrumental role in communicating information such as train schedules and equipment availability.

It quickly became evident that the telegraph system had a major shortcoming in that its speed was based on an operator's ability to interpret the incoming code and translate it into an understandable format. No specific time intervals existed between the characters sent, so messages were often misinterpreted. The introduction of the constant-length code devised by the Frenchman Emil Baudot in 1874 solved the problem. (Figure 2.2 illustrates Baudot code.) Baudot's name is still used to identify the communications code set for telex service.

Baudot devised a five-element, constant-length code (each character had five components to it). This code was combined with a method to indicate the start and end of the character, introduced by Howard Krum in 1910. The resulting communications procedure was an important step toward the automation of the telegraph system and a major step toward today's communications code sets and high-speed transmission methodologies.

The combination of Baudot's code set and Krum's start-and-stop technology paved the way for machines that could read holes punched in paper tape, convert them to electrical signals, transmit the electrical signals from point A to point B and create a new paper tape as an exact copy at the receiving end. (Figure 2.3 depicts the Baudot Telegraph.) To interpret the tape, another machine was developed that combined the elements of a typewriter with the components of a paper tape reader. This device could read the paper tape and produce an interpreted printed message.

In 1910, the U.S. Postal service started teleprinter service using this technique. The code developed by Baudot is based on Boolean logic; it consists of five binary numbers that,

Morse Code

A	• —	N	— •	1	• — — — —
B	— • • •	O	— — —	2	• • — — —
C	— • — •	P	• — — •	3	• • • — —
D	— • •	Q	— — • —	4	• • • • —
E	•	R	• — •	5	• • • • •
F	• • — •	S	• • •	6	— • • • •
G	— — •	T	—	7	— — • • •
H	• • • •	U	• • —	8	— — — • •
I	• •	V	• • • —	9	— — — — •
J	• — — —	W	• — —	0	— — — — —
K	— • —	X	— • • —	.	• — • — • —
L	• — • •	Y	— • — —	,	— — • • — —
M	— —	Z	— — • •	?	• • — — • •

Figure 2.1   Morse Code Set

Data Communications and Network Planning

Baudot Code

Character Case		Bit Pattern	Character Case		Bit Pattern
Lower	Upper	5 4 3 2 1	Lower	Upper	5 4 3 2 1
A	—	0 0 0 1 1	Q	1	1 0 1 1 1
B	?	1 1 0 0 1	R	4	0 1 0 1 0
C	:	0 1 1 1 0	S	'	0 0 1 0 1
D	$	0 1 0 0 1	T	5	1 0 0 0 0
E	3	0 0 0 0 1	U	7	0 0 1 1 1
F	!	0 1 1 0 1	V	;	1 1 1 1 0
G	&	1 1 0 1 0	W	2	1 0 0 1 1
H	#	1 0 1 0 0	X	/	1 1 1 0 1
I	8	0 0 1 1 0	Y	6	1 0 1 0 1
J	Bell	0 1 0 1 1	Z	"	1 0 0 0 1
K	(	0 1 1 1 1	Letters (Shift) ↓		1 1 1 1 1
L	)	1 0 0 1 0	Figures (Shift) ↑		1 1 0 1 1
M	.	1 1 1 0 0	Space (SP) =		0 0 1 0 0
N	,	0 1 1 0 0	Carriage Return <		0 1 0 0 0
O	9	1 1 0 0 0	Line Feed =		0 0 0 1 0
P	0	1 0 1 1 0	Blank		0 0 0 0 0

1 = Mark = Punch Hole
0 = Space = No Punch Hole

Figure 2.2   Baudot Code Set

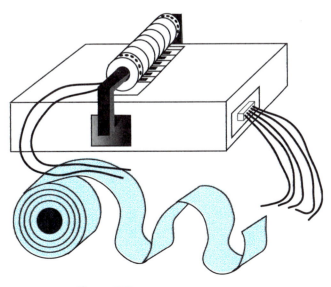

Figure 2.3   Baudot Telegraph

when combined, represent specific characters. These positional values are referred to as bit positions.

A specific character has a corresponding binary value. This code set was employed in a machine that used a paper tape having five columns, each of which represented a binary digit (positional bit). The presence or absence of holes in a particular horizontal row across the five columns represented the binary value for a character.

Modern data communications uses an expanded variation of Baudot's code due to the limitations placed on the number of combinations supported by only five positions. Even though the five-bit code covered all the letters in the alphabet as well as the basic numbers, no room was left over to expand the code set. Inclusion of start-and-stop indicators and other characters needed to communicate the status of the data being sent (such as sequence numbers, length of the data, etc.) were needed for a more extensive communications service.

Today, communications code sets have seven, eight and nine binary positions. Two of the most common communications code sets in use today are the American Standard Code for Information Interchange (ASCII) and the Extended Binary Coded Decimal Interchange Code (EBCDIC). ASCII is a seven- or eight-bit code depending on which version is being used, standard or extended. It is an extension of a code set known as the six-bit trans code that was used between 1910 and the early 1950s. The EBCDIC is an eight-bit code set. IBM developed both of these code sets. Figure 2.4 shows an ASCII code chart. Figure 2.5 shows an EBCDIC chart.

HARDWARE REQUIREMENTS

Originally, the data communications industry consisted of telephone company equipment and services supported by the existing Bell Telephone and American Telephone and Telegraph (AT&T) Company voice networks. Within the past 10 years, the need for data communications has grown to a point where the industry now has virtually thousands of independent suppliers and distributors. These vendors provide communications equipment and support services to any organization requiring data communications capabilities. The equipment and services that were once exclusively provided by the telephone network companies are now widely available and can be acquired from a multitude of private concerns.

Today, data communications is a multibillion dollar industry with an annual growth rate in excess of 35 percent. Most computer manufacturers incorporate data communications capabilities into their hardware and software product lines.

The primary catalyst for the tremendous growth of the data communications industry has been the data processing industry and the need to access information in an online, interactive environment. The basic need has been to transfer data economically from one location to another over long distances.

Today's complex and diversified businesses must have immediate access to information regarding their operations in order to serve customers and control business activities. With operations, sales offices and manufacturing spread all over the world, organizations must have methods to transfer vast amounts of data quickly and inexpensively.

The objective of data communications is to move data as quickly and as reliably as possible from one location to other locations that make up the network. From a hardware perspective, many different components are available for that purpose. Often, it becomes a time-consuming effort to evaluate and select equipment appropriate for a given situation.

Let's assume that we have nothing in place at this time and must start from ground zero in building our network. When we have determined what our data transmission requirements are and projected what the rate of growth will be, the first decision should

American National Standards Institute

b4 b3 b2 b1	row↓ column→	0	1	2	3	4	5	6	7
	b8→	0	0	0	0	1	1	1	1
	b7→	0	0	0	0	0	0	1	1
	b6→	0	0	1	1	0	0	1	1
	b5→	0	1	0	1	0	1	0	1
0 0 0 0	0	NUL	DLE	SP	0	a	P	`	p
0 0 0 1	1	SOH	DC1	!	1	A	Q	a	q
0 0 1 0	2	STX	DC2	"	2	B	R	b	r
0 0 1 1	3	ETX	DC3	#	3	C	S	c	s
0 1 0 0	4	EOT	DC4	$	4	D	T	d	t
0 1 0 1	5	ENQ	NAK	%	5	E	U	e	u
0 1 1 0	6	ACK	SYN	&	6	F	V	f	v
0 1 1 1	7	BEL	ETB	'	7	G	W	g	w
1 0 0 0	8	BS	CAN	(	8	H	X	h	x
1 0 0 1	9	HT	EM	)	9	I	Y	i	y
1 0 1 0	10	LF	SUB	*	:	J	Z	j	z
1 0 1 1	11	VT	ESC	÷	;	K	[	k	{
1 1 0 0	12	FF	FS	,	<	L	\	l	|
1 1 0 1	13	CR	GS	.	=	M	]	m	}
1 1 1 0	14	SO	RS		>	N	~	n	~
1 1 1 1	15	SI	US	/	?	O	_	o	DEL

ACK	Acknowledgment	DUP	Duplicate	GS	Group Separator	SBA	Set Buffer Address
BEL	Bell	EM	End of Medium	HT	Horizontal Tab	SF	Start Field
BS		ENQ	Enquiry	IC	Insert Cursor	SI	Shift In
CAN	Cancel	EOT	End of Transmission	ITB	End of Intermediate	SO	Shift Out
CR	Carriage Return	ESC	Escape		Text Block	SOH	Start of Header
DC1	Device Control 1	ETB	End of Transmission Block	NAK	Negative Ack	SP	Space
DC2	Device Control 2	ETX	End of Text	NL	New Line	STX	Start of Text
DC3	Device Control 3	EUA	Erase Unprotected to Address	NUL	Null	SUB	Substitute
DC4	Device Control 4	FF	Form Feed	PT	Program Tab	SYN	Synchronous Idle
DEL	Delete	FM	Field Mark	RA	Report to Address	US	Unit Separator
DLE	Data Link Escape	FS	File Separator	RS	Record Separator	VT	Vertical Tab

Figure 2.4 ASCII Code Set

Introduction to Data Communications: A Practical Approach

EBCDIC Bits				Controls				Characters											
				0				0								1			
				1				0				1				0			1
				2	0		1		0		1		0		1		0		1
				3	0	1	0	1	0	1	0	1	0	1	0	1	0	1	0	1
4	5	6	7	HEX	0	1	2	3	4	5	6	7	8	9	A	B	C	D	E	F
0	0	0	0	0	NUL	DLE			SP	&							(	)	\	0
			1	1	SOH	SBA							a	j	~		A	J	S	1
		1	0	2	STX	EUA		SYN					b	k	s		B	K		2
			1	3	ETX	IC							c	l	t		C	L	T	3
	1	0	0	4									d	m	u		D	M	U	4
			1	5	PT	NL							e	n	v		E	N	V	5
		1	0	6			ETB						f	o	w		F	O	W	6
			1	7			ESC	EOT					g	p	x		G	P	X	7
1	0	0	0	8									h	q	y		H	Q	Y	8
			1	9		EM							i	r	z		I	R	Z	9
		1	0	A					¢	!	:									
			1	B					.	$	,	#								
	1	0	0	C	FF	DUP		RA	<	#	%	@								
			1	D		SF	ENQ	NAK	(	)	_	'								
		1	0	E		FM			+	;	>	=								
			1	F		ITB		SUB		¬	?	"								

ACK	Acknowledgment	DUP	Duplicate	GS	Group Separator	SBA	Set Buffer Address
BEL	Bell	EM	End of Medium	HT	Horizontal Tab	SF	Start Field
BS		ENQ	Enquiry	IC	Insert Cursor	SI	Shift In
CAN	Cancel	EOT	End of Transmission	ITB	End of Intermediate	SO	Shift Out
CR	Carriage Return	ESC	Escape		Text Block	SOH	Start of Header
DC1	Device Control 1	ETB	End of Transmission Block	NAK	Negative Ack	SP	Space
DC2	Device Control 2	ETX	End of Text	NL	New Line	STX	Start of Text
DC3	Device Control 3	EUA	Erase Unprotected to Address	NUL	Null	SUB	Substitute
DC4	Device Control 4	FF	Form Feed	PT	Program Tab	SYN	Synchronous Idle
DEL	Delete	FM	Field Mark	RA	Report to Address	US	Unit Separator
DLE	Data Link Escape	FS	File Separator	RS	Record Separator	VT	Vertical Tab

Figure 2.5 EBCDIC Code Set

Data Communications and Network Planning

be what type of computer processing capability is necessary for acceptable performance.

Needless to say, a large number of computer manufacturers exist to satisfy this need. We have a large task ahead of us in simply selecting the computer system. When making such a choice, you'll need to consider the following major areas.

CPU Processing Capacity

Planners should make a detailed evaluation regarding the breadth of applications the computer will have to support. (Figure 2.6 shows a CPU capacity layout.) As a planner, ask the following questions:

- Will this machine be dedicated to online processing activities or will it need to support batch applications as well?

- Will the CPU directly support the terminal network or will a communications processor be required to assist the CPU due to the number of terminals it must manage on the network?

- How many online applications must be supported simultaneously on the computer?

- Will we need to have a hot backup (another computer waiting in standby mode if the primary processor fails)?

- Will our online applications be transaction based or interactive?

- Will program development occur on this machine?

- What is an acceptable response time for users?

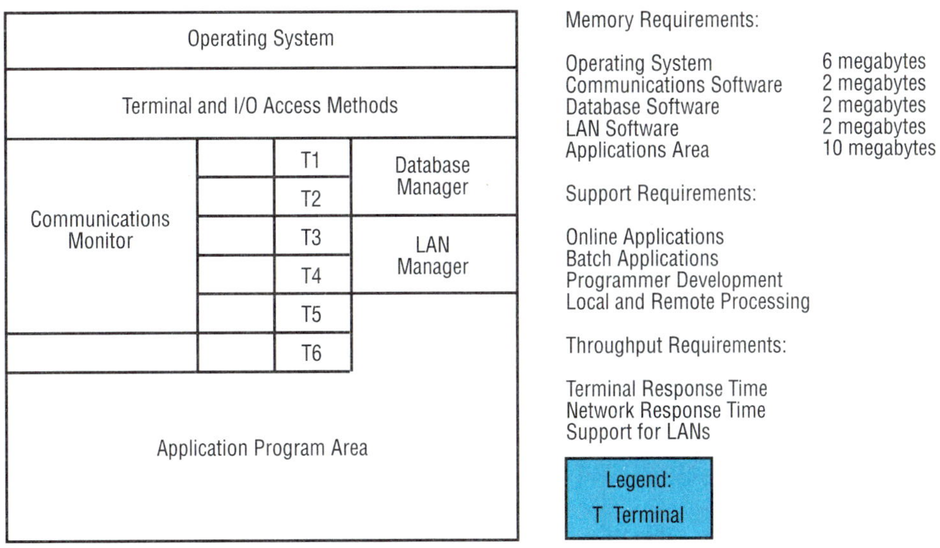

Memory Requirements:

Operating System	6 megabytes
Communications Software	2 megabytes
Database Software	2 megabytes
LAN Software	2 megabytes
Applications Area	10 megabytes

Support Requirements:

Online Applications
Batch Applications
Programmer Development
Local and Remote Processing

Throughput Requirements:

Terminal Response Time
Network Response Time
Support for LANs

Legend:
T Terminal

Figure 2.6   CPU Capacity Layout

Network Handling Capabilities

To determine network handling capabilities, you must determine the network's physical and logical organization. (Figure 2.7 illustrates a network layout.) Carefully weigh the answers to the following questions:

- Will the network need to support local (hard-wired) terminals as well as remotely attached terminals and workstations (terminals connected via telephone or other commercial links)?
- Are remote job entry (RJE) or network job entry (NJE) communications to be supported?
- RJE and NJE allow remote sites to use the remotely located computer as if it were a local computer. Should we plan for future growth in the equipment we purchase now?
- Will the network communications hardware support an interface to local area networks? (A local area network consists of computers restricted to a limited distance.)
- Will the system have to support a voice and video network?

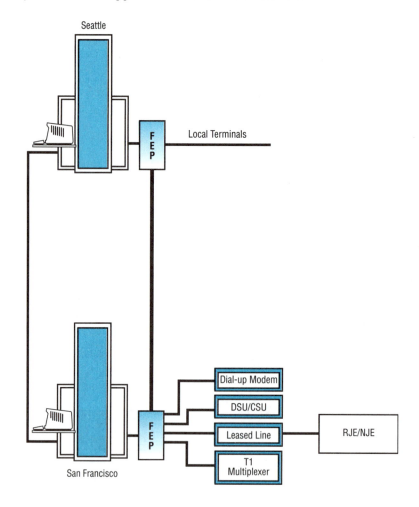

Figure 2.7 Network Layout

Communications Hardware Considerations

Communications processors and multiplexers assist the CPU in performing data communications activities, including terminal management and internetwork communications. If you are responsible for planning, you should review these requirements to determine whether a front-end processor or communications processor (CP) will be needed. Does the network require a CP due to the large number of terminals and printers on the network? Can future growth justify the acquisition of a communications processor even though channel and port capacities currently exist for the attachment of all terminal devices to the CPU?

Will the network require a remote communications processor in order to attach clusters of remote terminals resident in the same location? (Figure 2.8 depicts a communications processor.) Multiplexers can be used in place of communications processors, but can the remote terminal network grow using multiplexers? Should a network control center that manages the communications network be installed and what type of capabilities are required to support it?

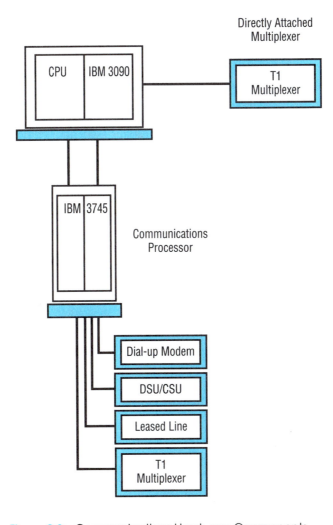

Figure 2.8 Communications Hardware Components

With respect to the transmission equipment, will a DSU/CSU (used for the movement of bits across the line) be required to support remote digital communications? Are modems (used for analog bit transmission over the telephone network) to be incorporated and, if so, what type and what transmission speed will be acceptable? Are multiplexing modems (which support multiple computers and terminals) suitable for this network so that modem pooling (sharing a single modem among several computers) can occur? When wiring the facility, what media or wiring types will the hardware support?

Transmission Links

Transmission link service options are also important to evaluate when selecting a data communications system. Costs associated with the selection of transmission link services should be carefully weighed. If a private microwave is considered, will the local laws support microwave transmission? Can FCC approval be obtained? Will enough capacity exist for future growth of the system? When using dial-up links, does the current public switched telephone network (PSTN) provide a high enough bit rate for reliable communications? Finally, what type of facility or service, if any, should be leased: satellite, wideband digital service provided by the telephone company, ISDN services also provided by the telephone company, or commercial microwave?

SOFTWARE REQUIREMENTS

At one time, the process of moving voice and data across a communications network was a mechanical as well as an electrical function. Eventually, telephone companies introduced electronic program control to the system through the use of computers. This became necessary due to the increased use of communications switching components required to manage data transfer. Because switches were provided with intelligence, software was needed for line control, multiplexing (line sharing) and management.

As the telephone networks were incorporating intelligence, computers were evolving to the next level of online processing. What was once a single application environment communicating with a few dedicated terminals became a multitasking, online application enterprise linking thousands of networked intelligent devices. New hardware provided the development platform for the complex software we need today for network communications.

Aside from business application software, several other types of software are needed. These other software classifications include management software for the control of the overall computer environment, software for the control and management of the terminal network and software for the management and control of internetwork communications. Monitoring and performance evaluation software for visibility into enterprisewide communications activities also is available, as are application program interfaces that manage terminal/program connectivity.

Decisions regarding acquisition of the software greatly depend on the hardware selected. Before selecting the software, you'll need to answer basic questions about how the network will function.

Application Control Software

This type of software controls the application-to-terminal processes to ensure error-free and timely access to data. Before choosing this software, consider these questions:

- Will the online environment require application control software to manage concurrent requests from multiple terminals? Or, will the communications activities be dedicated to a specific corporatewide function and have all terminals owned full time by a single application process?

- Does the control software need to provide password security, or will it be part of the application process?
- Should the control software support interactive or transaction-based activities?

Terminal Network Software

This software manages the physical terminal network and provides a method for controlling terminal access and availability. Depending on the size of the network and on the expected performance and the type of hardware and software used, it may not be required.

Network Control and Interface Software

If the planned network is to be part of a larger network, network control and interface software will be required to support gateway and bridging functions. The corporation must decide what capabilities will be acquired to support these activities. Will the network control and interface software be required to communicate with other manufacturers' computer environments running different control software? What are the interface requirements? Will the host computer that uses this software be used for routing and relaying data to other computers in the network and will they have compatible software?

Network- and Performance-Monitoring Software

Depending on the size of the network, network control may require a remote control center. When considering this type of software, ask yourself these questions:

- Will the network be large enough to support a network control and monitoring function at any level?
- Will funding and management support be sufficient for the purchase and use of the required software?

COMMUNICATIONS SERVICES

The need to move data between distant locations calls for a variety of equipment, software, services and expertise. Many methods exist for the transfer of data from one location to another, including telephone services (both leased-line and dial-up) provided by the various public telephone companies and private bypass services provided by alternate carriers and network services providers. In addition, an organization may install and maintain an on-site private network or share facilities with other organizations. The following types of services for the movement of data need to be considered.

Carrier Services

A large variety of carrier services exists worldwide for the transport of data, but in many countries, the telecommunications facilities are owned by the government. Where a choice is available, consider the reliability of the carrier, the variety and cost of the services available, the available bit rates, and the mean time to install and upgrade to another class of service.

Specialized Carriers

If the installed network is to support worldwide communications, consider whether specialized carrier services will be required or available at each of the locations. These may include satellite services, trans-Atlantic or trans-Pacific fiber-optic service, and others such as switched 56-Kbps service or packet-handling services.

Communications Service Providers

If the planned communications network is to consist of a heterogeneous mix of equipment (components from different vendors and companies), the network may require the services of a communications service provider. Such a provider reformats the data into an understandable form for reception by incompatible computer systems and other networks.

CASE STUDY (CONTINUED)

At the present time, a manual processing environment exists at each of the branches of the Bank of Scotts Valley. The bank now has more than 30 offices in California, and this method of processing cannot support efficient handling of the bank's business activities. Manual processing means that each branch periodically must batch all financial transactions throughout the day, reconcile them to the teller ledgers and forward them to the service centers. This activity is required for capture by a computer.

The bank has two regions, Northern and Southern, and two service centers support the bank's operations; however, very limited data communications lines exist between the service centers. This is because at the time of installation, it was determined to be an unnecessary expense. Each service center is responsible for processing batched data input from branches in the region it supports.

Interbranch banking is supported, but it is a slow, manual process involving the batching of transactions at the close of the business day. The transactions are taken to the service centers and then transported via computer tape delivery services between the centers. Transactions are processed overnight and returned, along with the appropriate listings, to each branch before the start of the next business day.

Because of the way the bank must handle its customers' activities, customer service is not competitive and suffers from a poor image. Customers wishing to make deposits must have a hold placed on the deposit until it clears. Withdrawals require a manual look-up and a telephone verification that the customer has sufficient funds to cover the amount requested. Account transfers as well as automatic deposits require manual entry by each of the tellers.

Each of the service centers has a Unisys mainframe and magnetic ink character recognition (MICR) equipment. This hardware is used to capture a variety of transactions that include checking account deposits and withdrawals, mortgage and loan payments and savings account deposits. Associated reports and tapes are prepared each night for the following day's activities and distributed to each of the branches before the beginning of the next business day. At the time the bank developed the initial data processing applications, data communications capability was not a requirement.

One objective for the new computer and communications environment is the use of teller terminals at each of the branches to provide employees with online access and update capabilities to the service centers. Additionally, automatic interbranch transfer activity for all accounts and transaction types will be needed. Another important objective for the bank is the elimination of paper and tape transfers between branches and service centers. Hardware required by the bank will include a new high-speed computer at each of the service centers capable of supporting a dynamic application environment for at least five years. Communications processors also must be considered to manage the overall network. The bank also must plan for communications transmission equipment to perform the data communications activities.

The bank requires a new software environment that will include a new operating system, specific banking application programs, communications control software and system programs for hardware and communications management.

A review of link service requirements will ascertain whether the data transmission capacity between the branches and the service centers will support existing and future business activities. Figure 2.9 depicts the Bank of Scotts Valley's planned network.

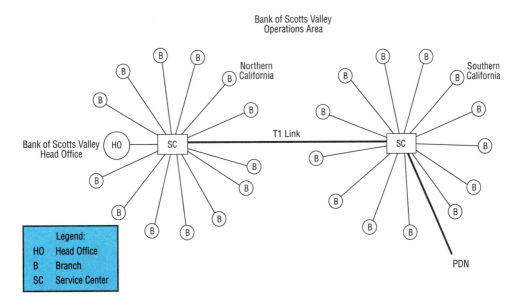

Figure 2.9 Bank of Scotts Valley Planned Network

REVIEW QUESTIONS

1. Data communications had its beginnings when Samuel Morse did what?
2. With what is Baudot credited?
3. Today, primarily what two code sets are used in data communications?
4. Name the code set that provides 256 character types.
5. What was the prime catalyst for the data communications industry?
6. Name the factors that must be evaluated when selecting hardware.
7. What software needs to be considered for data communications?
8. What function does application control software perform?
9. What do communications service providers offer?
10. What role does the telephone company play in providing communications services?

PART II

SOFTWARE REQUIRED FOR DATA COMMUNICATIONS

CHAPTER
3

Communications Software

INTRODUCTION

Many types of software exist, and many applications are designed to perform end-user processing such as developing payroll checks and maintaining inventory control. Some have system support responsibilities such as control, placement and organization of data on a disk storage device.

Within the past 10 years, manufacturers have incorporated many software activities and functions into computer and communications hardware. This incorporation is intended to take advantage of the advances in software that can be hard-coded and contained in read-only memory (ROM) semiconductor chips. There are still some activities better suited for inclusion into the software because these activities require modification of the code that direct hardware functions.

Data communications activities such as terminal management, network control, contention control and error detection require extensive software support. This chapter will concentrate on the two major categories of software, system and application software, as they relate to data communications. Subcategories for system software include operating systems, communications systems and network control software. Several subcategories of application programs exist; however, discussion is centered on online processing activities only.

ROLE OF SOFTWARE IN COMMUNICATIONS

Communications technology has rapidly evolved from early mechanical switching methods to the sophisticated third- and fourth-generation programmable digital computers we use today. However, due to the tremendous demand for speed and flexibility required by users, it is impossible to accomplish these communications functions solely within the hardware.

Communications and operating system software manage hardware resources so that all programs resident in the computer can share them. This software has many functions, including activities such as the provision and management of all communications between the host computer system and its remote sites, monitoring performance of the computer communications network and the provision of utility functions such as control and error resolution.

Many different types of system software are available from either the computer hardware manufacturer or from independent software manufacturers. An example of the use of system software would be the simple task of adding or deleting terminals to or from a network. Without system software to accomplish this task, physical wiring of the hardware switch would be necessary to add or delete terminals, making it a much more time-consuming and difficult activity. System and communications software responsibilities include:

- Network configuration and maintenance
- Network control
- Application management

Network Configuration and Maintenance

Network configuration and maintenance software ensures that all communications lines are correctly specified and uniquely identified as to their logical addresses, bit rates and types of service. These functions assist application programs in accessing specific terminals and lines when communications configurations are updated or changed. As an example, terminals must be uniquely specified in several software locations as to screen size, color and special features. Such specificity ensures that information transported to the terminal will be properly displayed. Another area requiring configuration and maintenance is network hardware. Many network components require information about the overall hardware environment to function properly. The role of network maintenance software is to manage communications and operating system software changes as well as to control update activities. Figure 3.1 illustrates line addresses and terminal address tables in memory.

Network Control

Control of the network is critical to acceptable network throughput and response time. Active network control software must be present to manage the overall computer and network resources. Network control software consists of many interlocking programs such as operating systems software elements, access methods and application program interfaces (APIs). These software components accomplish control by directing network and terminal routing and by providing error control and line/terminal congestion control for all processes requiring communications. Additional control activities include keeping track of active lines and terminals in the overall network and resolving contention and congestion.

Application Management

In today's complex multitasking environment, the many active online programs need to be supervised to ensure that they do not interfere with each other or cause contention problems. Application management software's primary responsibility is to manage the hundreds of application programs that may be resident in memory. This management activity ensures that conflicts do not occur between applications for terminal or other hardware resources. In the absence of application management, multiple communications networks managed on the same host computer would compete for the same scarce resources. Such an environment would create contention between two or more application programs by attempting to address the same terminal concurrently. Figure 3.2 illustrates a terminal-addressing conflict.

SYSTEM SOFTWARE

The term "system software" is frequently used to describe a vast number of general programs that perform a variety of functions. Basically, system software can be defined as software designed to perform interactively with application programs by managing them and providing a variety of services. The goal of system software is to provide acceptable throughput as efficiently as possible. As a rule, system software must be efficient in order to provide acceptable application program performance.

To achieve such efficiency, system software is typically written using a specific manufacturer's low-level computer language, generally the assembler language of the computer. The use of higher-level languages is less efficient because they often generate additional instruction code that adds processing overhead to the CPU. By using a low-level assembly language, the software programmer is given the most computer control because assembly language enables the programmer to direct a specific action by the computer, as opposed to a more general one that may include nonessential instructions.

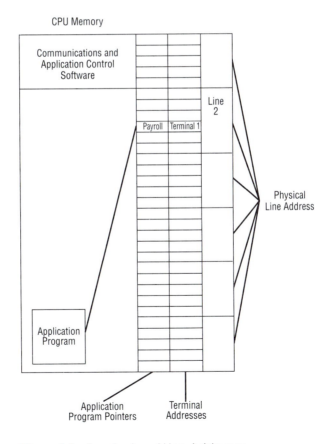

Figure 3.1 Terminal and Line Addresses

Introduction to Data Communications: A Practical Approach

Most system software currently in use is provided by the manufacturer, although some system programs may be written by the programming staff within an organization. This is so because it takes years of training and special skills to write system software. Almost all computer manufacturers provide communications network and application management software to support their computer products.

Vendor-provided system software is most often used because of the computer's need to handle the complex tasks associated with management of the required communications functions. These functions include:

- Allocation of access time for all tasks and programs desiring to use the hardware resources
- Management of tasks resident and active in memory
- Control and management of communications links
- Resolution of error conditions originating either from the hardware or from the software
- Checkpoint, restart and recovery activity when required

Figure 3.3 shows major software system components in memory.

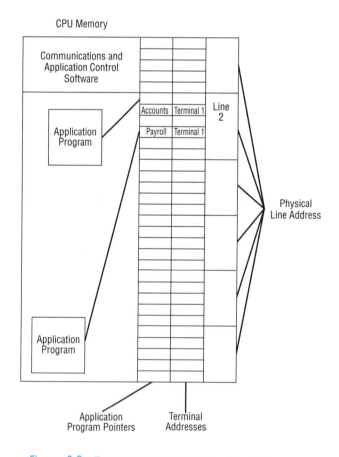

Figure 3.2 Example of an Address Conflict

Operating System Software

The foundation for all computers is the operating system software. This collection of programs is responsible for the use of memory, the management of all communications hardware functions and the control of all input/output devices attached to the computer. Overall, operating systems manage the use and availability of hardware resources so that all tasks (batch, online, communications control and system software) have access to the hardware in a timely and orderly manner. The operating system software performs several functions that are described below. Figure 3.4 illustrates an example of operating system components in an IBM processor.

The operating system must allow for interactive communications between operators and users. Operators require intervention to cancel executing programs, turn lines on and off, schedule output waiting for printer availability and a variety of other functions.

Operating systems also must provide scheduling management for application programs waiting for execution. They accomplish this by continuously monitoring memory for availability. When memory is available, the operating system accesses a list of programs waiting for execution, obtains the name of the next program to execute, fetches the program and loads it into the available memory.

Another function of the operating system is to manage the hardware resources and make them available to programs that require them. The operating system is responsible for managing channel access to I/O devices and will temporarily assign access use on a queue basis to any application process requiring it. The operating system also resolves input/output conflicts created by multiple programs requesting the same resources at the same time, and it attempts to detect and correct errors.

Operating system software manages programs in memory and temporary storage. Because the size of memory is usually large, many programs can reside together. However, the programs must be directed to avoid addressing conflicts. Remember, unless using multiple processors, the computer is capable of executing only one instruction at a time.

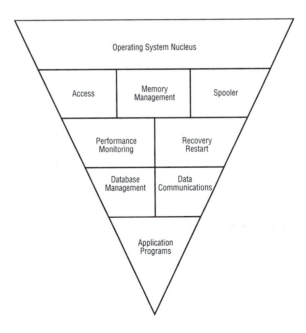

Figure 3.3 Major Software Components

The operating system must ensure that programs remain within their own boundaries. It also controls each program's active operations, limiting it to a specific number of instructions to be executed. Finally, the operating system ensures that all programs in memory have active CPU time.

If a failure or fatal error is detected, the operating system manages recovery and restart processes. The operating system attempts to identify and correct any error it can. The operating system may even be able to restart the entire system and each processing application. This is accomplished by frequently storing the contents of memory on disks or tapes and assigning identifiers to them. In the event of a failure, these snapshots of memory can be reloaded using a restart program within the operating system and processing can resume.

Communications System Software

Communications system software manages application and communications tasks, such as security and checkpoint activities that need system resources. This software provides control and access to the communications network and its terminals in an equitable manner. Many programs must interact to perform communications with terminals and other computer systems because of the complexity of the various activities that must be performed for successful communications.

In the IBM environment, programs that must communicate with terminals can communicate directly using logical access instructions written into the application program. (In other words, the code needed for physical access to the terminals is part of the application program.) This communications access code must interface to the operating system's

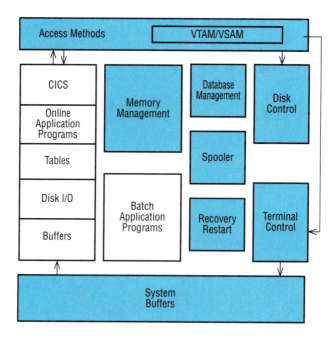

Figure 3.4 Operating System Components

access methods, which contain the specific code required to move data across the channels to the input/output devices or terminals. For other computer manufacturers, similar procedures must occur for accessing and controlling terminals and I/O devices. Two specific IBM access methods are the Basic Telecommunications Access Method (BTAM) and the Virtual Telecommunications Access Method (VTAM).

If application program code is to contain its own communications instructions, the program code must contain the hardware address of each of the terminals, as well as the instructions necessary to format messages to and from the terminals. The terminal display information along with the terminal address is passed by the application program's communications code to the correct operating system access method. Often, the access method code provided by the manufacturer is embedded in the application program code during its creation.

This method of direct hardware control creates an efficient application program. It is important to bear in mind that a specific terminal can be active only to a single application program at any point in time. This may create a major restriction unless some form of virtual terminal service is utilized. A virtual terminal is a terminal that can display multiple windows, each containing an active process or having the ability to switch between active sessions. Using this method of direct control communications, terminals are normally assigned to a single program during a specific time period.

As an alternative method, organizations can use commercial communications management software such as CICS (Customer Information Control System), an IBM product (see Figure 3.5). Communications management software is usually offered by the computer

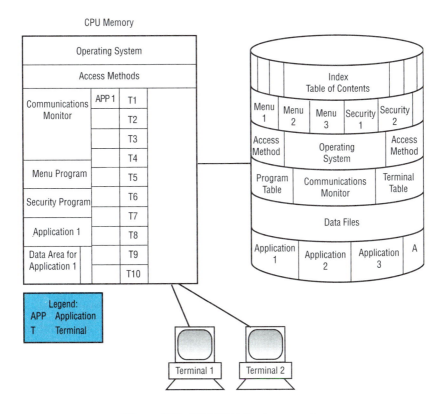

Figure 3.5   IBM CICS Environment

manufacturer and is designed to provide the same terminal access functions as user-developed application programs that contain embedded communications program statements. Several independent software companies provide communications management products that compete against software provided by the hardware manufacturers.

Communications products manufactured by Software AG, Cincom Systems Inc., Computer Associates International Inc., American Management Systems Inc. and other companies are designed to interface with the terminal access methods provided by the computer vendor. These products provide application program management, thereby making the program independent of the hardware. This means that the application program does not directly address a hardware device; instead, it uses logical addresses that are translated into hardware addresses by the communications software product.

Most organizations choose to use vendor-supplied communications management software because of the complexities involved in writing their own. This software is responsible for the management of communications functions, such as polling the line and each terminal to determine if any activity is present, or to see if a terminal wants to initiate a communications session.

When a user depresses the Enter key, a poll bit is set within the terminal indicating activity for that particular device. One of the roles of communications management software is to detect the poll bit and establish a session for the terminal. The software also must be able to select (indicate to the terminal it has something for it), broadcast (send to all terminals), or send data or messages to specific terminals on the link. Figure 3.6 illustrates the four stages involved in loading the CICS communications monitor and responding to an application terminal processing request.

Communications management software also schedules and loads online application programs into memory as requested by the terminal or another program. It is then responsible for transferring the message from the terminal across the link to the waiting program. It must be able to resolve any error conditions that may occur and to ensure that all users desiring terminal and program access have equal time.

Additional communications management software capabilities include the automatic broadcast of selection menus at start-up time or when sessions have been completed, and access-control validation to ensure that users have legitimate access to an online application.

Communications management software, when loaded, becomes resident in the computer's memory as a system task and provides services to all online applications requiring communications. Many vendors embed their communications support software into the operating system for this reason.

IBM's CICS and other communications management software products offer several distinct advantages. The software resolves contention between diverse applications without impact on programs or terminals. It handles polling, selection and program interrupts to ensure minimum response time. It resolves error conditions on both the data and line levels. And it becomes a memory-resident part of the computer system, enabling much faster access time to a single copy of the control software.

Network Support Software

Depending on the hardware and the size of the network, network support software may be required to physically manage the network, either from the CPU itself or from a supporting communications processor. This software manages the physical lines, the physical terminals and all internetwork communications. The functions of network support software are many and varied and include communications control and network control. Many vendors, such as Digital Equipment Corporation, Hewlett-Packard Company and Sun Microsystems Inc., have built these functions into their hardware and software as integrated components. IBM provides separate software packages to accomplish these activities.

Network communications controllers such as the IBM 3745 controller require software to send and receive data to and from local and remote terminals. (Figure 3.7 illustrates some of the software components found in an IBM 3745 communications processor.) Some of this software might be resident in the CPU, or it might be resident in the communications controller depending on the type of equipment available and the network defined. It can be downloaded from the host (transmitted across the communications link), or resident as part of the hardware in ROM (read only memory); this is known as device software. It can also be referred to as network control software. Some of the following are examples of network control software.

Network Control Program (NCP). This program is resident in the front-end processor (FEP) and is part of the IBM Systems Network Architecture (SNA) environment. The NCP software offloads many of the communications functions that normally would be controlled by the host computer, such as line control, network control and error resolution. This reduces the amount of processing time and memory that the host computer must allocate for communications activity, enabling it to better service the application processes.

Advanced Communications Facility (ACF). This IBM software assists VTAM in communications activity and enables the network operator or systems programmer to view and control the network. It can be classified as a monitoring and performance option.

Virtual Telecommunications Access Method. VTAM is an IBM access method resident in the CPU and is used to assist the communications monitor or other communications software to communicate across the network to the various nodes. It differs from BTAM in its ability to be terminal transparent. It can be modified (terminals added or dropped) without complex procedures, because it uses table entries that can be easily changed.

Basic Telecommunications Access Method. BTAM is similar to VTAM, but it is an older telecommunications access method. It is used primarily in pre-SNA networks and requires the hardcoding of terminal types and addresses into the program.

APPLICATION SOFTWARE

The function of application software is to address the business needs of an organization and to provide a data processing solution. This is accomplished by using the hardware, communications control software and system software to process the data and produce a desired product.

Typical examples of applications software are payroll programs designed to calculate payments and print checks, accounts receivable programs used to keep track of monies owed to a company and produce billing statements, and automated teller machine programs designed to dispense cash and handle other ATM transactions.

Application software is often written by an organization's programmers using one of the languages provided by the hardware or software manufacturer. Alternatively, application programs may be purchased from the many software developers.

Application program responsibilities include editing and verifying numeric and character data, manipulation of the various fields to form units of information, mathematical calculations and the preparation of the data into a format that the end user can understand. Another function of the application program is resolving error conditions that arise from the data or other programs with which it must interact.

Application programs, whether user-developed or vendor-supplied, employ one of two methods to provide online capabilities, depending on the needs of the user and how the

Introduction to Data Communications: A Practical Approach

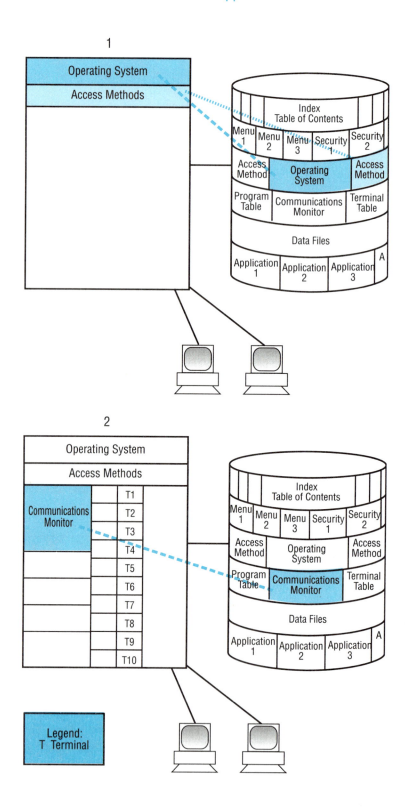

Figure 3.6   Four Stages of CICS Processing Activity

Communications Software

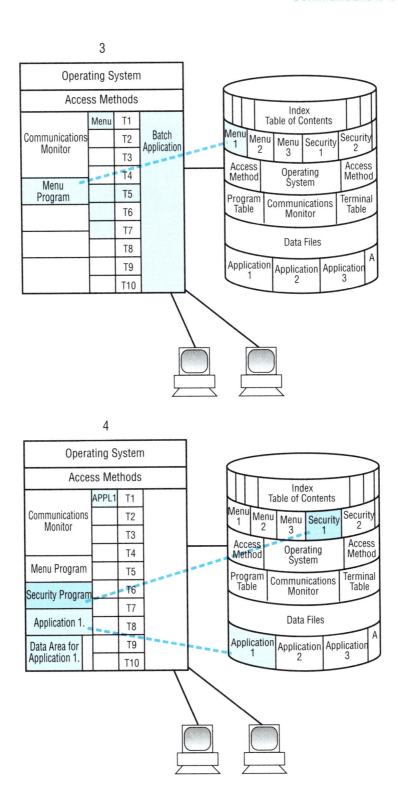

Figure 3.6 Four Stages of CICS Processing Activity (cont.)

applications are developed. Application programs used for data communications are written to use either the conversational or transaction-based method, as explained below.

Conversational Online Application Programs

Conversational online programs allow the user to establish and maintain a running dialog with the program. The conversational method is employed when the systems designer wishes to allow the user to converse interactively with the application (i.e., maintain a conversation and keep the application active until it is intentionally released by the terminal user). For example, financial application programs often require long periods of active time with the user. Conversational interaction is used when a number of options, such as questions answered on a screen display, determine what actions the application will perform.

In the conversational mode, the user controls the application until he or she wishes to release it. This type of access is used for continuous access to a specific application or task, such as a customer inquiry activity in an insurance or utility company.

Transaction-Based Application Processing

Transaction-based application methods are used for short, predetermined actions such as those found in automatic teller machines. This activity may include a variety of functions that are indirectly related to each other. The specific transaction is completed and the terminal is returned to an inactive status until the next user wishes to employ it.

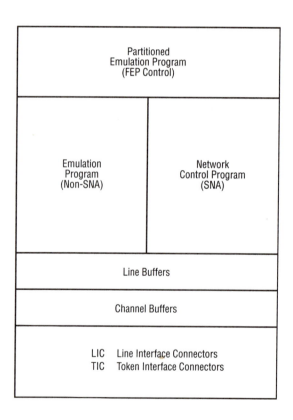

Figure 3.7   IBM 3745 Communications Controller

Neither of these two methods is superior to the other. They simply apply to different operational environments and each one has advantages for specific applications.

CASE STUDY (CONTINUED)

The move to a data communications networking environment by the Bank of Scotts Valley must be very carefully orchestrated. The implementation of new services and the methods for providing them represent a major change in the way the bank operates. These planned changes also represent a major financial investment and therefore must be cost justified to the stockholders. A key issue is that the hardware and software required to support the environment must be implemented in such a way as to allow the bank to continue operations during the transition period. This necessitates that the bank maintain two independent service center environments for both the Northern and Southern regions so that the conversion process is smooth and trouble free.

Because the bank has a Unisys system already installed, the bank performed an extensive evaluation to determine whether Unisys can provide solutions that will not require a total conversion process. At the conclusion of this evaluation it was determined that the existing systems located at the service centers do not have the capabilities to meet the new requirements. Both the hardware and software are inappropriate and cannot be upgraded to meet the objectives set forth in the evaluation study.

After careful review, the bank has decided to implement an IBM solution using an IBM 4341 mainframe and 3278 terminals. This decision was made based on the upgrade paths they think they will have to take, the availability of off-the-shelf components that will interface to the processor, the impact on the user community and the availability of system, communications and application software.

The bank has decided to employ IBM's CICS communications monitor because it does not have the resources to develop a custom monitor. CICS is a mature product in operation at thousands of locations around the world, and a large variety of banking applications run under its control. This last point is particularly important to the bank because it does not have a large or experienced programming staff to create either application or system software. The operating system will be IBM's OS-MVS because it is a mature operational environment for CICS and supports several database management systems. Database management is a requirement for online real-time data access.

The bank's management wishes to use commercial applications and system software as often as possible to expedite implementation of the network. Additionally, all applications must be written in the COBOL programming language because the bank will need to maintain the applications after a period of time.

It also has been determined that, because a communications processor initially will not be required, network control software also will not be necessary. This is not to say that at some point during the growth of the network, network control will not be needed.

REVIEW QUESTIONS

1. What functions does communications software perform?
2. What functions does system software perform?
3. What activity is application software responsible for?
4. Name four major functions performed by the communications monitor.
5. What does the term "conversational mode processing" describe?

6. BTAM and VTAM perform what functions for the communications monitor?
7. Network control programs perform what functions in the communications network?
8. True or false: Some overlap of functions exists between communications software and system software.
9. True or false: All software can be implemented into the hardware in ROM.
10. Communications and system software are usually purchased from the hardware manufacturer or a software vendor as opposed to the facility developing the software itself. Why?

CHAPTER 4

Application Development

INTRODUCTION

Chapter 3 covered data communications software requirements. This chapter expands on that information and provides a more detailed view of the various types of software required for online activities. It describes the different types of data communications management programs that can be employed for data communications activities and explores the differences between them.

One critical concept that must be understood is the detailed interaction needed between application programs and the controlling communications software. Interactions between multiple application and system programs are necessary because of the tremendously complex operational environment of online systems. It is essential to understand the activities that occur within this environment in order to plan, create, install and operate a data communications network.

Often, a communications environment requires millions of lines of code contained in several hundred programs to perform communications processing. Multiple programs are necessary because it is extremely difficult if not impossible for a single programmer to develop and maintain all the required code in a reasonable period of time. Many man years are often necessary to create the required application and system software.

To develop a data communications network, software systems must be designed, developed and put in place. The application processes (programs) also must be designed, tested and implemented. Rules for program interaction and operation are also important. Detailed rules governing program design must be followed for communications between online application programs and system software components. Rules are needed because all online programs must follow specific sets of procedures to accomplish their processing functions.

Application programs used in an online environment follow specific interactive activities in sequence when performing terminal processing activities. These activities provide orderly processing of the transactions and meaningful responses to requesting users.

Online application programs operate under the control of system software (the operating system and communications control software) when executing in the communications environment. As described in Chapter 3, this software controls and manages the hardware so that many programs can run concurrently. Remember, concurrent processing does not imply simultaneity, but the speed of the computer makes it appear so. Figure 4.1 illustrates a typical application program and communications system interface.

Interaction between the application program and the communications monitor is mandatory for data to be processed and transferred across the network to its destination in the correct order and format. This interaction is also needed because of the complexities of the hardware and operating environment. Online application program interaction with system software must be performed in a specific sequence due to the large number of activities that must take place. Interaction is also needed for error-free data communications in a multitasking environment where many programs must coexist.

MODES OF COMMUNICATION PROCESSING

Many methods can be used for creating an online environment. The simplest is to dedicate the computer to a specific set of terminals and application processes. It is important to note, however, that unless there is a budget to support this type of environment, the computer usually will have to support a mixed environment consisting of multiple batch processing activities, program development and testing, and one or more online environments.

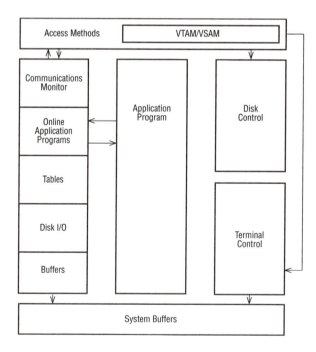

Figure 4.1 Application Program and Communications System Interface

Two types of online processing environments are *session-based processing* and *transaction-based processing*. Session-based processing is a conversational type of activity requiring continuous online interaction between the user and the program. This typically involves interactive conversational time-sharing management. Session-based communications is needed when long periods of time are required for interactive activities (e.g., program development).

Transaction-based processing is usually represented by interactions of short duration from many terminals. Transaction-based processing can be illustrated with products such as IBM's CICS communications programming system or Tandem Computers' Transaction Processing Facility (TPF). These products are designed for short, high-speed, burstlike types of multiple terminal activities such as those associated with ATM processing.

TRANSACTION-BASED COMMUNICATIONS

Online programs that require data transmission services to terminals and end users typically will use the services provided by the transaction-based communications management software. In some cases, custom communications software is used for the online application systems processing because of throughput demands. An example is the Programmed Airlines Reservation System (PARS). The design of PARS provides high-speed airline reservations processing using a subsystem called Transaction Processing Facility (TPF). Several banks also use TPF for their ATM networks because of the number of terminals that require support.

Online application programs running under the control of transaction-based system software use special commands to specify the activities the communications software needs to perform. These commands are communicated in the form of parameters passed on to the communications management software. The management software examines the values in the information passed from the application program to determine which type of activity is necessary. This information includes commands for passing display screens back to a specific terminal, retrieving a screen, and other parameters. Before exploring the online application program requirements for communications with the system software, let's examine the activities of typical communications management software.

Transaction-Based Communications Management Software

The communications management software is invoked (executed in the computer) by the computer operator at some point during the day. This activity usually occurs at the beginning of the work day. On systems that must provide 24-hour accessibility, the communications management software is resident and active 100 percent of the time.

One of the functions of the communications management software is to bring up or activate the communications lines that connect the terminals to the processor. It also monitors and maintains the lines to ensure that links are operating correctly. Additionally, the control software monitors each line and terminal for requests; this is known as *polling*. When the software encounters a line that has an activity indicator set (when a user enters a message at his or her terminal), the following events occur.

First, the communications monitor software identifies which online application program the terminal and user require. The monitor accomplishes this using some code or value located in the incoming message that arrives from the active terminal.

The next step is to transfer a message block received from the terminal into the communications management software's record buffers. A record buffer is an area of the computer's memory reserved for storing information from terminals and disk storage devices. A transaction code that identifies the terminal and application program will be contained in the received terminal's data block (part of the received message). The communications software uses this transaction code to look at an internal program name list that was made resident in memory when the system was activated. The communications software uses the input transaction code in order to determine which online program should be fetched from the disk-resident program library and loaded into memory.

The communications management software loads (fetches) the online program identified in the code table from its location on a disk device and places it into memory. If this is a highly active program, the management software might make the online program resident in memory for better response. Other programs with lower activity will be loaded when required and erased from memory when no longer needed. The communications software then informs the memory-resident online program where the terminal message is located and turns control over to that program so processing can begin.

In some cases, communications networks such as those used for ATM activities provide limited functions and usually require fast response times because of the number of terminals that require support. To provide acceptable response times, additional functions are often contained in the terminal or in the computer if it is dedicated to that one activity. In a dedicated environment, all application programs that service the ATM network would be made memory resident. A dedicated environment is one in which the terminal is designed for a specific activity, such as those used for airline reservations or bank teller activities.

Online application programs written for communications activities can transmit information using either transaction-oriented processing or conversational-oriented processing. Let's explore the differences between the two types by examining typical activities required for each method.

Transaction-Based Application Program Activities

The online application program accesses the transaction resident in the communications management software buffers and performs whatever action is necessary to respond to the message. That could include calculations, access to databases and data manipulation. Often, several interactive display screens are transferred between the computer and the terminal to complete the transaction. The application program either completes the activity or requests additional input from the terminal. It does this by passing another command back to the management software and requesting that the response be routed back to the sending terminal.

When the application program has completed processing the transaction, it informs the communications software so that the management software may use that memory space for another transaction-processing application if the space is needed. The application program must follow certain logical steps in processing transactions and messages.

Upon receipt of the initial request from the terminal, the application program begins to process the transaction. It acquires records to produce the information required as output to the terminal. Before the application requests a transfer of data across the link, the program must identify the templates, called mask and maps, it wishes the communications management software to display on the terminal screen for that data layout. See Figure 4.2 for an example of a typical terminal map used to identify display data.

Unless screen formats are to remain the same, this activity must take place for each formatted data layout to be returned to the terminal. The communications software transmits the screen map and then lays the data on top of it. The mask and maps create display formats for the data that make it comprehensible to the end user.

Prior to virtual systems concepts, when memory was limited, it was common for application programs to modify themselves to save memory. This was done by changing some of the branching or other instructions in the code that was already resident in memory. Another method for running large programs in limited memory was to overlay portions of the original code with new code. While this worked well, if the original code was required again, a fresh copy had to be brought in from disk. With the advent of multithreading methods, several terminals were able to access the same program. Of course, access must be at different times and in different program code locations. This allows the program to service several transactions and terminals concurrently. Multithreading allows several users to access the same program without conflict. The communications management software keeps track of the specific location of each user's program thread (see Figure 4.3).

In this environment, each of the active transaction context data blocks (this is the specific terminal data being worked on) must be saved by the communications software and be made available for restoration on demand by the online application program. This activity must take place whenever the online program switches from one active transaction or terminal to another. Switching of program control normally takes place when an online program needs system services such as requesting the retrieval of a record from disk storage. The program cannot continue processing the specific terminal transaction until it receives the requested records from the management software. At this point the program can begin processing another transaction if another terminal has an outstanding request. (This is analogous to placing someone on hold on the telephone while another call is serviced.) As a result, the application program must not modify itself.

A second reason that an online program must not modify itself is that it could be paged out (removed from memory to disk storage) while it is inactive and memory is needed by other programs. When the online program needs to become active in memory again because a new transaction requires processing, the communications management software will bring in a fresh copy of the program. Any counters, switches or total accumulators

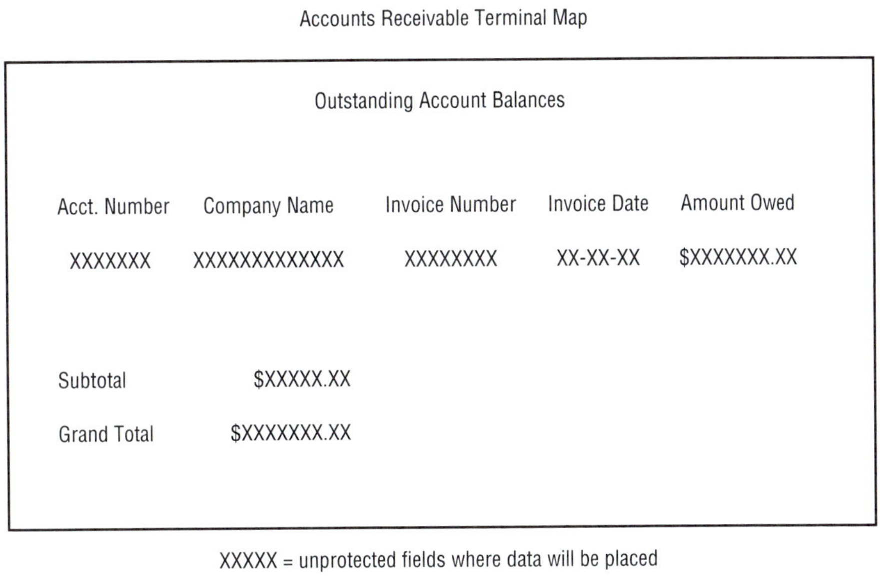

Accounts Receivable Terminal Map

Outstanding Account Balances

Acct. Number	Company Name	Invoice Number	Invoice Date	Amount Owed
XXXXXXX	XXXXXXXXXXXXX	XXXXXXXX	XX-XX-XX	$XXXXXXX.XX

Subtotal $XXXXX.XX

Grand Total $XXXXXXX.XX

XXXXX = unprotected fields where data will be placed

Figure 4.2 Application Program-to-Terminal Data Map

within the online program used for placement or mathematical activity will have a zero value. This program must be written in what is referred to as reentrant code.

The online program also should not engage in long record searches because system programs view the communications management software and its online application programs as a single activity. Long searches by one online application make all online programs, including the management software, wait. It also makes the end user wait an excessive amount of time for a response. This delay is nonproductive for the end user and it tarnishes the image of the computer department.

If the application program is a transaction-based program such as those used in ATMs, it normally will be designed to handle single transactions and may remain resident for the next transaction. This is opposed to low-volume transactions that do not need rapid response time. Typically, the latter will be dynamically loaded when required and then disappear until the communications software schedules it again.

Most communications monitors allow the application to be written in any programming language supported on the machine (COBOL, PL/1, BASIC, C, etc.). It is important to keep in mind, however, that processing efficiency is extremely important and throughput efficiency may require programs to be written in a low-level language such as Assembler.

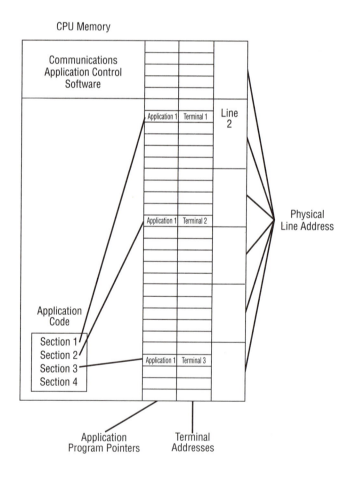

Figure 4.3 Example of Multithreading

CONVERSATIONAL COMMUNICATIONS

Conversational communications programs are written like transaction-based applications and interact with the communications management software in an identical manner. The major difference between transaction-based and interactive processing lies in the area of end-user interaction. Transaction-based programs are designed to service any terminal on the network in a surprise or random environment (i.e., the communications management software doesn't know when a transaction is going to arrive or what application program it is destined for until it is received). This creates a dynamic environment whose constant state of flux governs the way the online program is written. Transaction-based application programs break the connection to the terminal when finished processing one request and await requests from other terminals.

In the conversational environment, the application programs remain active and connected to the terminal until the end users at each of those terminals indicate they are finished. Typical conversational environments include customer service departments where customer information needs to be accessed on a continuous basis, as well as inventory look-ups, sales order look-ups and payroll. With these types of activities, a department's terminals remain online to the specific application until the user signs off.

Time-Sharing Communications

Most computer manufacturers base their primary communications software on time-sharing concepts. One example is the VMS operating system and conversational communications management system developed by Digital Equipment. Another time-sharing monitor is the VM operating system and conversational management system (CMS) provided by IBM.

Time-sharing communications management software is considered to be an integrated component of many operating systems. It is designed to offer a variety of user services on a time-sharing basis. You could look at the use of a time-sharing system as an alternative to the personal computer because the user interacts with the computer on a one-to-one basis using the software and services provided. This is not to imply that you cannot perform batch processing or provide interactive transaction-based processing in a time-sharing environment.

Many computer manufacturers offer specific time-sharing software in support of their hardware. Time-sharing software is usually user friendly and requires little or no knowledge of the hardware or software environments for many of its basic functions. Users can create private disk storage for their exclusive use or create public storage files that can be accessed by all users. Additionally, the user can employ community printers and access electronic mail software for communications.

Time-sharing management software is similar to transaction-based management software in that it provides hardware services and data communications to the end user on request. Time-sharing software is normally used by programmers and engineers for application development or utility activities, including file transfers, word processing, text editing and electronic mail. Transaction-based communications software is used to process data and communicate information to and from the end user.

The major difference between the two is in the method used to provide the hardware and software access by a user program. Most transaction-based communications programs operate on what is known as an *interrupt-driven* basis. In an interrupt-driven environment, the method of transferring control from one program to another (application to operating system or application to application) is governed by the specific processing program having control of the system at that time. The program in control voluntarily gives that control up when it needs operating system services or processing assistance from another program.

This is normally done when a program needs to perform some type of I/O request.

An example of this is a transaction-processing program receiving a request from a terminal for a customer look-up. The program takes the customer number from the incoming transaction and passes on an I/O request to another program designed to perform the record retrieval function. When the request for data is issued, control of the system is transferred to the data retrieval program and the transaction processing program is placed into a wait-state until the data is available.

The program performing the requested service (usually the access method) passes the request to a channel control program. On many machines, this is an independent activity operating within its own microprocessor-based environment. The channel control program then takes the request and tells the access method to come back in a little while to get the record.

Input/output activity is normally an independent program process in most computers. The requesting transaction-based application program is placed in a wait-state pending receipt of the retrieved data from the input/output access program. At that time, the communications management software can transfer control to another program to allow it to begin or continue processing. The communications management program also may have passed a record back to the waiting program, which will then be given control. The same process is repeated for each program operating under control of the communications management software. Although this may seem like a time-consuming activity, bear in mind that the hardware is capable of executing millions of instructions per second. A well-designed system can actually process hundreds of transactions per second.

Time-sharing communications management software, on the other hand, operates using a technique known as *time slicing*, whereby the communications software and operating system allocate to each application a preset amount of time. This permits an application to process a portion of its data. When the time expires for that application, the software passes control to the next application for a slice of time. All active users are serviced rapidly because the amount of time allocated to each user is minimal in the interactive environment. Remember, between communications activities, the user must review and act on the data transferred. Time-sharing techniques are also referred to as round robin techniques using quantums of time.

Selected Communications Software

Most communications software products are geared toward the IBM market since IBM and other companies making IBM-compatible computers require additional software for online processing. Following are some of the time-sharing communications products available for use on IBM systems.

IBM's Time Sharing Option (TSO). TSO operates as a system task under the Multiple Virtual System (MVS) operating system. TSO can also operate as a subsystem under the Virtual Machine (VM) operating system. TSO actually has its own subsystem, referred to as the Interactive System Productivity Facility (ISPF). These systems are designed to assist the programmer in program development, the computer operator in monitoring and managing the computer system, and the system programmer in maintaining the various software systems.

TSO with its ISPF subsystem provides many features and has an excellent text editor facility for program development. This software also allows users to access the computer system for status and program inquiries. It also enables programmers and users to access many utility functions. A unique feature of TSO and ISPF is that they provide an interface capability that allows other vendors' software to operate under its control. An example

Application Development

of this would be third-party software designed to monitor and tune the system's performance.

TSO and ISPF allow programmers to write small pieces of code to perform special functions, and they enable users to access and create data files. Both are extensively used by system support staff for software maintenance and provide a user broadcast and message-switching activity between various terminals on the network. Finally, TSO and ISPF provide a batch capability that allows programmers and users to execute batch programs and receive the program output on their terminals. This type of monitor is not used for transaction processing.

IBM VM and Conversational Monitoring System (CMS). VM/CMS incorporates several time-sharing options and treats every user as though that user were on the machine alone. VM provides user services by allowing users to access a number of subsystems that it controls. VM provides an editor (XEDIT) similar to the ISPF editor supported in TSO; this is part of CMS.

VM also provides for communications between end users on the same computer and end users on other computers connected to that computer. It does this by using a subsystem known as the Remote Spooling Communications Subsystem (RSCS). VM allows terminal users to execute programs from their terminals and permits the sharing of data and program files between multiple users.

In addition, VM and its subsystems create an environment where each user is provided with his or her own virtual machine. This allows users with little or no knowledge of computer hardware or software to use the facilities of the computer. One last point is that VM and its subsystems are user friendly and are not normally used for system programming activities. Figure 4.4 illustrates a VM software environment with an MVS guest operating system.

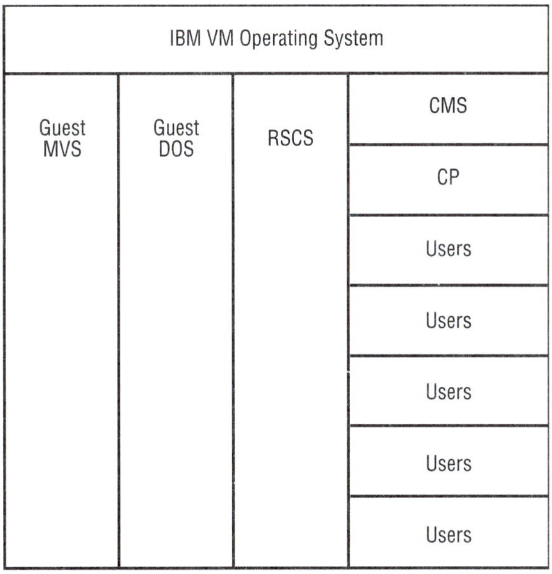

Figure 4.4 VM Software Environment with MVS Guest

CASE STUDY (CONTINUED)

For the Bank of Scotts Valley to meet the initial goal of providing online interactive systems to support its basic activities, it either must develop or acquire applications to provide the services required. These activities include demand deposit checking and savings, automatic teller machines, loans, mortgages, credit card transactions and other financial services. The necessary data will have to be accessible from both a teller branch online environment and a service center batch environment. (Figure 4.5 shows the Bank of Scotts Valley's CPU configuration.)

One of the bank's major objectives is to develop applications that will exploit data as a corporate resource. The bank wishes to use a database management system (DBMS) to manage and support the total operational environment. A DBMS will allow applications to share resources while reducing the time it takes to enhance or create new programs and systems.

The system planners believe that end users (tellers) will not need a free-form query capability because of the nature of the processing activity. Based on this information, the IBM Information Management System (IMS) DBMS is selected for managing the data.

The majority of the bank's data processing/data communications activities will take place in a transaction-based interactive manner; as previously stated, the IBM CICS communications monitor will be used for online processing. This communications monitor was selected because it is a transaction-based communications system that provides acceptable transaction processing throughput.

The bank's data processing organization also has determined that a conversational interactive communications environment is a critical requirement for access to systems and program maintenance. To satisfy this requirement, TSO and ISPF from IBM have been chosen.

The bank also hopes eventually to incorporate a production and development environment. However, the bank cannot, at this point in time, afford a separate development environment for programming and testing applications. To solve this problem, the bank

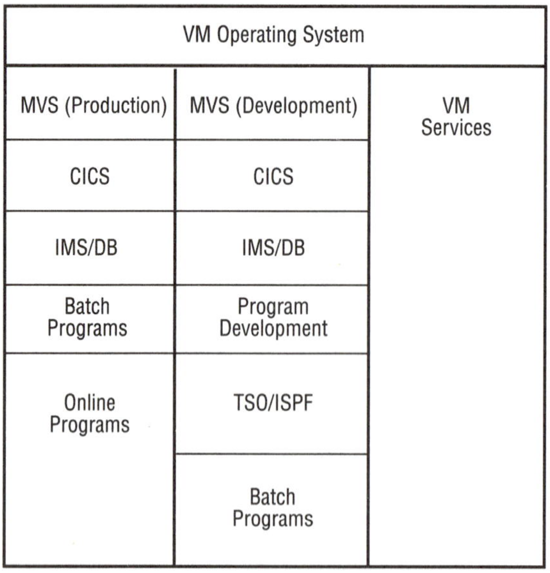

VM Operating System		
MVS (Production)	MVS (Development)	VM Services
CICS	CICS	
IMS/DB	IMS/DB	
Batch Programs	Program Development	
Online Programs	TSO/ISPF	
	Batch Programs	

Figure 4.5 Bank of Scotts Valley CPU Configuration

has decided to install the IBM VM operating system on the computers in each of the service centers. This system will be used to create multiple MVS environments on each machine, one for production and one for testing and development. While this creates a somewhat complicated environment, it will provide a safety net should a development activity get out of control and accidentally terminate the production environment.

REVIEW QUESTIONS

1. What are the differences between a communications monitor and a time-sharing monitor?

2. Can a time-sharing monitor be used in place of a communications monitor, and why would one want to do so?

3. What special considerations do application programmers need to take into account when writing programs that perform online functions?

4. What is the major difference between a conversational online system and a transaction-based online system?

5. What is a time-sharing system primarily designed to do?

Part III

Data Transmission Concepts and Communications Services

CHAPTER 5

Transmission Modes and Methods

INTRODUCTION

Establishing a network that is cost-effective and provides acceptable performance requires extensive planning. Important factors to consider include the bandwidth of the data transmission media (wire or cable) and the type of line required to support the desired bit rate. You also should consider the degree of reliability needed and the level of security required. Finally, the type of directional transmission necessary to accomplish the communications activity should be planned appropriately.

Although the cost for high-speed data communications has been falling rapidly, it is still expensive for the small user to incorporate and maintain high-speed links to remote sites. Small users either pay for capabilities they do not need or do not have the capabilities required due to high costs.

This chapter introduces transmission modes and grades of services to help you determine what type of service, mode and facility are required for a given communications activity.

BANDWIDTH CONCEPTS

Data communications concepts are built on a number of specialized terms used to describe certain functions and activities. An understanding of the following terms is a prerequisite to a solid data communications foundation.

Circuit. This term generally applies to an established medium such as wire, fiber-optic cable or radio frequency waves. A circuit can be impressed with a light or electrical signal to carry analog or digital transmission information.

Channel. This term describes the path for one-way transmission across a link. A circuit may utilize one or more channels.

Carrier. A carrier can be a constant signal on a channel or circuit at some fixed amplitude and frequency. This can be combined with an information-bearing signal such as a data signal of ones and zeros from a terminal. A modulation process within a modem creates a combined signal (carrier plus data signal) to produce output signals suitable for transmission.

Modulation. The term "modulation" refers to the variation of the amplitude (power), frequency or phase (angle) of the carrier in accordance with an input source to represent information, sound or video on a transmission medium.

Baud. Baud is an old term that denotes the number of sine waves or signal changes per second. It is frequently and incorrectly used interchangeably with bits per second to represent the number of bits that can be transmitted across a data communications link per second.

Bits per second (bps). Bits per second is a measurement of how many bits can pass across a data communications link in one second. The terms "baud" and "bits per second," although representing different activities, may in some cases be used interchangeably (see Figure 5.1). Keep in mind that they do not mean the same thing. Baud represents the number of signal changes per second or cycles per second (frequency of the link), whereas bps represents the bit rate of the link.

Decibel Measured (Dbm) Levels. Decibel measured is the strength or intensity of a transmitted signal placed on the communications circuit. Various standards govern the Dbm level for equipment compatibility.

Bandwidth. Bandwidth as it relates to modulation is the total frequency on the carrier available for modulation of the signal. (Figure 5.2 shows the total bandwidth available for the information signal and the signal overhead). The signal does not completely overlay the entire available bandwidth but does use most of it.

The term bandwidth implies some measured amount of frequency available on a channel. Two general bandwidth categories have been defined for communications: broadband and baseband. Figure 5.3 compares baseband and broadband transmissions.

Broadband Transmission

Broadband transmission is also referred to as wideband transmission because the bandwidth is usually wide on the transmission medium and can reach well into the gigahertz range (billions of cycles per second) depending on the media type. The available bandwidth is split (multiplexed) into a number of frequencies or channels by intelligent devices.

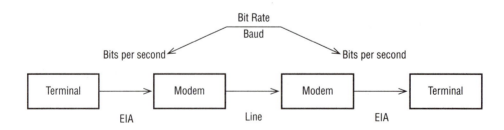

Figure 5.1   Example of Baud Versus Bps

Transmission Modes and Methods

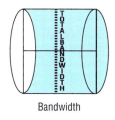
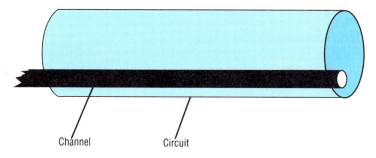

Bandwidth

Channel   Circuit

Figure 5.2 Bandwidth

Baseband Transmission

- Wideband single channel
- May be multiplexed

Broadband Transmission

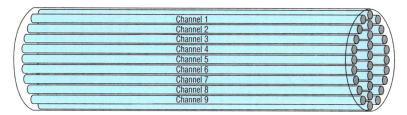

- Uses wide bandwidth medium such as coaxial cable
- Total bandwidth is divided into channels
- Guardbands are established between channels to eliminate crosstalk

Figure 5.3 Baseband and Broadband Transmission

Broadband transmission is employed in Community Access Television (CATV) cable systems and can carry analog as well as data (digital) signals. CATV cable is usually capable of handling a 500-megahertz bandwidth broken into six-megahertz channels. A single television channel requires that amount of bandwidth for video, audio and control information.

Baseband Transmission

Baseband transmission refers to one unit of information (a unit of information is data and control bytes) transmitted over a single channel one message at a time. Baseband transmission is extensively used in local area networks and consists of a single-channel, high-speed data path for the interconnection of workstations and computers. Because baseband transmission is used primarily for digital transmission under controlled distances, data transfer takes place at very high speeds, often well into the range of megabits per second.

MODES OF TRANSMISSION

For wired, cabled or radio frequency communications, three transmission modes exist for the transfer of information across a network link: simplex, half duplex and full duplex. Use of a specific mode depends on hardware requirements and budget constraints. Most installed lines are full duplex because carriers primarily support only full-duplex configurations. (Communications hardware and software also operate using these concepts.)

Simplex Transmission

In the simplex transmission mode, the operation of a channel or link is limited to one direction only with no capability of reversing the directional flow. The terminal will either be transmitting or receiving. Simplex transmission is analogous to one-way streets, escalators, doorbells and home security systems.

An example of the simplex transmission mode used in data processing and data communications is the remote station printer. This device is used to create printed output such as that used in airline ticketing systems. Most other types of printers require more than a simplex link to communicate status information back to the sending device. Bear in mind that some remote printers have large enough buffers to accept the entire transmission and do not need to communicate status information back.

A badge reader is another example of a device that can use simplex transmission. In some badge readers, the identification card is read and the data is transmitted to the intelligent device on a simplex link. The intelligent device validates the card and sends a signal to the door lock to open using another simplex circuit.

Card readers also use simplex links. CRTs without keyboards, like those found in airport terminals, are excellent examples of simplex transmission, because they are output devices only.

In modern data processing/data communications, simplex transmission is not frequently used because the receiver normally needs the ability to send error or control signals to the transmitter. Returning signals back to the transmitter is usually required for acknowledging receipt of the data or indicating that a problem has been encountered.

Half-Duplex Transmission

Half duplex is a transmission mode in which the channel operates in either direction, but not both directions at the same time. In most communications environments, half duplex is the predominant transmission mode in use today. It is important to note, however, that with the speed of lines rapidly increasing and the costs correspondingly decreasing, most lines are in fact full duplex. Half-duplex operation is largely due to the capabilities and costs of the communications equipment and the type of data communications taking place. In a conversational environment, in which one side will be listening while the other is sending, this probably would employ the use of a half-duplex link.

A major disadvantage of half-duplex transmission is the time required to change the direction of the data flow so that the other end can respond. In a typical half-duplex operation, line reversal can add up to 500 milliseconds of delay time on some types of links. This is referred to as line turnaround time and can range from 50 to 500 ms, depending on the distance the signal must travel.

An example of the use of half-duplex transmission in data processing and data communications is the line printer. Most printers operate using half-duplex transmission because they must send control and status information back to the sending device. For example, a printer with a paper jam needs to inform the CPU it cannot accept any more data at the present time. Terminals also typically operate in half-duplex mode because they normally either are sending or receiving but do not perform both functions concurrently.

Some modems actually transmit in full-duplex mode using half-duplex facilities by splitting the channel in half. Each side of the link uses one of the subchannels. The only problem with this technique is the reduced speed of the link in each direction. It is usually half of the total available speed because only half of the bandwidth is available for each direction.

Full-Duplex Transmission

Full-duplex transmission is considered bidirectional in that data communications occurs in both directions at the same time. Two simplex channels are required for full-duplex transmission; each channel carries signals in one direction. One might look at full-duplex channels as two paired simplex channels.

One example of full-duplex transmission in data processing and data communications is the channel-to-channel interface between two processors. This is required when the processors are in continuous communications with one another. The Tandem fault-tolerant computer system and its communications network operate in a full-duplex environment. Terminal controllers that interface to multiple terminals may also operate in full-duplex mode, which would allow them to send and receive data to and from their terminals and the processor at the same time.

Full-duplex lines are often used to support half-duplex terminals so that no turnaround time delay is encountered when reversing the direction of the data flow. While this is more expensive because of full-duplex line charges, it reduces the amount of time required for a device to acknowledge receipt of the transmission, which can be considerable over long distances.

GRADES OF SERVICE

An incredible number of link service providers support the world of data communications. Standards have been established by both the industry and international standards organizations to ensure worldwide compatibility between communications providers. Various types of services are offered by American Telephone & Telegraph, Microwave Communications Incorporated, the regional Bell operating companies and the independent operating companies. In addition, other private companies also offer competitive services for data transmission.

The communications line, whether it be wire, fiber-optic cable, microwave circuit or other types of circuits, is the physical portion of the communications link. The physical link normally is divided into two or more channels depending on its rated bandwidth. A channel is a logical path through the physical link over which information and data flow.

Channels are described in terms of transmission type or transmission mode. Grade of service, or the link's information-carrying capacity, refers to the volume or speed in bits per second that a channel can handle. Grades of service as discussed here refer to the various types of service offered by most telephone operating companies.

Bit transmission speed is determined by the available frequency bandwidth of the channel. Bandwidth is one of several important characteristics that you must consider when configuring a communications link. Bandwidth is the difference in hertz (or cycles per second) between the lowest and highest available frequencies of that channel. This available frequency bandwidth determines the overall carrying capacity of the transmission link.

Be careful to analyze bit rate requirements when ordering and installing lines. It would be foolish to install a megabit capacity wideband line for personal computer communications; that would be comparable to a truck driver who uses an 18-wheel truck to transport two trash cans to the dump. Capacity planning is vital to the design and implementation of a data communications network. It often can take extended periods of time and a great deal of money to install or upgrade line capabilities if future usage projections were not accurate.

The major telephone companies generally offer three basic grades of telephone service — subvoice, voiceband and wideband — but in some cases, only voiceband and wideband services are available. Specialized grades of services such as Digital Dataphone Service (DDS) and T1 are usually offered to organizations that need bulk or high-speed data transmission capabilities. The three grades of service are generally defined in terms of available bandwidth:

- Subvoice, also referred to as narrowband service, is a low-speed service with a bandwidth of 0 to 300 hertz for a total bandwidth of 300 hertz. Bit transmission speeds range from 45 bits per second to 150 bits per second. A subvoice channel is also referred to as a telegraph or telex service channel, because it is used primarily for telex and telegraph activities.

- The voiceband grade is considered a medium-speed service with a frequency of 300 to 3300 hertz, for a total bandwidth of 3000 hertz. This is also the bandwidth of a standard voice-grade circuit used between homes and central telephone offices. Bit transmission speeds range from 60 bits per second up to 19,200 bits per second. Speeds over 4800 bits per second are possible with modems using advanced modulation techniques on leased or dial-up lines. This grade of service is primarily used for dial-up switched facilities.

- The wideband or broadband grade is considered a high-speed service and extends from 3300 hertz into the megahertz range. Transmission speeds range from 19,200 bits per second to greater than 1.544 million bits per second. It may be implemented for multiple voiceband channels that are multiplexed into groups, supergroups or portions of line groups. It is used for the transmission of large amounts of data over high-speed links.

Not all hardware links support all grades of services, so be sure the lines selected support the entire geographic network. This is particularly true for the faster links because they are designed more for high-speed multiplexed service that may not be available in certain locations. Slower links, associated with most grades of service, are usually more widely available.

TRANSMISSION METHODS

As was previously stated, transmission modes apply to the direction of the transmission and the channel. Additionally, there are two basic transmission methods — asynchronous and synchronous — for moving the information across the link. Each of these methods is used with specific network architectures, hardware, transmission speeds and transmission protocols.

Asynchronous Transmission

Asynchronous transmission is really an offshoot of the old telegraph system and the Baudot code. This method operated by inserting start and stop bits in front of and behind the data bits to indicate the beginning and ending points of a binary-coded character of data. The telegraph system transmitted a number of timed electrical on or off pulses that, when combined in groups, made up a character. Because each character was sent randomly (no order or sequence to the letters or numbers), timing was essential for the duration of the electrical pulses that made up that character.

This transmission method migrated to the data communications environment and is referred to as asynchronous transmission. Because of the higher speeds associated with data communications, start and stop pulses (bits) are required to separate each character. The asynchronous transmission method follows this principal and is also referred to as start/stop transmission (see Figure 5.4). The addition of start and stop bits for each byte transmitted adds up to a 20 percent to 30 percent overhead, which reduces the number of data bits transmitted.

Synchronous Transmission

Because of the inefficiencies associated with asynchronous transmission, another procedure was devised to allow for higher transmission speed with better error detection and correction capabilities. The synchronous transmission method is the principal transmission method currently used for high-speed communications (see Figure 5.5).

The synchronous transmission method does not use start and stop bits to denote the beginning and ending of each character being transmitted. The data is framed (blocked),

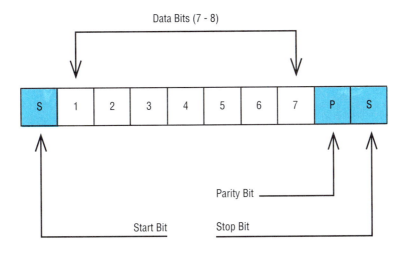

Figure 5.4   Asynchronous Transmission

and a synchronization character or bit pattern is used to synchronize the frame of bytes being transmitted. The synchronous transmission method requires this synchronous sequence to be transmitted in order for the receiving terminal to understand and accept the data being sent. The receiver must know when to expect the first bit of each data block being transmitted. This is also known as *character* or *byte synchronization*. In addition, the bit stream to be transmitted must be sent at a fixed clock rate to ensure that the transmitting circuits are sending bits out at the same time that the receiving circuits are taking them in. This is known as *bit synchronization* or *clocking*.

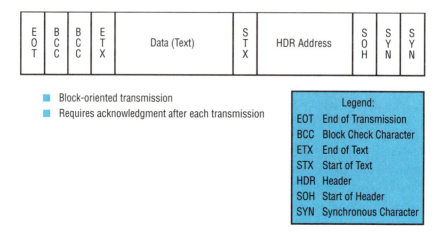

Figure 5.5 Synchronous Transmission

CASE STUDY (CONTINUED)

Up to this point, the bank has not had to support a communications network other than to perform batch file transfers between service centers. It has accomplished this by using standard, low-speed telephone facilities. The link that connects the two service centers is a half-duplex, low-speed line that operates asynchronously because there was no need for full-duplex, simultaneous transmission. The bank uses a voice-grade link and asynchronous half-duplex transmission method because of the cost associated with the transmission components and telephone facilities. (Figure 5.6 shows the evolution of the bank as it implements a data communications network.)

The new implementation plan for the bank mandates extensive communications capabilities to support all of its operations. This calls for a variety of high-speed wideband and low-speed voiceband and baseband links to interconnect the branches and service centers. Each branch will have a full-duplex, voiceband synchronous link to its regional service center, and a second link that will be used for backup in the event of a failure.

The service centers will be synchronously interconnected using high-speed, full-duplex wideband links. Multiple lines will be installed to ensure that backup capabilities are available in the event of a line failure. Within the branches, each terminal will be hard-wired to a central transmission point within the building via half-duplex, synchronous low-speed links.

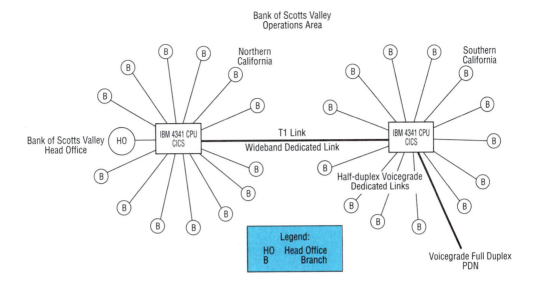

Figure 5.6 Bank of Scotts Valley Network

REVIEW QUESTIONS

1. Define the term "channel."
2. What is baseband transmission?
3. True or false: Simplex transmission is transmission in both directions but not simultaneously.
4. True or false: Full-duplex transmission is the most common transmission mode.
5. True or false: Half-duplex transmission allows two-way communication at the same time.
6. What are the three grades of transmission service available for data transmission?
7. What type of transmission, analog or digital, are current telephone transmission networks designed to support?
8. What type of transmission mode are most types of data communications equipment designed to support?
9. What are the two transmission methods available for data communications?
10. Which transmission method requires clocking information?

CHAPTER
6

Communications Services

INTRODUCTION

Carrier communications link services offer the media by which data is transported from one point to another. Such services vary depending on organizational needs.

Most telephone service companies that provide data communications in North America have a wide selection of methods available for the transportation of data. Larger organizations are more likely to install dedicated links because of large capacity requirements, whereas smaller companies often use the services of a link provider. Even those companies that install dedicated links must, to some extent, follow the conditions set by the carrier. Table 6.1 lists types of carrier services.

Many smaller organizations elect to use the dial-up telephone network for data communications because their transmission requirements are such that acceptable performance can be realized with this type of service. Other organizations find that hard-wired dedicated links provide improved conditions for error detection and correction, increased speed capabilities and multiplexing flexibility.

PUBLIC AND PRIVATE CARRIERS

Data processing and data communications services are provided by two types of carriers: common (or public) carriers and private carriers. Common or public carriers are companies that provide voice or data communications services to the public. They include organizations such as telephone companies, computer hardware vendors, time-sharing service vendors and data carriers. Many of these companies offer similar services that will be discussed later in this chapter.

Common Carriers

While there are more than 3,000 telephone companies in the U.S., over 95 percent of all revenues are generated by the regional Bell operating companies (RBOCs), AT&T, MCI Communications Corp., Sprint and General Telephone. These, as well as most other telephone companies, offer a full range of services from dial-up voice networks to value-added public data networks. Figure 6.1 illustrates the public switched telephone network carriers and the areas in which they operate

Other Carriers

Western Union Corp., founded as a telegraph company in 1851, generates a substantial portion of its revenues from custom-built private wire networks, TWX, Telex and data services. Telex service was introduced in the U.S. in 1958 and currently has more than 150,000 subscriber terminals in its domestic network and more than 500,000 terminals worldwide. Users also can access other Western Union services such as Data Com, a low-speed channel service for subscribers on a point-to-point basis.

Another available service is Info Com. This is a computer-controlled store-and-forward message-switching system that allows users to have their own pseudo-network using the Western Union communications links. Other services include mailgram, satellite links and hot-line telephone service.

The Southern Pacific Communications Company (SPCC) offers three separate types of communications services: Sprint for voice transmission, Speedfax for facsimile service and data dial for data transmission. SPCC has established a nationwide network consisting of microwave, cable and satellite facilities and offers a complete line of services.

Satellite Services

Over the past few years, satellite communications have become more popular for certain transmission activities because of the reduction in costs and greater circuit availability. This form of transmission service is excellent for long-distance and high-speed communications. Several telephone companies offer satellite service either by connecting subscribers through

Type of Service	Bit Speed	Standard
Switched	to 19.2 Kbps	North America
Dedicated	to 56 Kbps	North America
DDS	to 64 Kbps	North America
DS-X	up to 800 Mbps	International
ISDN	up to 2 Mbps	International

Table 6.1 Types of Carrier Services

their land line (surface) facilities or, in some cases, through the placement of on-site uplink and downlink equipment installed at the subscriber's various locations.

Value-Added Carriers

Value-added carriers provide services using transmission facilities leased from common carriers such as AT&T and MCI. Value-added carriers such as Tymnet, McDonnell Douglas Network Systems Company provide network facilities that are connected through the use of computers and other specialized equipment designed to enhance the ability to transfer data. These enhancements include extensive error detection, code conversion and encryption using data packets that are switched (transferred) from one computer to another until they reach their final destination. This is referred to as a *public packet-switching network*. Packet switching is a cost-effective method for transmission of data by small computer users because packets usually consist of a number of pieces of data.

International Record Carriers

International voice and data communications between the U.S. and other countries have been provided within the U.S. by such common carriers as AT&T, MCI, RCA Global Communications, ITT World Communications, Western Union International, TRT Communications and FTC Communications. These organizations follow the guidelines issued by the Consultative Committee for International Telephone and Telegraph (CCITT) for interconnection. While they cannot directly have point-to-point international communications links in many locations, companies have formulated agreements with their international counterparts to provide end-to-end service to their subscribers.

Figure 6.1 Common and Long-Distance Carriers

Public Data Network Services

In many cases, using a value-added carrier service is less expensive than the services of the various common carriers; however, both provide public data network (PDN) services. Use of a public data network provides an advantage in that error control and routing are usually features of the PDN. Typically, users of PDN services must provide their own packet assembly/disassembly devices (PADs) to convert their data into synchronous packets. The PAD can be viewed as a minicomputer that creates high-level data link control frames of data that originate from user terminals and devices.

Public data network providers usually have large support organizations and provide a variety of additional services. One such service is education in the use of network services and available systems. The PDN vendor also may provide communications networks for the user's offices. Public data networks are generally implemented according to CCITT standards such as those described in X.21, X.25 and X.29. (Refer to Appendix A for a list of standards.) The carriers are regulated by the U.S. Federal Communications Commission and follow guidelines established by the International Standards Organization (ISO). Expenses associated with use depend on the types of lines and services required.

Time-Sharing Service Providers

Time-sharing services are provided by independent data communications and data processing companies to users who want to control their own processing or communications activities. These companies usually are not large enough to have their own data processing operation. They also may wish to use an outside service for security or convenience. Some time-sharing vendors have value-added services such as packet switching or protocol conversion that facilitate communications from one computer format to another. This feature allows the user to take advantage of software available on other manufacturers' hardware.

With the arrival of small, inexpensive, powerful personal computers and minicomputers, typical users of time-sharing services include organizations requiring services such as supercomputer activities. Service providers normally will include terminals and lines to a subscriber's location. Additionally, service providers make available certain types of application programs and, for a fee, will provide consulting and design services. Fees usually include a monthly service charge as well as additional charges for connect time, number of lines printed and number of bytes of disk storage used.

Time-sharing service vendors generally implement their systems according to international standards such as X.21, X.25 and X.29, which are identified in Appendix A, and use software provided by the hardware supplier. Time-sharing service vendors are regulated by the U.S. FCC and generally follow guidelines established by the ISO.

Packet-Switching System Services

Many PDN vendors provide an inexpensive, efficient method of transferring data called *packet switching*. Companies use this type of service to transfer data nationally and internationally without having to lease lines or pay for telephone company services they do not need. Using the concept of packets of data, which is the encapsulation of the data with communications control information, store-and-forward techniques can be used for data transmission. Store-and-forward techniques imply that the data can be temporarily stored at some intermediate point within the PDN. This may be needed if the circuits are in use at the final destination.

Packet-switching system vendors normally provide value-added services to users such as code set conversion, data encryption services, communications format conversion and error detection. The PDNs provide end-to-end data transmission regardless of format or hardware. The user need only send the data in the format it was created and the packet-switching software or hardware assembles the data into packets and disassembles the packets back into the user's format. Companies providing packet-switching systems generally provide the end links to subscriber sites. This is an excellent alternative for transferring large amounts of data not required for immediate processing.

TRANSMISSION SERVICES

One issue that must be addressed when planning a network is providing sufficient capabilities to satisfy all of the organization's users without having a large amount of unused line capacity going to waste. To understand this problem fully and provide an acceptable solution, we need to look at how capacity has been provided in the past.

In the past, if an organization wished to implement a data communications network, the first step was to determine the required number of lines and the desired capacity. The next step was to install the lines and bring the network up. Planners needed to ensure that enough capacity was available to satisfy peak-period time demands; yet this often translated into excess capacity in low-load situations. This is a problem of today as well.

Excess line capacity is wasteful in terms of the costs associated with having unused resources. It is important to note, however, that as line costs decrease, many companies do not consider this as great a problem. Also, in many locations around the world, waste is not an issue because the only link capability available is obtained from the government's telecommunications authority. How, then, does the telecommunications authority ensure that the links it is providing are being used to maximum availability and return on investment? One way is for the link provider to define different types of data communications service, as has been done in Europe by the various communications authorities.

The various levels of service provided in Europe have evolved into a worldwide series of standards used for the movement of data across internationally shared lines and facilities. This involves a data transport method that formats data into packets. Packet switching is widely used by PDN vendors and common carriers around the world.

A packet is a self-contained entity that includes a variable amount of data as well as any addresses required to deliver it to its destination (see Figure 6.2). Packets are very efficient for moving data across public links because each packet is a self-contained entity. This allows packets to be mixed (multiplexed) from multiple sources onto the link. Each packet contains sending and receiving addresses that are used by the packet network hardware and software for routing and delivery. Several types of packets have been defined and are offered to accommodate a variety of services.

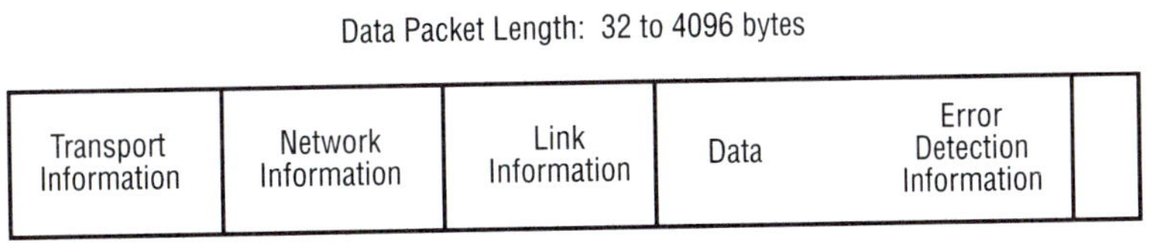

Data Packet Length: 32 to 4096 bytes

Transport Information	Network Information	Link Information	Data	Error Detection Information

Figure 6.2 Typical Data Packet Format

Datagram Packet Service

As mentioned earlier, packet services originated in Europe to support transborder data communications. The first defined packet format was referred to as a *datagram packet*. A transborder network, the X.25 packet-switched network, was defined by the various European telecommunications agencies to support the datagram concept. X.25 is a CCITT standard designed to provide a packet delivery service across multiple networks. The original standard covers basic services and does not guarantee that the packet will arrive intact if corrupted during transport. Arriving packets are not delivered in any predefined sequence and no capability exists for acknowledgment of the received packet to the sender. Figure 6.3 shows an example of an X.25 network in Europe.

Datagram services have improved as they have matured. Now it is possible to obtain error correction and routing services, which are provided by other supporting software in the network. Basic datagram service was primarily designed for videotext (video information service) activities, but because of widespread use of X.25 types of networks around the world, two types of datagram packets now exist: unreliable datagrams and reliable datagrams.

Unreliable Datagrams

The unreliable datagram service does not guarantee delivery of the data packet to its destination. If end-to-end confirmation of delivery is desired, it must be provided by higher-layer protocol software. This level of packet service does not ensure that delivery will be without error or that packets will be delivered in the same sequence in which they were transmitted. Unreliable datagram service was originally developed to provide an inexpensive delivery service for data, text and videotext information. Videotext is a television- or computer-based service provided to subscribers. Because videotext data is transmitted on a repetitive basis, a damaged or lost packet would be resent automatically on the next transmission cycle.

Reliable Datagrams

Reliable datagram service provides improved capabilities over unreliable datagram services. It ensures that data packets delivered to the network interface from user sites will be delivered to their addressed destinations. Additional levels of service include improved routing and error detection, as well as notification back to the sender that the packet was received intact. Most public networks provide reliable datagram service.

Virtual Circuit Service

While datagram services were a step in the right direction for the occasional user or transaction-based activities such as interbank communications, another type of service was required for the dedicated or interactive user. The service for the interactive user, referred to as *virtual circuit service*, is designed to provide end-to-end delivery, error detection and correction and delivery confirmation of the data packets across the network. A virtual circuit is a temporary dedicated channel between the sender and the receiver for a specific amount of time. This is similar to the type of circuit established for a telephone call. Virtual circuits guarantee sequenced, acknowledged delivery of each packet transmitted from the sender to the receiver. Virtual circuit services follow international specifications that are provided in vendor-specific software. This software is defined to follow and support several layers of the ISO's Open Systems Interconnect (OSI) architecture.

Communications Services

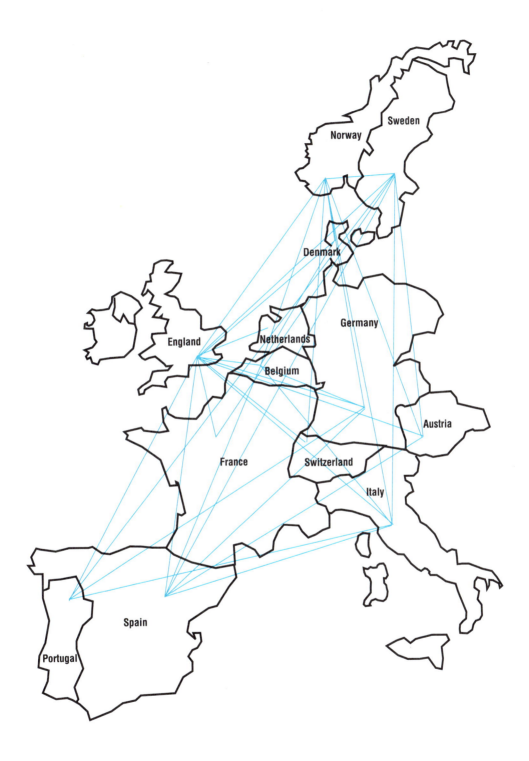

Figure 6.3 X.25 Network in Europe

Switched Circuit Services

Switched circuit service is similar to dedicated links or to virtual circuit service except that it eliminates the need for source or destination addresses after the connection has been established. There is no need to packetize data because the circuit is always available for the exclusive use of the two communicating stations. This type of service is usually found in networks that are self-contained (no internetwork communications activity is supported) and is not really considered a network service. Figure 6.4 illustrates a virtual circuit service contained within a switched circuit service.

TYPES OF COMMUNICATIONS SERVICES

Most worldwide carriers offer five basic types of services and options to ensure compatibility between foreign networks. The five basic services are:

- Dial-up service (public-switched telephone network)
- Dedicated or private-line service with or without conditioning to improve performance
- All-digital service (DDS)
- T-level and DS-level high-speed wideband service
- ISDN (Integrated Digital Services Network), an all-digital network service

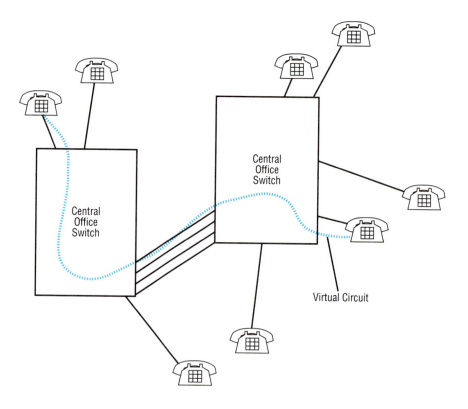

Figure 6.4   Virtual Circuit on the Telephone Network

In addition to the five basic types of services, each carrier offers a variety of other services. Two examples are AT&T's 800 data transmission service and MCI's VNET service. Figure 6.5 illustrates a network using all of the five basic communications links.

PUBLIC SWITCHED TELEPHONE NETWORK

Transmission links — including most of the local loop telephone circuits to central office connections — currently are designed to transport analog signals rather than digital signals. A local loop can be defined as wires running from the central office to a residence or business (see Figure 6.6).

With the development of new digital technologies, a rapid conversion has begun to take place and digital circuits are now encountered more frequently. This is mainly due to the availability of fiber optics and its superior transmission characteristics. Additionally, the digital conversion and switching equipment required to support this type of transmission are more readily available. Bear in mind that analog transmission is still used and will be for some time to come because of its lower costs, wide availability and adequate capabilities for many activities.

Digital signals do not travel very far over standard telephone wires without expensive pieces of hardware called digital repeaters that reamplify the signals at periodic intervals. However, they can travel extensive distances without reamplification when converted to the analog format and modulated to emulate a digital format. A modem is needed to convert the digital signal from a computer or a terminal into an analog signal.

The public-switched telephone network is also referred to as the direct distance dialing network (DDN). This network uses a variety of cabling methods to interconnect the various independent telephone company central offices with the subscriber sites. (Figure

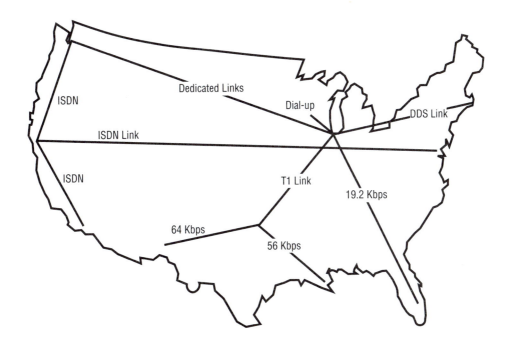

Figure 6.5   A Network Using Different Types of Links

6.7 shows an example of the public-switched telephone dial-up network.) The majority of these links can be referred to as local loop links that define subscriber-to-central office connections. This wiring consists of a two-wire pair from the home and four-wire pairs from newer buildings that house businesses. Both types of wiring are referred to as *twisted-pair wiring* because the two wire strands are wrapped around each other to reduce attenuation and echo that appear as crosstalk in a telephone conversation.

Many regional telephone companies that provide end-point connections are beginning to install fiber-optic cable rather than twisted copper pairs because the former has tremendous advantages over twisted pairs. The use of fiber optics solves the principle problems of noise and speed restrictions inherent in the PSTN.

DEDICATED TELEPHONE SERVICE

Many organizations require the full-time services of a communications link that operates at higher speeds and is more reliable than the PSTN. Network providers have developed a solution to this problem by offering hard-wired dedicated links between customers' locations. These dedicated or leased telephone lines are also known as private facilities; a dedicated circuit is permanently in place between two end points or shared among multiple

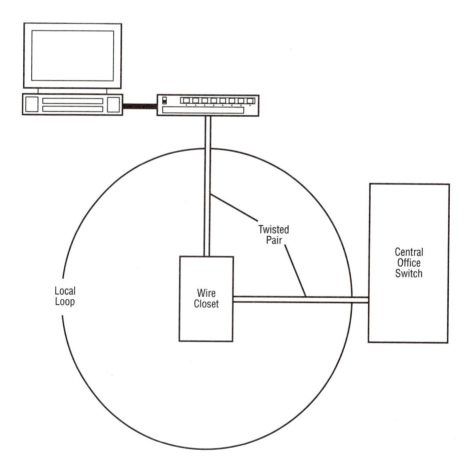

Figure 6.6   Local Loop Telephone Network

points. Dedicated lines usually provide service on a point-to-point or multipoint line configuration. This type of line is called a type 3002 line and normally consists of four-wire twisted-pair circuits that support half-duplex or full-duplex operations. Dedicated links also can support microwave, satellite or fiber-optic transmission.

The subscriber has sole use of the link, which is a permanent circuit. Line availability is guaranteed, along with some base level of service. The base level of service can include maximum acceptable values for delay distortion, impulse noise hits and bit and frequency error rates. Data transmission is normally accomplished using one of the synchronous transmission methods. Leased lines can support speeds in excess of 64 Kbps.

Conditioning

Standard dedicated links often do not provide sufficient noise and transmission control for high-speed data communications. Lines can be tailored for better performance using a feature called *conditioning*. AT&T, MCI, Sprint and the various Bell operating telephone companies provide leased analog lines suitable for data transmission based on specifications established by the FCC that define signal-to-noise ratios and permissible signal strength gain from the transmitter. Table 6.2 lists parameters associated with conditioning.

FCC Tariff No. 260 defines additional capabilities for a basic voice channel that is intended for use with data applications. These additional capabilities, referred to as *line conditioning*, include five levels of C conditioning and two levels of D conditioning.

C-level conditioning controls attenuation and envelope delay distortion by providing equalization of the circuit. (Refer to Chapter 7 for more information on attenuation distortion and envelope delay.) Equalization capabilities allow both ends of the link to be balanced to each other in terms of noise and signal strength. This is accomplished by inserting equalizers on the line between the customer's site and the central office.

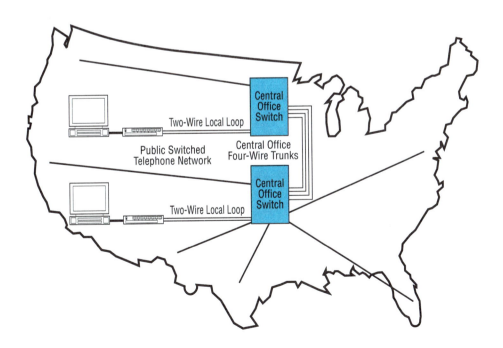

Figure 6.7 Example of a Dial-up Telephone Network

D-level conditioning controls nonlinear distortion and signal-to-noise ratios. D conditioning is accomplished by matching the modem's signal strength, noise levels and distortion parameters to the line specifications.

HIGH-SPEED WIDEBAND SERVICES

A variety of wideband digital and analog services may be offered by public carriers depending on location. An analog service is usually incorporated for speeds up to 1.544 Mbps because analog circuits can manage reliable data transfer into the millions of bits per second. One problem with analog circuits, though, is that they experience a higher bit error rate than digital circuits. High-speed analog circuits come in various bandwidths suitable for various equipment and requirements.

Carriers also offer a variety of digital services. Techniques have been developed to carry a digital representation of on and off bits across analog facilities at very high speeds. This transmission technique provides improved error detection and correction and is a much more reliable data transfer method.

Of major importance are the T-type carrier services. These are also referred to as DS-x services. Two categories of T services are DS service and fractional T1 service. Both of these services can employ either analog or digital facilities.

	Nonconditioned 3002 Channel		With C1 Conditioning		With C2 Conditioning		With C4 Conditioning		With D Conditioning
Frequency Range in Hertz (Hz)	300-3000		300-3000		300-3000		300-3200		
Attenuation Distortion (Net Loss at 1000 Hz)	Frequency Range	Decibel Variation	Frequency Response	Decibel Variation	Frequency Response	Decibel Variation	Frequency Response	Decibel Variation	
	300-3000	-3 to +12	300-2700	-2 to +6	300-3000	-2 to +6	300-3200	-2 to +6	
	500-2500	-2 to +8	1000-2400	-1 to +3	500-2800	-1 to +3	500-3000	-2 to +3	
			300-3000	-3 to +12					
Delay Distortion in Microseconds (µs)	Less than 1750 µs from 800 to 2600 Hz.		Less than 1000 µs from 1000 to 2400 Hz. Less than 1750 µs from 800 to 2600 Hz.		Less than 500 µs from 1000 to 2600 Hz. Less than 1500 µs from 600 to 2600 Hz. Less than 3000 µs from 500 to 2800 Hz.		Less than 300 µs from 1000 to 2600 Hz. Less than 500 µs from 800 to 2800 Hz. Less than 1500 µs from 600 to 3000 Hz. Less than 3000 µs from 500 to 3000 Hz.		
Signal to Noise (dB)	24		24		24		24		28
Nonlinear Distortion Signal to 2nd Harmonic (dB)	25		25		25		25		35
Signal to 3rd Harmonic (dB)l	30		30		30		30		40

Table 6.2 Conditioning Parameters

DIGITAL SERVICES

Dataphone Digital Service

Dataphone Digital Service (DDS) was originally an AT&T service, but it now more generally describes a digital service provided by most major carriers and regional telephone operating companies (see Figure 6.8). DDS services consist of leased digital line circuits that provide direct-connection synchronous transmission of pure digital sources. DDS provides network timing and synchronization using a master clock and slave subordinate clocks, which keeps all clocks on the various network nodes operating at the same rate. Timing signals are also provided to subscribers for synchronization within the network.

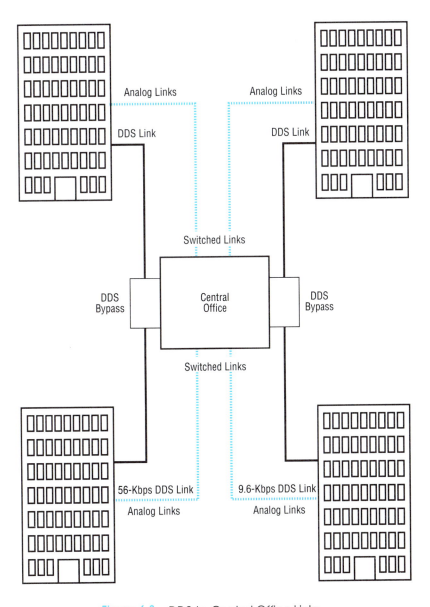

Figure 6.8 DDS-to-Central Office Links

AT&T's DDS network access is provided to end users at over 120 local access and transport areas (LATAs) serving more than 400 cities in the U.S. It can be connected to Canada's Data Route service at four border crossings and connects to more than 70 locations throughout Canada.

DDS operates at rates from 4800 bits per second to 64 kilobits per second. DDS also requires a DSU or CSU, which are similar to modems except that they operate digitally. DDS is primarily a full-duplex service but can be operated in half-duplex or simplex mode if necessary. The transmission rate is set at the telephone company's central office.

A DDS centralized testing facility provides dynamic testing and automatic rerouting of the data upon circuit outage or network degradation. DDS is usually guaranteed to provide 99.5 percent error-free transmission seconds at 56 Kbps with 99 percent transmission availability. This type of service is implemented using a hierarchy of multiplexers within the various telephone company's systems. Typically, DDS supports high-speed links such as intermediate length regional lines (T1, T2 carrier [64 Kbps]) and long-haul microwave facilities.

DDS service requires the removal of loading coils from the local loops (the computer site and the central office), thus providing an unloaded leased line capable of carrying digital pulses to and from the customer's location. DDS also requires the use of regenerative repeaters every few thousand feet. Repeaters are needed to take the incoming digital signal, refresh it and pass it along to the next repeater or switch. DDS service is somewhat expensive, but the cost is rapidly decreasing in response to competitive service offerings. (DDS must compete against the newer high-speed digital services and fractional T1 digital services.) An important point to remember is that DDS can operate over a twisted-pair configuration.

High-Speed Digital Service

In addition to DDS, many other high-speed wideband voice and data transmission services operate digitally. To provide digital transmission, the carriers had to develop a method to manage and control the digitized channels. Channel information (data or voice) is carried within data frames, also known as DS-1 signal frames, that can contain 192 user information bits and one control frame bit. Twelve DS-1 signal frames are grouped together to create a D4 superframe (see Figure 6.9).

Each superframe contains information for signaling and synchronization (in addition to the 12 DS-1 signal frames). DS superframes are designed to be carried across all types of DS links. All U.S. domestic and some international carriers follow the DS specifications, but in some cases the available bit rates vary from carrier to carrier. This is mainly due to the carrier's need to maintain timing and control on the link.

DS links usually consist of customers' time-division multiplexed traffic channels. Time-division multiplexing (TDM) is the sharing of a single line between multiple devices by allocating time on the line to each device. (Figure 6.10 shows DS links and multiplexer connectivity.) Digital service is divided into categories based on the speed of the link. A DS-0 link is equivalent to one voice circuit of 64 Kbps. A traffic channel (DS-0) may carry either voice or data and will contain signaling information to identify the data carried.

DS-1 is a 1.544-Mbps link that is usually multiplexed into 24 64-kilobit channels. DS-1 is generally referred to as a T1 carrier. While DS-1 is rated as a 1.544-Mbps link, unless the carrier offers clear-channel capability, only 1.344 megabits per second are available to the end user. This is primarily due to the various carriers' need to maintain timing on the network using what is referred to as *one's density*. One's density uses 192 Kbps to maintain proper timing between nodes on the network.

DS-1C operates at 3.152 Mbps and consists of two T1 TDM lines. It can be broken into 96 traffic channels of 64 Kbps each. This is referred to as a T1C carrier.

DS-2 is referred to as T2 carrier service (6.312 Mbps) and consists of four T1 TDM links providing 96 DM-0 channels (64 Kbps).

DS-3 service (T3 carrier) operates at 44.736 megabits per second and provides the capacity for 28 T1 channels supporting 672 DS-0 voice channels.

DS-4 service (T4 carrier) provides 168 TDM T1 lines for a total capacity of 4032 DS-0 channels of 64 Kbps. The total speed of DS-4 service is 274.176 Mbps.

Many types of service support the links described above, such as fractional T1, insert, drop and bypass services. Fractional T1 allows customers to use a portion of a T1 link for end-to-end dedicated services; this can be provided by the carrier company. Insert and drop capabilities allow the user to specify insertion and drop-off points for parts of a leased T1 circuit.

DS services are offered worldwide. However, in Europe, T-span services use a different channel allocation that creates some bit rate incompatibility between global networks. In North America T1 rates are 1.544 Mbps spanning 24 channels and in Europe, 2.048 Mbps spanning 30 channels.

Today, many carriers are offering clear-channel signalling, which allows the user to bypass the framing conventions normally found with DS-0 and DS links. Clear-channel capabilities provide the user with the entire available bandwidth minus a small amount of bit overhead needed for timing control.

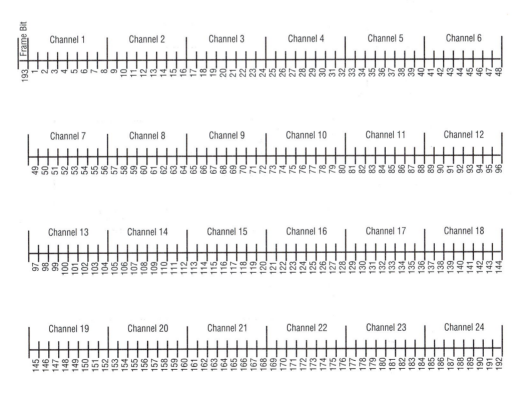

Figure 6.9 DS-1 Frame Formats

ISDN

The design criteria and specifications for ISDN were based on the rapid and uncontrolled growth of digital services using the analog facilities provided by worldwide carrier services. These carrier services typically provide a mixture of links that consist of two-wire twisted pairs, four-wire twisted pairs, coaxial cable, microwave, satellite links and fiber-optic cable (see Figure 6.11).

Many different types of cable are now installed as a result of the millions of miles of links put in place during the past 50 years and the evolution of the technology over that time. User requirements and expenses also have played a major role in dictating the services offered by the telephone companies. In examining the capabilities of these services, three problems become apparent:

- Different speed restrictions exist for each type of link.
- Different error rates apply to the different types of media used.
- Different types of support equipment may be required.

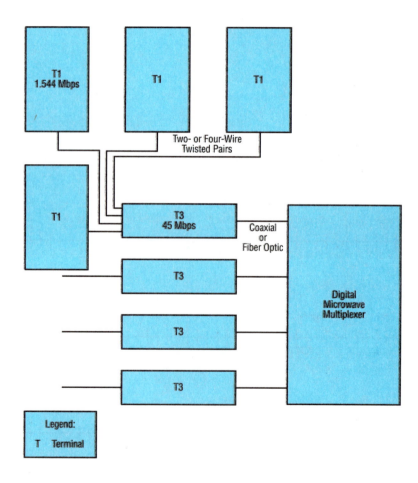

Figure 6.10   Example of High-Speed Transmission

Communications Services

While these problems present little difficulty for low-speed links, high-speed data transfer places a greater strain on existing media and facilities. As the world becomes increasingly digitally oriented, the multitude of existing techniques will not be able to handle demands efficiently. All-digital technologies are needed for the effective integration of digital voice, high-speed data, video, private branch exchange (PBX) and local area networks.

In order to meet such network demands, the development of an all-digital network standard was proposed to the CCITT by its membership. The result was ISDN, which is designed to provide an all-digital, end-to-end pathway for the transmission of various types of digital signals. It comprises a series of 29 pending standards referred to as the I.400 series. (Refer to Appendix A for a list of these standards.)

ISDN is partially implemented now but will require years to be fully implemented. It will provide multiple conversions of the data along the transmission circuit, avoiding distortion and processor delays, and will make possible the concurrent transmission of voice, data, video and text over the same digital pipeline. Intelligence and capacity are two key features of ISDN (see Figure 6.12). ISDN standards have not been formally approved to date, primarily because the U.S. and European countries still differ as to the number of channels a primary access connection should have.

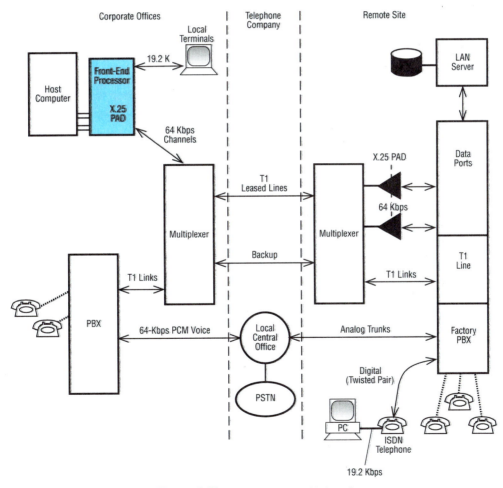

Figure 6.11   Mixed-Media Network

ISDN Specifications

ISDN standards specify an all-digital transmission pathway from end to end regardless of the data source, be it video, voice or data. They also specify lower error rates as a result of new techniques for moving and controlling the digital information, as well as new hardware. Error rates will be reduced over conventional data transmission error rates because of end-to-end control using ISDN specifications, not link-to-link error specifications.

ISDN will provide greater overall carrying capacity than the network to be replaced as a result of the new technologies it employs. ISDN also is designed to provide standardized bit rates for the various levels of service offered worldwide. Cost reductions will result from a worldwide standard approach to network communications.

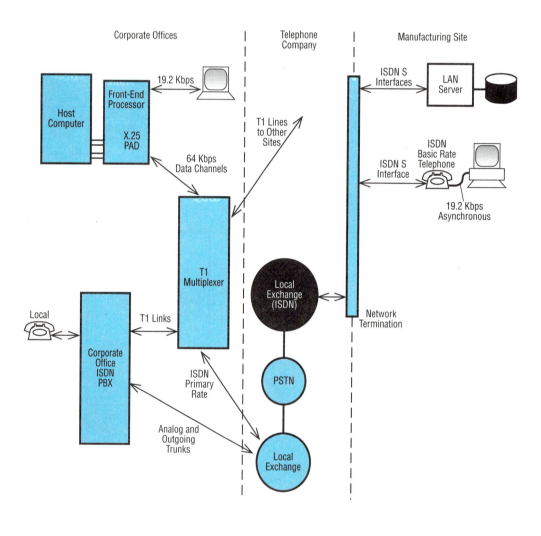

Figure 6.12 Example of an ISDN Environment

Standard Interface Connections

Standards for user interface connections are also part of the ISDN system. These standards include those described in the following sections.

Terminal Types. Two ISDN terminal types exist: TE1 and TE2. TE1 is an ISDN-compatible terminal. TE2 is a terminal type incompatible with ISDN recommendations and requires a terminal adapter (TA) for conversion and connection to a basic rate interface.

Terminal Adapters. Terminal adapters can be implemented as standalone devices or as personal computer expansion cards and may support both circuit-switched and packet-switched services. The terminal adapters provide the electrical/mechanical interface signal conversion and bit rate adaptation between a non-ISDN user terminal device (TE2) and the ISDN network. The terminal adapter also provides synchronization and auto-dial/auto-answer functions as well as manual call control functions for either voice or data circuit-switched services.

One of the major tasks of a terminal adapter is to adapt the CCITT V series bit transmission rates to the ISDN B channel rate. This function is performed by rate adaptors (RA) located in the TA. The Rate Adapter type 1 (RA1) converts CCITT V series voiceband bit rates to intermediate bit rates of either 8, 16 or 32 Kbps. The Rate Adapter type 2 (RA2) converts the intermediate rate of CCITT V series wideband modems to 64 Kbps.

Network Termination Devices. Two network termination devices exist for connection to ISDN. Network termination device type 1 (NT1) is used for basic rate (2B+D) direct device connection, as required by personal computers and other small intelligent devices. Network termination device type 2 (NT2) is required for interconnection of multiple line devices, such as a PBX and a LAN that require a primary interface (23B+D).

As previously mentioned, some ISDN standards have been implemented while others are pending approval. Interface standards pending approval include the following.

R Interface Proposal. The R interface proposal describes the methodology for adapting bit rates for the RS-232 interface, the V.35 interface, X.21 networks and X.25 networks to 64-Kbps ISDN channels.

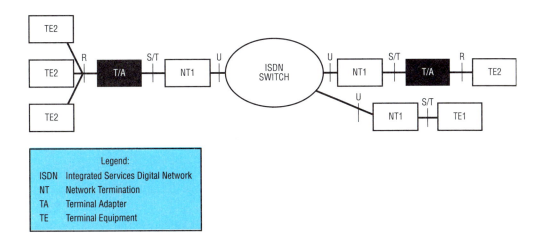

Figure 6.13   ISDN Terminal Interfaces

S Interface Proposal. The S interface proposal delineates a standard four-wire plug, the connector for the basic rate interface (2B+D).

U Interface Proposal. The U interface specification describes the central office connection to subscribers' locations using two-wire connections.

Figure 6.13 illustrates an example of ISDN interface connections.

Out-of-Band Signaling

Within the existing non-ISDN telephone network, much of the routing and billing information is considered to be in-band. The term "in-band" implies that a single transmission pathway exists and both control and user data must coexist within that single pipeline. One of in-band signaling's drawbacks is the amount of time required to establish an end-to-end connection (known as call-setup time). Telephone network communications require many components for the transfer of digitized voice or data. One of the components already mentioned, the ISDN control channel (the D channel) associated with 2B+D and 23B+D, is used to transport signaling information among all telephone switching nodes separate from the voice or information signal.

Within an ISDN network, control information generated by each switching node can be placed on the D channel. This will provide a noticeable improvement in connection time. It will also provide capabilities for other activities, including those required for establishing routing, connections and timing and for generating billing information. At the present time, the technique for handling this activity is known as Common Channel Signaling #7 (SSN#7). Figure 6.14 illustrates out-of-band signaling and the use of CCS#7.

CCS#7 is in the process of being implemented by all major carriers. An advantage of using the ISDN signaling technique is that call connections are faster because control information regarding routing and billing travels on its own channel (D channel) and arrives before the data on the B channel.

Signaling System #7 (SSN#7) is a common channel signaling protocol that is being adapted worldwide to support voice and packet switching. SSN#7 defines the basic digital communications support required for advanced telephone services. It provides for the exchange of digital trunk information between telephone switches via data links instead of in-band (mixed with the data) on a per-trunk basis.

With SSN#7, common channel signaling can be used by many different information channel (B channel) activities at the same time. SSN#7 is defined as part of the ISO ISDN standards and is compatible with the ISO seven-layer architecture and methods used for data communications.

SSN#7 provides a high degree of flexibility in that future services such as call number identification can be implemented. Call number identification allows the receiver to view the sender's telephone number. This feature has also been implemented outside of ISDN, and although ISDN is not a requirement, it does provide some additional benefits.

SSN#7 is internationally compatible because there is agreement among international telephone companies to support 64-Kbps digital transmission.

CASE STUDY (CONTINUED)

The plans for implementing a data communications network at the Bank of Scotts Valley are progressing nicely. To date, the group responsible for planning the service centers' hardware and software and defining the network has had considerable success. It has completed the definition and selection of the computer centers' mainframe computers, which will be IBM 4361 processors. It has defined and identified the required operations, applications and communications software needed by the bank. Also completed is a general plan for the operational mode and types of lines required by the service centers and branches. (Figure 6.15 shows the Bank of Scotts Valley's progress to date.)

The bank's planners are now ready to begin defining the different types of communications link services needed by each of the locations that make up the bank's network. Communications between the branches and the service center consist of teller, administrative and ATM activities. Each of these activities requires different capabilities.

Teller and administration activities involve continuous communications to and from the service center in support of teller functions such as check cashing and savings transactions, and administrative activities associated with loans, stocks and investments. Communications requirements include random-sized data packets from several terminals at the same time or in rapid succession. This dictates the need for lines that will provide enough throughput rate to ensure acceptable response time. The bank's planners have decided to install two 19.2-Kbps analog dedicated conditioned links to provide this service. The bank will contract with the local telephone company for the links. The bit rate selected is based on the perceived requirements at the present time and for anticipated growth.

The ATM terminal needs a dedicated primary communications link because it will support random activities 24 hours per day. The ATM also will require a backup link should the primary link fail. Data requirements between the terminal and the host computer are minimal because each transaction will carry only about 35 bytes of information. This is because many of the basic user interface functions, such as the PIN validation, are contained within the terminal. The planners have determined that a low-speed, 1200-bps dedicated and conditioned analog link between each ATM terminal and the service center will be required. This link will be provided by the local telephone company. Since a back-up link is required, an internal modem within the ATM will be used should the

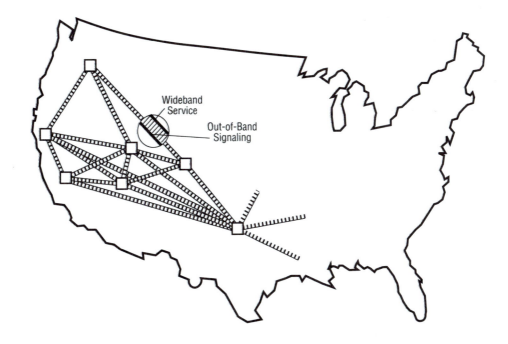

Figure 6.14   Out-of-Band Signaling

primary link go down. It will be programmed to call a number at the service center and reestablish the connection.

Each service center will require facilities to support multiple dedicated 19.2-Kbps links. They also must have high-speed dedicated links between each other to support interbranch banking activities. The planners initially considered incorporating ISDN service but decided not to go in that direction because ISDN is still an emerging technology and has not been fully implemented throughout the state. Instead, they have decided to use digital T1 links provided by one of the long-distance carriers because several different telephone companies operate throughout the state. Two T1 links will be installed to support both voice and data traffic.

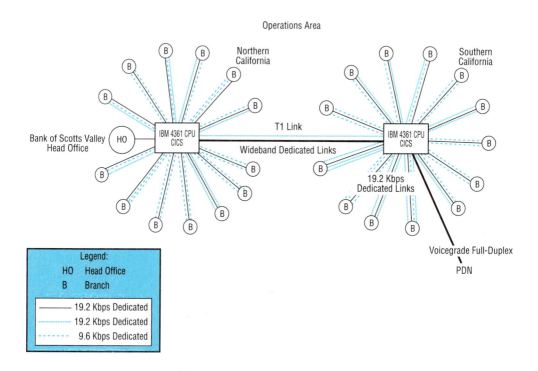

Figure 6.15   ISDN Terminal Interfaces

REVIEW QUESTIONS

1. What three companies provide 95 percent of all carrier services in North America?
2. What services do international carriers provide?
3. What services do public data network vendors typically provide?
4. What types of packets are available for use in packet-switching networks?
5. What does PSTN refer to?
6. What is a type 3002 line?
7. Name the two types of conditioning available with leased lines.
8. What digital transmission service do most common carriers support?
9. The design criteria for ISDN were based on what?
10. What is 2B+D considered to be?
11. What activity is the D channel used for?
12. What is the bit rate for the ISDN 3H0+D channel?

CHAPTER

7

Transmission Concepts

INTRODUCTION

Several methods are available for moving data across a communications link, including radio frequency broadcast transmission, infrared radio transmission and modulated land-based transmission over a wired media such as coaxial cable or twisted-pair wire. The process of converting the digital ones and zeros into a form suitable for transmission and placing them onto a link is known as modulation.

This chapter introduces basic modulation as it relates to wired media and radio frequency transmission. Several standard radio frequency modulation techniques are currently in use by international modem manufacturers. These modem standards, which are governed by the CCITT, permit compatibility between different vendors' products.

For low-speed communications, modems use simple modulation techniques because they work well, do not require extensive error detection and correction logic, and are inexpensive to manufacture. High-speed modems use more complex modulation techniques because the circuitry provides better error detection and correction and is more efficient.

The radio frequency spectrum is the principle vehicle for transporting modulated information. Figure 7.1 shows the frequency spectrum associated with hearing and the human ear. This graphic represents the bandwidth, or range of frequencies, associated with human hearing. Although the audible frequencies are limited, there is no real limit to the overall frequency spectrum available for use in communications, except that of the equipment.

Initially, the limitation imposed by the audible frequency spectrum dictated the frequency range available for transmission because it was governed by the bandwidth of the voice-based telephone network. While this narrow range of frequencies no longer governs the available bandwidth for electronic communications, the voice frequencies did establish the basic foundation for modulated transmission. Data communications bit rates originally were limited to the voice bandwidth (300 Hz to 4000 Hz) of the telephone network, but with wideband circuits currently available, no practical limitations exist.

Modulated transmission bit speeds are directly related to several additional factors, including the physical properties of electrical transmission, network limitations and hardware. A correlation between data rate and available bandwidth governs overall transmission capabilities. For data communications, a frequency spectrum (channel bandwidth) broad enough to handle the required data rates must be available to support the bit rate requirements.

For many years, two theories governed radio frequency transmission activities: the Nyquist theorem and the Shannon theorem.

Nyquist Theorem

In 1933, a theory was developed by Harry Nyquist that stated that a maximum bit rate cannot exceed twice the frequency bandwidth of an allocated channel. This suggested that a frequency bandwidth of 2400 Hz could handle a maximum bit rate of 4800 bits per second. The theory applies to a simple binary signal applied to two different amplitudes or two different frequencies.

Shannon Theorem

C.E. Shannon developed a formula that relates transmission speed to signal power and error rates. Very simply put, Shannon stated that as the power level increases, so does the noise level. This combination created a limitation on the speed at which the link could operate.

Both theories are still valid today, with some modification. However, the derived modulation techniques that incorporate error correction assume a much different technological approach. This approach mitigates the impact and restrictions set forth by Shannon and Nyquist in their respective theories.

Table 7.1 defines the general frequencies allocated worldwide for radio and communications activity.

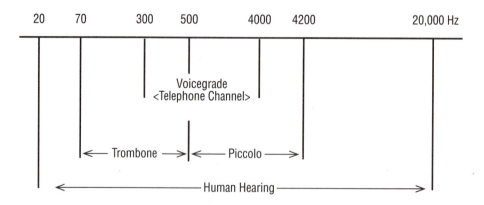

Figure 7.1 Human Hearing Frequency Spectrum

Transmission Concepts

Frequency	Band Designation	Usage
3000G Hz – 300G Hz	Unassigned	Unassigned
300G Hz – 30G Hz	EHF Extremely High Frequency	Satellite Communications Microwave Transmission Radar-Amateur Radio
30G Hz – 3G Hz	SHF Super High Frequency	Satellite Communications Radar Microwave Transmission
3G Hz – 300M Hz	UHF Ultra-High Frequency	Microwave Transmission Amateur Radio/Pub. Svcs. UHF Television
300M Hz – 30M Hz	VHF Very High Frequency	Amateur Radio (HAMS) VHF Television Broadcasts FM Radio 88 MHz--106 MHz
30M Hz – 3M Hz	HF High Frequency	Citizens Band Radio Diathermy Machines
3M Hz – 300K Hz	MF Medium Frequency	Radio Navigation AM Radio 500 KHz--1.6 MHz
300K Hz – 30K Hz	LF Low Frequency	Radio Navigation Maritime Communications
30K Hz – 3K Hz	Very Low Frequency Upper End of Hearing Range	Navigation, Weather Communications Piccolo
3K Hz – 300 Hz	Voice Frequencies	Human Voice Base Violin
300 Hz – 30 Hz	Extremely Low Frequency Low End of Hearing	Power Lines Submarine Communications

Table 7.1 Frequency Allocations

MODULATION

Modulation is the mechanism or technique that "pushes" the data-bearing signals across the link. Modems modulate the digital data into a form suitable for transmission over analog lines. Technically, modulation is the process of varying the characteristics of a wave in accordance with another wave or signal. The modulation of a carrier (a carrier is an unmodulated electrical signal on the link that can be modified to carry data bits) on a channel produces an information signal that can be sent from one location to another.

A carrier is used to establish a logical connection from point A to point B. The carrier is created by applying voltage or current to the communications link (transmission circuit) at a specified frequency. (Figure 7.2 shows an unmodulated carrier and a modulated carrier.) Modulation of that carrier can be accomplished by one of the following techniques:

- By keeping the voltage or current constant on the link from point A to point B and then varying the signal timing to create different frequencies representing one or zero bits

- By keeping the frequency (signal timing) constant and varying the amplitude (voltage) up or down in order to represent one or zero bits

- By varying both the frequency and the amplitude of the signal at the same time

Figure 7.3 illustrates a signal as it attenuates outward from its center point.

BASIC MODULATION TECHNIQUES

Three basic analog modulation techniques (amplitude, frequency and phase) are available for data transmission (see Figure 7.4). Several derived modulation techniques are also available, but because of their complexity, they will not be discussed in detail in this book (though most CCITT modems in use today employ derived modulation techniques). A derived modulation technique is one that combines the three basic techniques in order to form a derivative. The derived technique has the ability to carry more data than the basic technique. Additionally, some modulation techniques use encoding schemes to pack more bits into the transmission and then decode them at the receiving side.

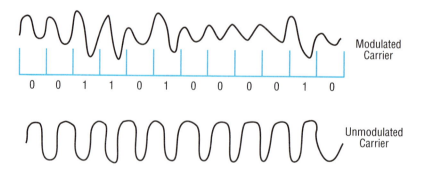

Figure 7.2 Modulated and Unmodulated Carriers

Amplitude Modulation

Amplitude modulation (AM) is a descendent of the telegraph system in which a circuit attached to a battery was keyed on or off. This keying activity created a current that represented dots and dashes defined as characters of the Morse Code character set.

A basic method of transmitting analog signals, amplitude modulation operates by varying the amplitude or magnitude (voltage) of the carrier signal according to the input data source (see Figure 7.5). To put it simply, the voltage is modified up or down depending on whether the input digital signal is a one or a zero bit. In amplitude modulation, the carrier signal timing remains constant; that is, 1200 cycles per second, 2400 cycles per second, and so forth. Only the voltage (amplitude) is changed.

On a 2400-baud line, the amplitude or current will change 2400 times to indicate zero and one bits coming from the digital source. This results in a communications rate of 2400 bps sent over a 2400-baud line.

Since amplitude modulation increases the noise level as the signal level increases, it is no longer used extensively by itself. However, amplitude modulation is still used in combination with other modulation schemes.

Frequency Modulation

Frequency modulation (FM) is a method of data transmission in which the frequency of the carrier changes to correspond to the changes in the information signal (see Figure 7.6). In frequency modulation, the number of cycles per second (hertz) varies according to the source (more cycles per second for one bits and fewer cycles per second for zero bits). Unlike amplitude modulation, the bits per second and the number of cycles per second are not the same with frequency modulation.

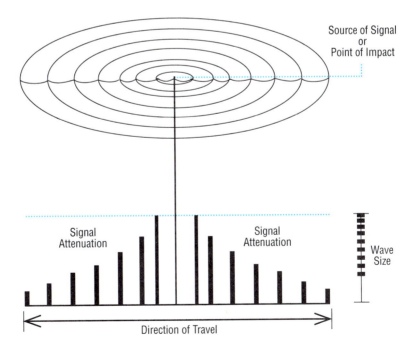

Figure 7.3 Wave Travel and Attenuation

Amplitude: The peak value of a varying quantity

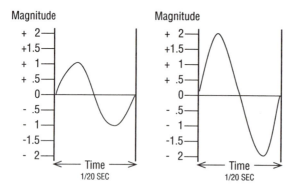

Frequency: The number of complete cycles per unit of time

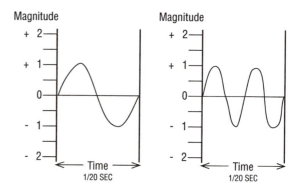

Phase: The relative position in time where a cycle begins

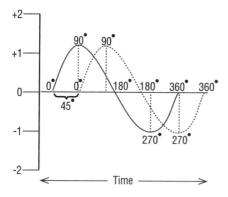

Figure 7.4 Three Basic Modulation Techniques

If you were able to listen to the analog signal of ones and zeros in frequency modulation, one bits would sound a higher tone than zeros bits. Generally speaking, two sets of frequencies are used for FM transmission; 2025 Hz and 2225 Hz are used for the first set of carrier frequencies, while 1025 Hz and 1225 Hz are used for the second set. Note that although these are the commonly used frequencies, some manufacturers elect to use other frequencies.

Until recently, frequency modulation was the most popular modulation technique because it is less prone to interference than amplitude modulation techniques. Modem manufacturers have begun replacing FM with newer derivative modulation techniques because of their ability to handle higher bit rates on the same type of lines. Nevertheless, frequency modulation is still used extensively because of the low noise aspects of the signal. Its primary use is in low-speed modems having transfer rates under 2400 bps.

Phase Modulation

Phase modulation (PM) is often referred to as multibit modulation because it is used in modems that have the ability to produce more than one bit per cycle of signal (see Figure 7.7). In PM, the angle or phase of the carrier signal can vary (change its shape). This change occurs based on the ones and zeros of the digital signal. There are many types of phase modulation, but phase shift keying (PSK) is normally used for data transmission. Phase modulation is considered to be a derivative modulation technique and has many variations. This discussion addresses PM in its simplest form; explanations of more complex variations are beyond the scope of this book.

As already discussed, the carrier signal transporting data on a communications circuit operates at a specified set of frequencies or cycles per second. If one cycle of a carrier is viewed as a 360 degree circle, that cycle can be divided into degreed sections. Phase modulation is accomplished by shifting the phase at certain degrees within the circle to represent one and zero bits.

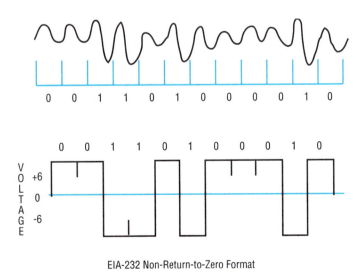

Figure 7.5   Amplitude Modulation

Phase modulation is accomplished by interrupting the amplitude (voltage) for a duration of time that corresponds to the degreed position defined for combinations of zero bits and/or one bits assigned to and predefined in the 360 degree circle. When the phase is shifted, the carrier begins again at zero degrees. By controlling the timing, one bits and zero bits can be represented at the specific degreed locations in the circle.

Thus, it is possible, using phase modulation techniques, to create two bits per cycle (dibits), three bits per cycle (tribits) or four bits per cycle (quadbits). With this modulation technique, the rate in bits per second can exceed the baud rate.

Variations

There are many derived modulation techniques that permit more efficient transmission of data across analog communications lines. Examples include double vestigial sideband (DSB/VSB), frequency shift keying (FSK), phase shift keying (PSK), quadrature/differential phase shift keying (QPSK/DPSK), quadrature amplitude modulation (QAM), Trellis coded modulation (TCM) and pulse code modulation (PCM). All of these derived modulation techniques use combinations and variations of frequency, amplitude and phase modulations.

Trellis Coded Modulation. TCM is used by higher-speed modems because it employs forward error correction techniques and provides a more reliable high-speed data transmission rate. Because of the complexities of TCM, specific technical information is not presented here; however, this modulation technique uses an extra bit per cycle per second (cps) and encodes the bits into a transmission pattern for decoding at the other end.

Quadrature Amplitude Modulation. QAM uses two carriers of the same frequency that are 90 degrees apart and added together. It is a derivative of phase modulation and has the ability to create multiple bits per cycle.

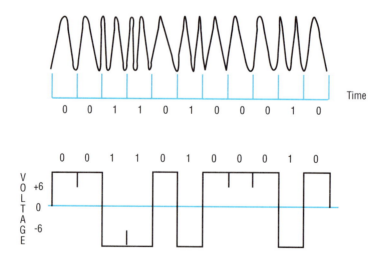

Figure 7.6   Frequency Modulation

Transmission Concepts

The use of derived techniques increases the bit rate of the line over that provided with basic modulation techniques. At higher bit rates, trade-offs must be considered due to variables such as line quality and signal-to-noise ratios.

Several modulation schemes using phase encoding techniques are designed for the conversion of voice signals into a digitally encoded analog form. The two most common are pulse-code modulation (PCM) and adaptive differential pulse-coded modulation (ADPCM).

PCM functions by sampling the voice signal 8000 times a second, quantizing each signal sample into a numeric digital value and creating an eight-bit word for each sample (see Figure 7.8). This creates a 64,000-bps signal that encodes the entire voice spectrum (300 Hz to 3330 Hz).

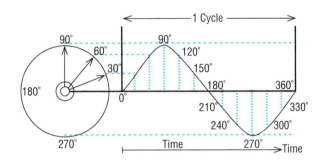

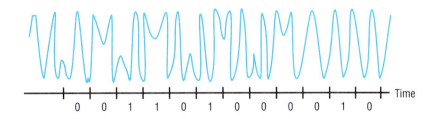

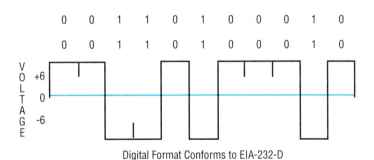

Digital Format Conforms to EIA-232-D

Figure 7.7   Phase Modulation

ADPCM operates similarly to PCM but encodes only a four-bit sample that represents the difference between the serial samples (current and next waveform sample). If there is no difference between samples created by pauses or silences, a two- or three-bit sample is formed. This technique allows ADPCM to create a full spectrum signal in 32,000 bits per second.

DIGITAL TRANSMISSION

Pure digital transmission is represented by changes in voltage on the communications media. (Figure 7.9 depicts a digital transmission signal.) Some digital signals are nothing more than the voltage turning on and off. Other digital methods use a constant voltage having positive and negative values that represent one and zero bits. At the transmitting side, the voltage polarity changes from positive to negative depending on whether one or zero bits are coming from the computer. At the receiving side, the voltage is monitored and, when it makes the transition from a positive to a negative value, one and zero bits are derived.

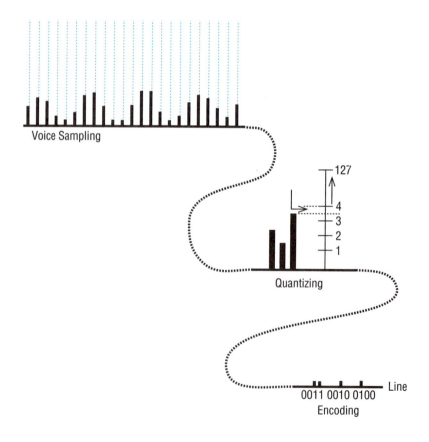

Figure 7.8 PCM Digital Process

Transmission Concepts

Typically, digital signals from a computer or terminal are not in a form suitable for direct placement onto the media partly because of the low power levels used in the computers. Even though the signal from the computer is a pure digital signal, it often must be changed or shaped to be transmitted. This requires a DSU/CSU.

Some of the digital transmission techniques currently used are bipolar, return-to-zero (RZ) and non-return-to-zero (NRZ).

Bipolar Current Loop

Bipolar digital transmission uses positive and negative voltages to represent digital information. (Figure 7.10 illustrates a bipolar signal in which one bits are always a negative voltage and zero bits are represented by a positive voltage.)

Return-to-Zero (RZ)

RZ digital transmission uses a self-clocking transmission method. Data bits operating at a given bit rate begin on the link at a zero reference level regardless of value and go through a transition during bit time or signal period. (Figure 7.11 presents an RZ digital signal.) Zero bits begin at a zero reference level and go negative for half a bit time or signal period. During the second half of the signal period, the signal turns positive and then returns to a zero reference level. For one bits, the exact opposite signals occur. Two different RZ signals can be used and care must be taken to ensure that both devices are using the same form of return-to-zero transmission.

Non-Return-to-Zero (NRZ)

NRZ also can be referred to as differential encoding and is unique in that transitions only occur when a one bit is present. (Figure 7.12 illustrates an NRZ digital signal.) The first one bit encountered causes the signal to go positive; the signal remains positive until the next one bit causes the signal to go negative and remain there. When the next one bit is encountered the signal will go positive. One bits may be represented by either a positive or negative signal; therefore, synchronization must occur between the communicating devices because it is the transitions in the signal that represent bit values, not the signal value itself (positive or negative).

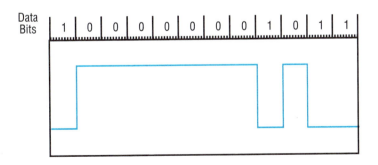

Figure 7.9 Digital Transmission Signal

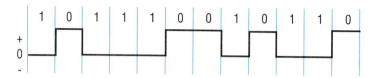

Figure 7.10   Bipolar Digital Signal

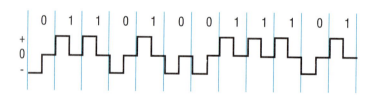

Figure 7.11   Return-to-Zero Digital Signal

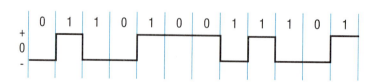

Figure 7.12   Non-Return-to-Zero Digital Signal

CASE STUDY (CONTINUED)

The Bank of Scotts Valley uses many types of data transmission equipment on its data communications links. As stated earlier, the bank will use both dial-up and dedicated links for communications with the service centers. Modems using TCM and operating at 19.2 Kbps or 9600 bps will be used over the dial-up or voice-grade dedicated links. The bank's digital links used between the service centers will employ the telephone company's signaling and digital transmission formats.

REVIEW QUESTIONS

1. Name the three basic modulation techniques used in data communications.
2. Describe frequency modulation.
3. Describe amplitude modulation.
4. What is the difference between baud and bps?
5. What are dibits, tribits and quadbits?
6. What is phase modulation?
7. Does TCM include a coding technique?
8. Can a digital signal be sent using any of the defined modulation techniques?
9. What is PCM?
10. Name two digital transmission techniques.

Part IV

Hardware, Media and Interfaces

CHAPTER 8

Hardware Links

INTRODUCTION

Various types of wiring are available for video, audio and digital information transport. A point of emphasis is that most communications systems today are designed to support voice transmission or analog data communications. This is rapidly changing, however, due to new technologies such as ISDN, low-cost DDS links and new equipment that supports pure digital transmission. Nevertheless, traditional cabling that maintains analog network facilities is still the most predominant media in use.

The type of cable link best suited for a user's application is usually dictated by specific requirements, which include but are not limited to environment, security, bit rates and availability of transmission and support equipment. These should be carefully evaluated by both data communications planners and personnel responsible for the facilities prior to cable link selection. The availability of network connections and the need for high-speed or low-speed capabilities also play an important role in the decision-making process.

Another consideration is the integration of voice and data onto the same transmission link. The types of services to be combined (e.g., digital voice) may dictate what is required. In reality, it is common practice among most carriers to incorporate a variety of different links in situations where distances are great. This is not necessarily by the user's choice, but rather because of the various telephone circuits that are available from the carrier.

COMMUNICATIONS MEDIA

Two- and Four-Wire Twisted Pairs

Two-wire and four-wire twisted pairs used for telephone circuits are referred to as single-ended or unbalanced circuits. This is because the signal strength is not balanced from end to end. The signal is carried over one wire with the ground return on the other wire of the pair. Two-wire twisted pair circuits are usually located between the home and the central office or between an organization's facilities and the central switching office. This type of link is a local loop between the location of the handset and the local telephone office.

Four-wire twisted pairs are the wiring scheme of choice for many organizations that need wiring for data communications. This is primarily because newer communications equipment can better resolve error conditions associated with the transmission media. Four-wire twisted pairs also allow higher data rates and a wider bandwidth than two-wire twisted pairs and can provide full-duplex transmission.

Twisted-pair wires are manufactured in many configurations, including unshielded wire, shielded wire and multiple conductors. Twisted-pair wire found in the telephone network varies in size from 19 gauge to 28 gauge, but the most common size used is 24 gauge. While the telephone companies generally limit bandwidth (mainly due to the equipment used), twisted pairs can accommodate much higher bandwidths than those required for telephone communications. Many companies reduce wiring costs by installing twisted pairs and using them to transmit data at rates in excess of 2 megabytes per second.

Recent technology breakthroughs are now allowing very high bit rates to be transmitted over shielded and unshielded twisted-pair wiring for limited distances. This becomes ideal for use with local area networks (LANs). LAN bit rates can go as high as 16 Mbps using twisted pairs.

Four-wire circuits are commonly found between many of the older central offices (telephone offices) for long distance transmission. This is rapidly changing, however, as a result of the rapid conversion taking place among many telephone carriers to fiber-optic cable. There are usually 24 twisted pairs of wire grouped into each twisted-pair cable, but this may vary from four to 28 conductors. The use of twisted pairs for long distance circuits is rapidly diminishing with the introduction of the newer high-speed transmission methods mentioned earlier.

Four-wire transmission is also used for most business telephone systems because four-wire circuits have superior full-duplex capabilities compared to two-wire circuits. It is also possible to create several channels over a four-wire circuit by using a form of multiplexing.

The conversion of two-wire to four-wire transmission in order to transmit data over long distances must take place at the telephone company's central office. This is done using hybrid coils that transform the signal on the two-wire circuit into one that can be placed on the four-wire circuit.

Standard telephone lines (twisted pairs), when used in the public switched network, are considered to be switched lines that are unconditioned. Data transmission using the PSTN is generally limited to a maximum of 4800 bits per second for long distances. Speeds greater than 4800 bps over standard telephone links are prone to high error rates. This is not to say that future communications components will not be able to detect and correct errors at higher speeds. Newer modems use variant modulation techniques such as Trellis Coded Modulation so that higher speeds are now much more common on the switched network.

The term "switched" simply means that the connection is established manually or dynamically. Manually implies the act of a mechanical switch actually moving and making contact. Dynamic switching is accomplished via an electronic device and no mechanical activity takes place.

The type of circuit (the medium) and line availability are not guaranteed by the telephone companies. Line busy/circuit busy signals may be encountered at any point in the network. This is due in large part to contention between users who want to use the network at the same time. In addition, variable noise levels may be frequently encountered.

Switched lines operate on a point-to-point basis. This means that routing is determined by the availability of lines from one telephone central office to another. Line contention can occur because a much smaller number of circuits exist between central offices than between central offices and homes or businesses. The central-office-to-central-office circuits are available on a first in, first out, basis which means that circuits are assigned sequentially based on incoming requests. Line contention usually results in a busy signal or reduced signal quality due to the excessive distance the signal must travel as a result of alternate routing from CO to CO.

Contention is frequently encountered on holidays such as Mother's Day or Christmas due to the sheer volume of traffic on the network. Since limited capacity is dictated by two-wire and four-wire connections, busy signals are often encountered at the area code, city code or country code entry points. The lack of available circuits is responsible for this overload situation.

Coaxial Cable

Coaxial cable consists of an unbalanced pair of wires, an inner conductor, usually copper, surrounded by a grounded outer conductor, which is either solid or braided. The inner and outer conductors are held in a concentric configuration by a dielectric material, usually Teflon or PVC.

Coaxial cable can handle more than 10,000 voice-grade channels (300 Hz to 3400 Hz) using a variety of multiplexing techniques. It is used extensively for terminal-to-terminal controller connections, LAN connections and cable television connections because of its superior noise control.

Coaxial cable requires signal repeaters (a type of line amplifier) for transmission over long distances. It can support bit rates well in excess of 1.544 Mbps and is superior to two- and four-wire circuits with respect to noise control due to the shielding placed around the signal conductor. Coaxial cable has a wide frequency bandwidth, in excess of 500 MHz.

Coaxial cable can be configured with multiple center conductors for increased transmission capability. Care must be exercised when using PVC coaxial cable because it may violate some fire regulations.

Fiber-Optic Cable

Fiber-optic cable is rapidly becoming common for digital transmission. Virtually all of the telephone companies — local, long distance or government operated — are implementing or expanding fiber-optic cable networks each year. The availability of fiber-optic local area networks and the emergence of the Fiber Data Distributed Interface (FDDI) standard have made it desirable for users to incorporate fiber-optic cable into their wiring plans.

The concept of using light pulses transmitted from a laser or light-emitting diode (LED) source is really nothing more than an extension of the concept employed by Samuel Morse and the telegraph system. The major difference is in the technology, using pulses of light instead of electricity. Moreover, fiber optics represent a major advancement beyond electronic transmission because a single fiber has the potential to carry incredible amounts of data in the future.

When fiber-optic cable was introduced, it was very expensive because of rigid manufacturing requirements and the special handling needed. As new and improved splicing techniques and mass production of the cable have evolved, prices have rapidly decreased. The reduction in costs has enabled fiber-optic cable to be competitive with other types of transmission media.

Fiber-Optic Technology

Fiber cables are composed of hair-thin fiberglass or other light-conducting fibers. The fibers are covered by a light-reflecting opaque material referred to as cladding. The multiple fibers are then wrapped in an outer protective sheathing, usually Kevlar, which is an extremely tough material (used in the construction of bullet proof vests). This rigid protective covering protects the cable from stretching. (Figure 8.1 shows a cross-section of a typical fiber cable.)

Three fiber-optic technologies are now in use (see Figure 8.2). The oldest is multimode step-index transmission, which works by bouncing the light along the fiber cable path to its destination. This technology is primarily used within a building because of the limited distances normally encountered. A second fiber transmission technology is multimode graded index, which is typically used in a campus or multibuilding environment because it performs most efficiently within a limited distance. The fiber-optic technology with the greatest potential is known as single-mode transmission. This technique uses a very narrow core and causes the light pulses to travel in a straight line down the center; it is suitable for greater distances. Various core sizes are used in all three methods. Typical core and cladding sizes are 8.3/125 microns for single-mode fiber and 62.5/125, 50/125 or 100/140 microns for multimode fiber. Each type of cable is designed for specific applications based on the distances and bit rates supported. Fiber transmission uses one cable for each direction of transmission because fiber cable operates in a simplex mode.

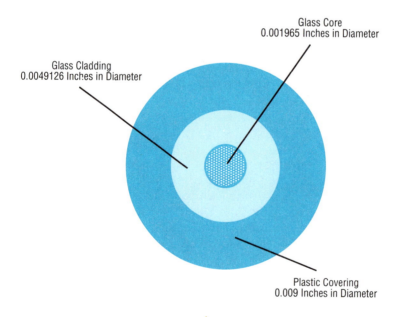

Figure 8.1 Cross-Section of a Typical Fiber-Optic Cable

Nominal transmission speeds are in the range of 300 to 500 Mbps using a single-frequency laser. Much higher data rates can be achieved using the newer coherent communications transmitters because the coherent technology provides multifrequency laser capabilities (parallel lasers transmitting laser light pulses of different colors at the same time). Recent tests by Bell Laboratories using multifrequency laser capabilities have achieved speeds in excess of 50 billion bytes per second over a single fiber.

At the present time, distances are limited to less than 50 miles without repeaters. Repeaters are placed enroute and reamplify the light pulses received on the input side. The repeater then retransmits the amplified light signal across the next segment. For long-distance fiber applications, the fiber cable contains an electrical wire that carries power for the repeaters. Ongoing testing at Bell Laboratories and other organizations has achieved distances of more than 3,000 miles without the use of repeaters, but these experiments have been conducted in highly controlled environments using special test equipment.

Many regional telephone companies, long-distance companies in the U.S. and various private and government telecommunications companies in Europe are switching to fiber-optic networks because of their speed, capacity and reduced error rates. Ongoing research and development of new LED and laser technologies will continue to enhance fiber-optic capabilities.

One of the many advantages of fiber-optic cable is that it eliminates crosstalk commonly found in twisted-pair transmission. It also is not subject to electromagnetic interference (EMI), and it provides a high level of security because it is difficult to tap without detection.

Extensive fiber-optic networks have been installed in North America as well as overseas with trans-Pacific (Haw-4/TPC-3), trans-Atlantic (TAT-8) and trans-Caribbean (TCS-1) undersea cables. (These cable designations are defined by the carriers for the Pacific, Atlantic and Caribbean circuits.) Fiber-optic potential is nearly unlimited; the only real restriction is the transmitting and receiving speed of the equipment.

Microwave Transmission

Microwave is a form of radio transmission using ultra high frequencies in the gigahertz (GHz) range. Microwave is considered to be a line-of-sight transmission method because the transmission and reception facilities must be within a line of sight. Distance is usually limited to less than 50 miles because of the curvature of the earth's surface.

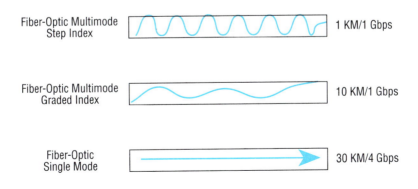

Figure 8.2 Types of Fiber-Optic Technology

Microwave towers and transmission facilities act as amplifier stations to refresh the signal and retransmit it. Microwave transmission can provide multichannel transmission in excess of 6 Gbps. Thousands of channels can be integrated into a single microwave circuit because microwave transmission can make use of multiplexing techniques.

This type of transmission is used extensively for short-haul, point-to-point communications. It is, however, expensive due to the equipment required to handle the transmission. Microwave may be subject to interference by passing airplanes, rain and other weather-related phenomena. Microwave transmission and reception sites must employ extensive error correction technology to ensure acceptable performance.

Satellite Links

A satellite link is a channel connection using radio frequency waves between an earth station transmitter and a device on a satellite called a transponder. Satellites act as relay stations for very high-speed communications from one point to another. Typically, a satellite consists of multiple channels, each having the capacity to handle in excess of 1.544 megabits per second. The transponder is a receiver and amplifier coupled to a transmitter which receives the incoming signal, amplifies it and then retransmits it to another receiving earth station or satellite. Figure 8.3 illustrates a geosynchronous satellite in orbit around the earth.

Data communications connections using a satellite link require ground stations for transmission and reception of the high-speed signals. Like microwave, satellite transmission is considered a line-of-sight transmission method. However, because of the distance involved and satellite location and placement, its signal can cover a wide area. This wide area is referred to as its footprint and is determined by the altitude and position of the satellite.

Two sets of frequencies are used, one set for uplink activity and the other for downlink activity. The CCITT has designated two frequency bands for satellite communications. These bandwidths are allocated by the various governing agencies; the C band uses the 4 GHz to 6 GHz range and the KU band uses 14 GHz to 16 GHz. A typical user on the KU band would use 16 GHz for uplink activity and 14 GHz on the downlink.

The cost of a satellite link was expensive in the past, but with the placement of additional satellites in orbit and new technology to increase the speed of transmission, the cost appears to be dropping rapidly. One disadvantage of satellite use is the propagation delay of the signal (it must travel 22,300 miles up and then return the same distance), which causes potential timing problems with certain transmission protocols and frequencies.

Equipment may be expensive for companies that want on-site links because both uplink and downlink transmission facilities must be acquired and installed. Typical costs for leasing equipment for a private ground station range from about $3,500 per month to over $8,000 per month. Most companies that want to use satellite transmission use a satellite ground station service for link accessibility. Data to be transmitted using this service is carried over dedicated high-speed links from the customer site to a ground station called a satellite port. For improved performance, some vendors provide a digital technique called Demand Assigned Multiple Access (DAMA), which results in better service and more efficient circuit use than the standard analog links. Time-share satellite service is available from a number of value-added suppliers of data communications services.

DATA TRANSMISSION ERRORS AND IMPAIRMENTS

Many types of data transmission errors and impairments apply equally to wire transmission and radio frequency transmission. However, certain types of error conditions apply specifically to wired forms of data transmission, while microwave and satellite transmissions

Hardware Links

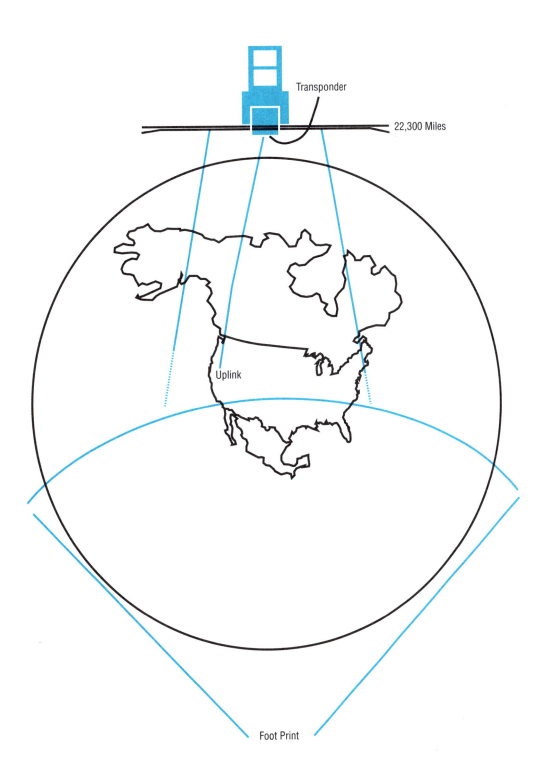

Figure 8.3 Satellite Transmission Example

are especially subject to others, most notably propagation delay. Detailed explanations for certain error types are not provided here due to their extreme complexity. Figure 8.4 shows the effects of distortion on a digital signal.

Wired Switched Networks

Distortion. Signal distortion is a general term resulting from multiple conditions. As a current travels through a circuit, it encounters a resistance or opposition known as impedance which acts as a partial barrier to the signal's flow. Distortion, also referred to as attenuation, is caused by loss variations (power, speed) at different frequencies. Two of the primary causes of distortion are signal attenuation and delay.

The installation of smaller gauge wire will reduce some distortion, but this solution is good only for short distances and is expensive. Another method for controlling distortion is to add electronic components called inductors uniformly spaced along the line to ensure that the circuit remains stable. This process is referred to as loading; however, this technique will increase delay distortion. Insertion of attenuation equalizers in conjunction with hybrid coils will partially correct this problem.

Reflection (Echo). Reflection is produced by impedance (resistance at certain frequencies) due to irregularities along a transmission line or at its end points. This irregularity causes a portion of the signal's energy to be reflected back toward the originating end. Reflection can be corrected by the insertion of echo suppressors into the line. Be cautioned that although echo suppressors work well and are required with voice transmission, they have an adverse effect on half-duplex data transmission.

In data communications, echo suppressors located in the satellite or central office can be disabled by the user via the answering modem, which can transmit a high-pitched tone at a frequency of 2000 to 2250 hertz. This must be maintained for a duration of 400 milliseconds. Echo suppressors will remain disabled provided that the carrier signal is not interrupted for more than 100 milliseconds. Echo suppression is required in data communications because an echo distorts the forward bound signal and creates data errors.

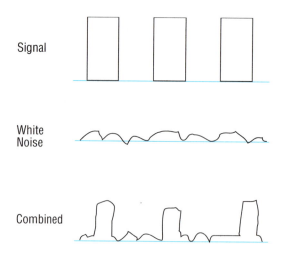

Figure 8.4   Digital Signal with Noise

Noise. Background, white or steady-state noise is the average noise power on a voice channel and usually maintains a constant level. The presence of this type of noise often causes problems in voice transmission and, to a lesser extent, data transmission. Another type of noise, referred to as impulse noise or line hits, is characterized by very short bursts of high amplitude (i.e., power surge). Impulse noise produces major problems for data transmission because the pulses are of very short duration. This activity can alter bit values and even block out the entire data signal for short durations of time. At the present time, little can be done to eliminate noise on switched lines.

Propagation Delay. Propagation delay is a variation in the time it takes for a signal to travel from the transmitter to the receiver. Such a delay can be viewed as a slowing down or speeding up of the transmission signal. On switched networks, the propagation delay is not controlled and creates problems at higher speeds. In addition, propagation delay in switched networks can vary greatly depending on the routing within the network. This can cause problems because the delay may exceed line turnaround time (the time it takes to reverse the line in a half-duplex environment in order for the receiver to acknowledge a response). This type of delay can disable echo suppression circuits in the central office switch and can prevent the line turnaround from occurring. Often, the only solution to data transmission problems of this nature is to terminate and reestablish the connection.

Wired Dedicated-Line Networks

In addition to the transmission errors discussed for switched links, data transmission over leased or private facilities can also experience signal degradation. In addition to attenuation distortion and envelope delay, which already have been discussed, several others also create problems. These include nonlinear distortion, phase jitter, line transients, poor signal-to-noise ratios and impulse noise.

Nonlinear Distortion. Nonlinearities in amplifiers and other electronic devices can cause the generation of signal components (distortion) along with the original data signal. This distortion is harmonically related to the fundamental frequency of the base signal. These added components can reshape the transmitted signal to such an extent that the data signal is difficult to detect.

Phase Jitter. This random distortion of the transmitted signal's phased sine wave results in the intermittent lengthening and shortening of time related to the transmitted signal.

Line Transients. Transient phenomena (unexpected and very rapid) are a major cause of transmission problems in data communications. They include impulse noise, phase hits, gain hits and dropouts. Phase and gain hits are similar to voltage spikes that momentarily will increase the carrier voltage to a higher level. This can change the value of the data bits being transported at the point of the hit.

Poor Signal-to-Noise Ratio. The signal-to-noise ratio (SNR) represents the difference between the noise level on the link and the information signal, expressed in decibels measured. If the SNR exceeds the rated specifications for the link, the receiver will not be able to distinguish between the noise and the signal.

Impulse Noise. As stated previously, impulse noise is characterized by short bursts of high amplitude. This can be caused by a variety of things, including telephone switching equipment, lightning and other electrical surge activities. Impulse noise creates problems in data transmission because it may cause bits to change their value during transit. A one bit could become a zero bit, thereby altering the composition of the data. If this problem occurs, the only solution is often to retransmit the entire block of data after the receiving station returns a negative acknowledgment.

CASE STUDY (CONTINUED)

The Bank of Scotts Valley uses several types of communications links between the two data centers and the various branches. This is because most of the dedicated links are provided by the telephone carriers contracted with for link services.

Within each branch, the bank planners have decided to use twisted-pair wiring for terminal connections. This decision was based on the fact that distances are limited and unshielded twisted-pair wire will support standard terminal connections at rates in excess of two million bytes per second. Twisted-pair wiring also was selected because, at some point in the future, the bank probably will convert its terminals to personal computers with local area network capabilities. Twisted-pair wiring is ideal for this type of connectivity. Fiber-optic cable will also be placed into each of the bank's branches because it will be quite expensive to convert to fiber in the future.

For connection between the branches and the service centers, the local telephone carrier has provided a coaxial cable link from each of the branches to its central offices. The telephone carrier is in the process of installing fiber links throughout its access area but has not yet completed the conversion.

Communications between each of the service centers through a dedicated telephone link employs fiber for its primary link and coaxial for its secondary links (see Figure 8.5). The fiber links terminate at a telephone company central office and are then placed on a digital, long-haul microwave circuit.

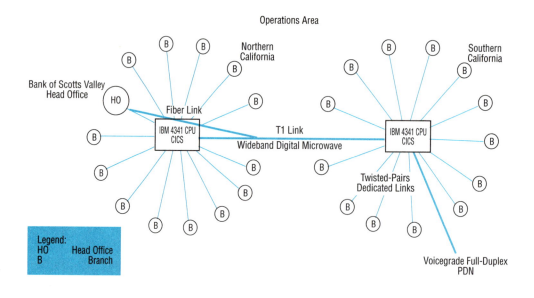

Figure 8.5 Types of Links Employed by the Bank of Scotts Valley

REVIEW QUESTIONS

1. Name some of the basic transmission media used in data communications.
2. What is the main advantage of coaxial cable over twisted-pair wire?
3. Why is fiber optics considered the wave of the future?
4. Are microwave and satellite transmission considered line-of-sight transmission methods?
5. What transmission medium does "cladding" refer to?
6. What function does a transponder perform?
7. What connections are twisted pairs primarily used for?
8. What does line-of-sight transmission apply to?
9. In what manner is distortion a problem in data communications?
10. True or false: Distortion is really a general term for many types of errors.

CHAPTER
9

Data Communications Hardware

INTRODUCTION

A major part of planning and implementing a data communications network is evaluating and selecting software and hardware components. Myriad products with the same or similar capabilities are available, manufactured by a multitude of vendors. The process of reviewing hundreds of products is time-consuming but absolutely necessary to produce an efficient, cost-effective system. Expensive mistakes can occur if the network components are incompatible or cannot be upgraded to communicate with newer equipment. It is important to determine if vendor claims of compatibility and field upgradability are valid. Vendor claims of performance and compatibility are usually correct, but the test cases they use are highly controlled, with only a limited number of configurations used to perform the validation.

Questions frequently asked when planning for network and hardware communications components include:

- Will they meet our basic communications and networking needs?

- Do we have to acquire additional equipment or convert to new equipment when our network expands or when we need to replace older equipment?

- Are we buying capabilities we do not need at the present time, and is it cost-effective to do so?

Choices often are limited because of an organization's need for specific hardware configurations. This also applies when equipment is to be placed in remote locations where the vendor's support policies may not cover it. Equipment to be installed in remote locations and operated in a self-attended mode (unattended operation) requires higher mean time to failure parameters for a higher degree of reliability. The self-attendance requirement usually adds to the product's cost and generally limits selection to a few products. Another factor to consider is the vendor's minimum configuration product purchase requirements. Frequently, these policies force the buyer to purchase equipment that has more capabilities than required, thereby driving up the costs of network implementation and maintenance.

The term data communications hardware generally describes equipment designed specifically to support a computer data communications environment. It is important to recognize that the equipment also may be required to support a digitized voice environment. This chapter addresses the nonvoice digital environment that is used primarily for computer-to-computer or terminal-to-computer communications. However, it is unwise to assume that digital data and voice reside in separate worlds; such an assumption can create future problems because a combined environment might be a requirement further down the implementation path. (Figure 9.1 illustrates various types of equipment in a typical IBM network.)

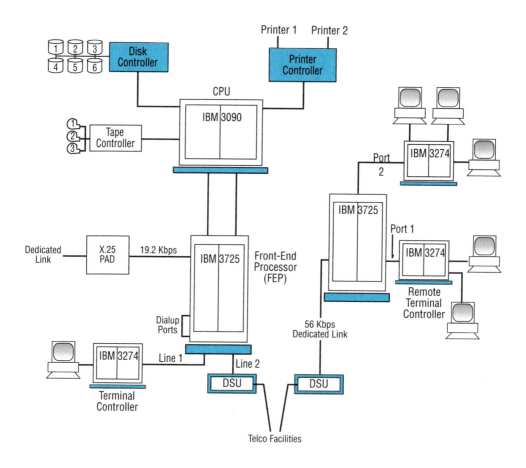

Figure 9.1 Typical IBM Data Communications Environment

As data communications evolved, the computer or central processor of the past was set up to manage communications software, multiple concurrent tasks and the physical communications lines. In many cases, the same situation still exists today. In small networks where traffic is moderate, this arrangement still works well. However, there is a price to pay for this arrangement because a processor with a somewhat high MIPS (millions of instructions per second) rate is required to support the combined data processing and communications activities. This high MIPS rate requirement is primarily due to the tremendous overhead needed for both memory-resident software resources and CPU processing cycles needed to achieve acceptable performance for communications activities.

COMMUNICATIONS PROCESSORS

One solution to the aforementioned problem is to use a communications processor (CP) specifically designed to function as an assistant to the central processing unit (CPU). This CP is used exclusively for data communications and can be interfaced in either of two environments. When the CP is placed local to the host computer system it is referred to as a front-end processor (FEP). The term "local" implies that the device is hard-wired to the CPU. (Figure 9.2 shows a communications processor and some of its components.)

When the communications processor is placed at a remote location and communicates with either an FEP or host computer using modems or digital service units, it is called a remote communications processor, or remote CP. A remote location is any location that communicates via telephone lines or other communications links back to the host site. The remote CP handles all terminal or communications activities at the remote site and between the remote site and the host system.

Before the introduction of the FEP the host computer performed all communications functions using memory-resident software. These communications programs had to

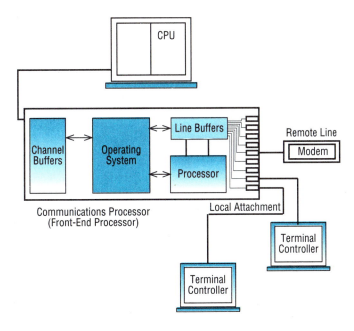

Figure 9.2   Communications Processor Environment

compete with applications and system programs for processing time and hardware resources. The use of front-end processors may reduce host computer use up to 50 percent by offloading system communications programs that normally would reside in the CPU. This increases host efficiency by having less overhead to conflict with other program operations. An FEP also increases the amount of CPU memory available for other programs to use.

Many companies manufacture communications processors. Among them are IBM, which produces the 3725 and 3745 type processors and NCR Corp., which manufactures the Comten communications processors (which support the IBM environment). Other manufacturers such as Digital Equipment and Hewlett-Packard provide communications processors designed primarily to support their own hardware.

Because channels attached to the host computer are considered to be high speed (1.5 to 5 megabytes per second) they are usually limited in number. This suggests that it is not practical to attach directly low-speed user terminal devices (9600 bps) to the host because low-speed devices will substantially slow the host. The front-end processor performs concentrator functions for the terminal network to take advantage of the high-speed input/output channel links. Local area networks also may be directly attached in the newer communications processors, such as the IBM 3725.

The communications processor, when channel-attached directly to the computer as an FEP, relieves the host of network and terminal communications duties. This gives the host more time for application-processing activities. This does not imply that the CPU does not perform communications activities; in fact, the CPU has extensive responsibilities for managing applications and system programs involved in communications.

The front-end or communications processor software is normally downloaded from the host computer at initial program load (IPL) time, when the operator boots the computer. The communications processor also may contain an optional disk storage device for self-loading the required communications software when power is turned on. When the communications processor is used as a front-end processor, it is channel-attached directly to the computer and also connected to the physical links. These links include twisted pairs, coaxial cable, dial-up or dedicated telephone links, and digital service (DS) links. The communications processor acts as the interface between the outside world and the computer.

The FEP is responsible for link control, which includes connections to the physical communications lines and management of the logical and physical terminal identification (ID) activities. Each terminal has a software-defined ID assigned to it when it is active as well as a permanent hardware address. The hardware and software use these IDs to locate specific terminals in the network.

The FEP also is responsible for establishing the logical links that allow terminals to communicate with the host. Logical linkage is the process of connecting an end-user terminal to a processing program by creating a path from the terminal to the program. This includes all of the physical lines, the system software and the application process. The establishment of a logical link is also referred to as session establishment.

In environments where different types of lines and terminals with different bit speeds and modes (duplex, half-duplex) are attached to the FEP, the communications processor must be able to recognize the bit speed and type of service required by each terminal in the network. Another important responsibility of the CP is polling and selection. This is the process of looking for and recognizing service requests from the terminals on the networks.

The CP can detect certain types of bit and frame errors and either will correct them or request retransmission from the sending device. Some CPs are able to perform data compression and expansion on the data transmitted by reducing the number of bits in a frame on the sending side and expanding the frame back to its original form on the receiving side. The CP may also support multiple binary code sets, such as the Extended Binary Coded Decimal Interchange Code (EBCDIC) and the American Standard Code for Information Interchange (ASCII), and provide code sets conversion suitable for host processing. Most FEPs can handle message switching between terminals and broadcasting of messages to all terminals. Often this can be accomplished without the involvement of the host computer.

The FEP also can contain several additional pieces of software to control the interface to other networks. Operating system software to manage communications is also required for the front-end processor. This software is considered to be communications control software and consists of network control software, partitioning supervisors, performance monitoring software and emulation programs.

Communications processors are often used for local area network control as well as the more traditional wide area networking activities.

MULTIPLEXERS

As the need for networking in an organization is evaluated, it becomes evident that a communications processor is not always cost justified because of the network's small size or the limited number of devices or lines it supports. Such a situation creates an opportunity for devices that are inexpensive, support a limited number of devices and provide functions similar to those of the FEP. In the past, a concentrator was used to enable multiple devices to use a single line. The concentrator has all but disappeared, and has been replaced by the multiplexer.

Multiplexing refers to the combining or interleaving of several data streams (data from multiple terminals) to form one composite data signal. This can also be accomplished by allocating time segments to each device wishing to use the link. The major advantage of incorporating a multiplexer into a network is cost. It is generally less expensive to use a multiplexer than to use direct links or a communications processor line for each terminal.

Multiplexing generally requires either pairs of multiplexers or a multiplexer and a communications processor capable of communicating with each other. A paired arrangement is needed because the composite data signal must be demultiplexed at the receiving end. Multiplexing devices may be found as standalone devices, combined with modems, or as part of a vendor's specific terminal controllers or communications processors.

Multiplexers utilize the total bandwidth available on the communications link. They operate by dividing the bandwidth into multiple channels or multiple time slots, which allows a group of terminals to communicate with the host computer or communications processor over a single line. Multiplexing techniques can provide a substantial savings in communications link charges by reducing recurring monthly line costs, which can be quite expensive.

Multiplexers interface terminals to communications processors via coaxial cable, or to host computer sites via modems or digital service units. They can perform a variety of functions, depending on which type of multiplexer is acquired and how much it costs. In many instances, a multiplexer can eliminate the need for other devices such as concentrators and modems.

The basic function of the multiplexer is to interface many low-speed devices onto a single line that provides a high-speed pathway to the host or communications processor. Very high-speed multiplexers are also used extensively by telephone carriers to handle their large traffic requirements. Many types of multiplexers are offered by a variety of vendors such as Network Equipment Technologies Inc., IBM, StrataCom Inc., AT&T and Paradyne. These devices use a variety of multiplexing methods that are generally compatible.

Operational Characteristics of Multiplexers

Multiplexers come in a variety of configurations and can support up to 32 terminal devices depending on the manufacturer and type of multiplexer required. Multiplexers are either intelligent or unintelligent. However, there is little difference between the two. In many cases the multiplexer can be custom configured from basic four-line support to comprehensive support for up to 32 devices. The configuration and operation vary from manufacturer to manufacturer, but they all provide compatible interfaces. The following options are available.

Terminals or computers are cabled to the multiplexer using a connection referred to as a port. The multiplexer is usually microprocessor controlled and programmable to allow technicians to access the configuration parameters. The object of multiplexing is to hold input from the attached devices in a memory buffer for a very short period of time (microseconds) and then, either using time- or frequency-division methods, combine them onto the outbound link. The receiving multiplexer separates the incoming data into its original parts and stores the parts in a port buffer for transmission to the attached device.

Most multiplexers are designed to support low- or medium-speed links (2400 bps to 19,200 bps). However, with the advent of ISDN and the availability of higher-speed links as well as reduced line costs, many multiplexers support speeds up to DS-3 (45 Mbps). The higher-speed multiplexers may also support fractional T1 links.

Many multiplexers provide individual port configurations that allow installers and technical support personnel to specify explicit character structures (code sets) and bit speeds. Several multiplexers can automatically detect and enable echo suppression on dial-up lines, as well as provide modem holding of the connection upon loss of carrier.

Each port on the multiplexer can be configured for a specific maximum transmit frame rate (the number of frames per second that can be transmitted), which depends on the type of line and the terminal or computer. The multiplexer's memory can be configured for the input queue size and output buffer size for each device. This may be necessary if a retransmission is required because of frequent errors on the line.

Many multiplexers allow for the attachment of a control terminal to provide the support staff with an interface to the multiplexer. The multiplexer contains software to provide statistical capture of operational and performance information via the control terminal and status panel. This information may include:

- The number of free buffers (memory or devices not in use) available
- The number of errors experienced by each port
- Trunk block error rate (the number of errors experienced by line reject commands)
- Trunk frame error rate (the number of frames requiring retransmission)
- Traffic density (the overall bps rate specified in percent of capacity busy)
- Frame-per-second rates

Multiplexers generally include link diagnostics and test capabilities to check remote and local trunk loopback, which is an end-to-end validation. In addition, tests for remote and local port loopback are used to ensure that the connections to the terminal or computer are intact. Control signal monitoring is also provided along with start-up diagnostics.

Multiplexers offer many additional features, including auto-speed capabilities that constantly monitor the lines for quality, then increase or decrease the bit rate depending on the values detected. High-Level Data Link Control (HDLC), which is an OSI protocol, and Synchronous Data Link Control (SDLC), which is another IBM protocol, are the most widely used protocols and almost all multiplexer manufacturers support them. Many multiplexer manufacturers support the Binary Synchronous Communications (BSC) protocol for the attachment of BSC terminals. BSC was developed by IBM for communications between terminals and computers, as well as from computer to computer. Many other computer manufacturers have incorporated BSC-type terminals as well.

Most multiplexers can be configured to support both asynchronous (one character at a time) and synchronous (clocked bit strings) terminals in the same environment. An additional feature, referred to as piggybacking, enables multiplexer ports to be connected to another multiplexer. This is required when a series of stepdowns to reduce the bit rate are needed because of the high speed of the primary link.

Frequency-Division Multiplexers

Frequency-division multiplexing was one of the first multiplexing techniques to be used in the data communications industry. Its technology was taken from the telephone industry. The frequency-division multiplexer is an analog device and is used primarily in broadband local area networks where different channels are needed. The LAN requires the use of a frequency-agile modem in a decentralized environment to access specific channels. The frequency-division multiplexer will divide the total available input/output bandwidths into the same number of channels on the link, depending on the number of ports and devices supported. The total input bps rate of all terminals or devices connected to the multiplexer must not exceed the output line bps rate.

If a device attached to the frequency-division multiplexer is taken off line (turned off), no reallocation of the available frequency is made in order for the other attached devices to take advantage of the additional bandwidth. This means that the multiplexer does not have dynamic reallocation capabilities to use all available bandwidth. FDM multiplexers have built-in digital-to-analog converters, so the need for modems at both ends of the link is eliminated.

Each channel designated within the total bandwidth is separated from other channels by guard bands. These are subchannels designed to prevent information channels from interfering with one another. This is a waste of bandwidth but is required with analog transmission to prevent crosstalk and interference. The amount of frequency assigned to a given channel depends on the speed of that channel: Higher speeds require greater bandwidth. Frequency shift keying is the most common modulation technique used in frequency-division multiplexers. Frequency-division multiplexing is normally used for digitized voice applications and not data. (Figure 9.3 illustrates a frequency-division multiplexer with all channels active and shows what happens to the bandwidth when one of the channels becomes inactive.)

Time-Division Multiplexers

Time-division multiplexing (TDM) is more efficient than frequency-division multiplexing because it uses the high-speed link more effectively. Time-division multiplexers are digital devices that combine several digital input signals from a computer or terminal into one composite digital output signal. Several time division multiplexers permit attachment of DDS digital links, but a digital service unit or channel service unit is required to interface the multiplexer to the link.

Time-division multiplexers operate by allocating time slots to each terminal attached to the port. Usually the total bit rate for all devices cannot exceed the output line bps rate; however, a higher level of throughput efficiency can be achieved by using data compression. Compression/recompression techniques, if employed, must be present in each of the multiplexers. To compress the data, the multiplexer uses a binary algorithm to reduce the total number of bits to be transmitted by some percentage factor. The receiving side uses a reversing algorithm and restores the received bit string. In most cases, as with frequency-division multiplexing, the time slot for a device out of service or not currently sending is not reallocated.

Some time-division multiplexers allow for the establishment of a fixed order for transmitting and receiving data. The multiplexer can accept as little as one bit or one byte of data from each terminal or computer and assemble the data into a blocked frame within the buffer for transmission. This is referred to as bit or character interleaving. Some newer TDM devices can process packets in a packet-switching environment. Figure 9.4 illustrates a time-division multiplexer servicing four terminals and what the bandwidth will look like when one of the devices is taken off-line.

Similar to frequency-division multiplexers, some time-division multiplexers can support both asynchronous and synchronous devices at the same time but will usually operate in a synchronous mode. As stated earlier, some TDM devices require modems to convert the digital signal into an analog form. However, some time-division multiplexers incorporate modems into their design. Many communications processors and front-end processors include multiplexing circuits, thereby eliminating the need for a multiplexer at the host computer side.

Statistical Time-Division Multiplexers

Statistical time-division multiplexing (STDM) is one of the newer multiplexing techniques. The statistical time-division multiplexer provides the same capabilities as the time division

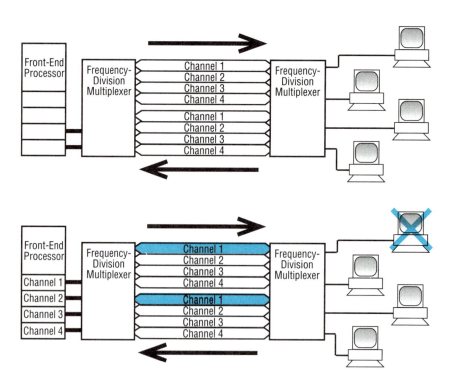

Figure 9.3   Frequency-Division Multiplexing

multiplexers but it contains additional intelligence to provide time-slot duration allocation dynamically. If a device becomes inactive, the multiplexer will reallocate its time slot to another attached device; this allows the remaining active devices to operate at a higher speed. A major drawback to using statistical multiplexers is their high cost. Although the cost has been steadily declining, STDM multiplexers are still expensive.

The statistical time-division multiplexer like many time-division multiplexers, has microprocessor-based intelligence and manages all buffering, blocking and data framing for input/output operations. It may also provide an operator interface for monitoring line performance and configuring lines and ports.

Often, when two or more high-speed devices are linked together, frame flow control management is required. Two types of flow control are used in statistical multiplexers, internal and external. Internal flow control enables the statistical time-division multiplexer to stop the port-attached terminal or computer from sending any more data. This is used primarily when the multiplexer's buffers are full and it cannot accept any more data from a port. Flow control is accomplished by sending an x-off hexadecimal character to the terminal or by lowering the clear-to-send (CTS) signal between the data communications equipment (DCE) and the data terminal equipment (DTE). This is pin 5 on the EIA-232 interface cable. When the statistical time-division multiplexer is ready to receive data from the terminal once more, it will send an x-on hexadecimal character or raise the CTS signal. Figure 9.5 illustrates a statistical time-division multiplexer servicing four terminals and what the bandwidth will look like when one of the devices is taken off-line.

In external flow control, the terminal or computer sends the statistical time-division

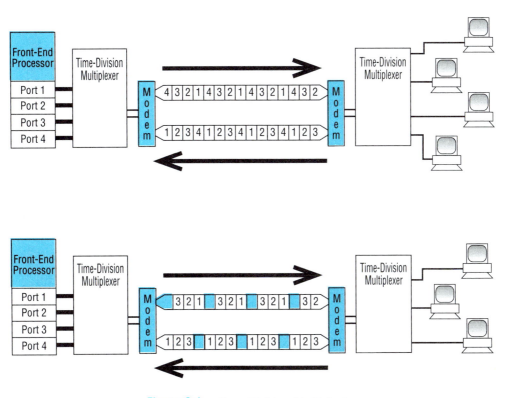

Figure 9.4   Time-Division Multiplexing

multiplexer a signal to indicate that it cannot receive any more data. It accomplishes this by either using the x-off capability or by lowering the data terminal ready (DTR) signal, which tells the multiplexer to stop sending data. When the terminal is ready to receive again, it performs the reverse operation. Some statistical time-division multiplexers can pass some of the EIA-232 control signals to remote multiplexers or modems. These signals are used to control what are referred to as tail circuits, which allow a local CPU (host computer) to control a remote multiplexer.

Wave-Division Multiplexers

Wave-division multiplexing (WDM) is currently under development and is undergoing consideration by the Institute of Electrical and Electronics Engineers as a standard to support multiplexing on fiber-optic cable (see Figure 9.6). WDM permits the use of different wave lengths of light representing different data channels on the same fiber-optic cable. This technique is similar to frequency-division multiplexing. WDM may be viewed as laser beams of different colors crossing each other. Each beam can be distinctly identified even though combined with the other light waves.

WDM technology will require new transport techniques to manage data flow. A proposed standard, the Synchronous Optical Network (SONET), is under development by the CCITT to handle the very high speeds (in the billions of bits per second range) associated with multifrequency fiber optics. The basic building block of SONET is the

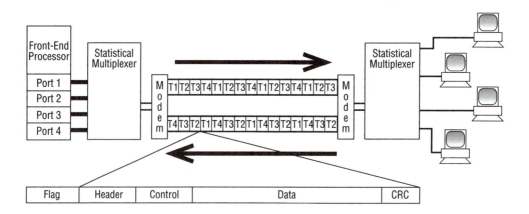

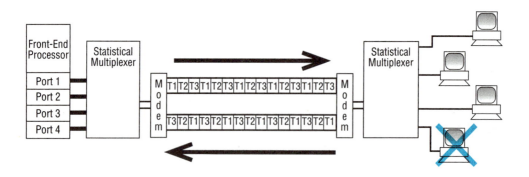

Figure 9.5   Statistical Time-Division Multiplexing

Synchronous Transport Signal Level 1 (STS-1). STS-1 is a protocol that employs a synchronous frame alignment allowing DS-1 bit rates to be extracted from the STS-1 frames without the frame being disassembled and reassembled. Most of the STS-1 frame consists of the SONET payload envelope, a large data field that allows STS-1 to carry a clear-channel DS-3 signal or a number of lower bit rate links.

Multiplexer Framing

In a straightforward statistical multiplexer, the data to be multiplexed from a particular terminal or device is collected and temporarily stored in a terminal buffer. The multiplexer creates a transport frame from each of the terminal buffers. Each frame is n bytes in length and contains several pieces of information such as the location of the sending and receiving devices. The actual framing of the data may employ a standard protocol such as HDLC, described in detail in Chapter 15.

Each frame may vary in length (number of bytes of data) depending on the number of characters accumulated from a particular terminal since the last transmission. If no data is present from a device, no frame is sent. If a single character is present, the frame is transmitted because holding a frame with only a few data characters can cause transmission delay. Some statistical multiplexers allow channel priorities to be established. Typical signals that are passed include request to send (RTS), carrier detect (CD), data terminal ready (DTR), data set ready (DSR) and ring indicator (RI).

Error Control

Most multiplexers provide end-to-end error control and use a technique referred to as cyclical redundancy check (CRC) detection (CRC-16, CRC-32, CRC-64). This error detection field is resident in each information frame and contains the results of a complicated formula for error detection. At the transmitting multiplexer, the CRC bit value is calculated using a series of algebraic calculations based on the total number of data bits in the packet to be transported. The CRC is then transported along with the data inside the transport frame behind the data. At the receiving end, the same formula is used to recalculate

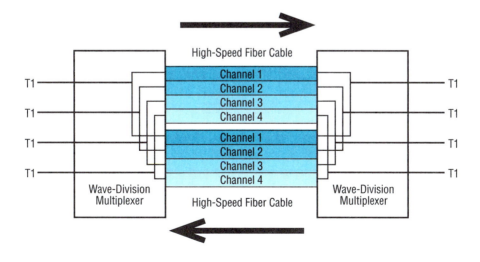

Figure 9.6   Wave-Division Multiplexing

the CRC on the received data and the results are then compared to the original CRC sent. If they differ, the receiving multiplexer requests that the frame be retransmitted and discards the data in error.

PACKET ASSEMBLY AND DISASSEMBLY DEVICES

Public data networks (PDNs) are an alternative to dedicated links. They provide error detection, routing and switching functions, relieving the user of those responsibilities. If a PDN is used, it is the responsibility of the user to format the data into packets or frames suitable for transfer over the PDN. If the PDN is used only for carrier activity, computer software in the processors most likely will accomplish the framing activity. Many organizations are not large enough to have a computer dedicated for PDN terminal activity, so they use outside sources. Several manufacturers provide packet assembler/disassembler (PAD) devices to perform the framing and conversion functions. The most common is the X.25 PAD, which provides an interface with an X.25 public data network (see Figure 9.7).

X.25 is a CCITT standard for interfacing DTE and DCE devices. DTE equipment comprises terminals and computers, and DCE equipment consists of PADs, modems and multiplexers operating in a public data network environment. A PAD may be purchased by the end user or provided by the public data network or hardware vendor. Some

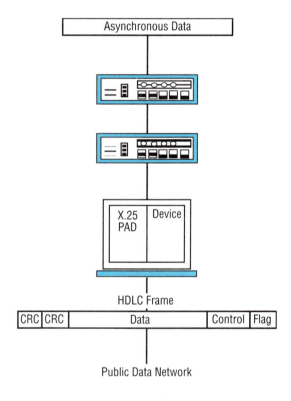

Figure 9.7   X.25 PAD

telephone companies in Europe and Asia allow the use only of equipment provided by themselves. The output from a PAD looks like an OSI-defined HDLC frame and contains a minimum of 128 data bytes, in conformance with the 1980 HDLC standard.

As with most types of communications equipment, there are many options for PADs. For example, many PADs support multiple asynchronous devices and terminals. The PAD communicates via synchronous transmission methods at speeds up to 720 Kbps. All PADs are designed for specific network standards and adhere to one or more of the CCITT standards, including X.3, X.25, X.28 and X.29, as well as the X.121 (universal addressing) extensions.

Many PADs contain intelligence for activities such as password control and security; several PADs also provide statistical and performance reporting. Often a company will use the computer services of the PDN in place of resident computers because of the extensive support provided by the PDN. In this case the company will have only a PAD and asynchronous terminals on-site.

NETWORK CONTROLLERS

As networks grow and become distributed to remote locations, it is increasingly important for data communications technical support to have a clear view of network performance. This ensures that quick action can be instituted if the network begins to experience problems. Along with visibility requirements, network managers also must have the ability to modify configuration parameters that govern the operation of the network.

Network performance determination, as well as problem detection, are often difficult tasks to accomplish because of the number of devices making up the network, their locations and the wide variety of media in use. Several vendors have developed a type of communications processor for network monitoring and line control referred to as a network controller. Network controllers are designed to provide local and remote monitoring of the communications network and to allow quick detection of errors and rapid problem resolution. Before the introduction of network control centers, substantial degradation of the network had to occur before users or technical support staff had any indication that a problem existed.

Figure 9.8 illustrates a multinational network headquartered in London that requires a network controller. It provides the routing and control for processing and communications nodes at key locations within Europe.

Often the network controller is located in a remote network control center and is designed to act as a hub for all network links. Depending on the size of the network, the controller may support multiple control terminals and enable the setting of definable alarm threshold values. This means that the network controller will notify a control terminal when a programmed value, such as the acceptable retransmit on error rate, is exceeded. Program values can be established by the technical support department for the number of packet retransmissions in a given period of time, parity errors, number of lines active, number of lines idle or other important operations that should be monitored.

Comprehensive circuit quality monitoring is another function of the network control monitor. Many controllers can monitor links and dynamically shift link resources when errors are encountered. This is accomplished by constantly monitoring and testing all point-to-point and multipoint lines in the network. The controller also can provide a status report on all terminals in the network on demand.

Often, a network controller functions as a value-added device, providing gateway functions for different code sets and protocols. This allows the network to function in a heterogeneous manner without substantial degradation. Many companies (including AT&T,

Codex Corp. and Racal Vadic Corp.) offer network controllers that can be configured for specific networks and terminal types.

TERMINAL CONTROLLERS

Direct attachment of terminals to a host computer is not usually considered efficient because of the wide disparity in bit rates between the channel (megabits per second) and the terminal (hundreds of bits per second). Most computer manufacturers provide either device-level or board-level connectivity for terminals.

The terminal controller device or board is designed to support a variety of terminal types and printers in a local or remote environment. In the non-IBM world, the boards or terminal control devices may be referred to as asynchronous or synchronous terminal adapters. Terminal controllers associated with the IBM world are referred to as cluster controllers. The terminal controller can be viewed as an intelligent microprocessor-based device having specific dedicated responsibilities. Figure 9.9 shows the internals of a typical terminal controller.

The terminal controller performs a number of functions depending on the manufacturer and how it is to be configured. The controller is primarily responsible for establishing and maintaining connectivity to individual terminals or groups of terminals. The role of the terminal controller also is evolving because many are being used for additional activities such as the control of local area networks.

One of the controller's basic functions is to maintain the physical addressees for all terminals it manages. Another is performing link control framing and deframing for data transmission between itself and the host computer or front-end processor. A third function is error detection. If an error is encountered, the controller is responsible for coordinating and requesting retransmission.

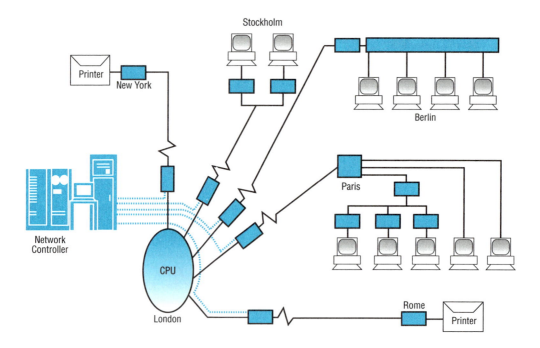

Figure 9.8 Example of a Network Control Center Headquartered in London

A terminal controller normally contains memory and allocates buffer space for blocking and deblocking of messages between the terminal and the host computer. It controls the transfer of data between the computer link and the terminals and ensures that all terminals have equal access to the host.

The controller is hard-wired to each terminal and manages polling and selection requests to and from each terminal after it has received the poll/selection request from the FEP or host computer. When the controller is installed or the terminal configuration changes, the controller needs to be configured (set up for the types and numbers of terminals it will control). This is normally accomplished using vendor-supplied software loaded from an installed diskette or hard disk drive.

Identical in operation to the terminal controller is the value-added terminal controller manufactured by such companies as Memorex Telex Corp., Televideo Systems Inc., Telex Communications Inc. and Charles River Data Systems Inc. The value-added terminal controller offers features greater than those found on the original manufacturer's equipment. Usually this device is designed for a specific configuration and is able to perform protocol conversion. It also may be designed to handle character set conversion (ASCII to EBCDIC) and to support a larger number of terminals than the original manufacturer's equipment.

Many of the newer controllers provide emulation for asynchronous and synchronous terminals at the same time, allowing the user to have a mix of low-cost and high-end terminals. Some controllers can link to multiple host computers and provide its terminals with a selection capability at the touch of a key.

Speeds up to 19.2 Kbps are standard, but several controllers operate at higher speeds (up to 56 Kbps) than the original equipment available with the system. Many value-added controllers contain additional intelligence and memory and they support enhanced color displays and graphics.

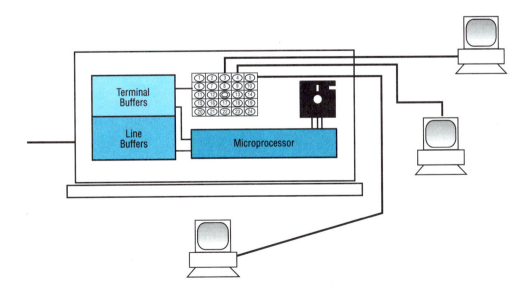

Figure 9.9   Terminal Controller Internals

TERMINALS AND PCS

Terminals enable users to interact with a computer. Excluding those designed for specific activities, terminals are considered to be input/output devices that usually have a keyboard for input, a cathode ray tube (CRT) or video screen for output and possibly a cable-connected printer for hardcopy output.

Several types of terminals in a variety of shapes and sizes are manufactured. Most CRTs are generally configured for 25 lines vertically and 80 characters horizontally, or 43 lines vertically and 133 characters horizontally. The twenty-fifth line is usually reserved for communicating status information between the computer system and the user and may be used to indicate that the system is busy, disconnected or available. Some terminals provide a greater number of resolution widths and lines, but these must have enough intelligence to execute a screen image sizing program.

Terminal functions can also be performed by personal computers equipped with terminal emulation hardware or software or both.

Dumb Terminals

A terminal described as "dumb" (as opposed to "smart") is a terminal that has no microprocessor or memory. The internal equipment of this type of terminal is usually nothing more than a video display tube with several wires. Almost all terminal configuration is performed by the software in the attached computer. Most dumb terminals function asynchronously, sending one character at a time, and are considered to be low-speed devices. Because they have few components, they generally cost less than terminals with some intelligence. This type of terminal is also referred to as a scroll-mode terminal because each byte is transferred immediately on being entered at the terminal. Dumb terminals are generally used as low-cost inquiry and data entry devices. They usually do not provide enough capability for the interactive end user.

Several terminal manufacturers produce dumb terminals with limited intelligence. These terminals contain microprocessors and memory and operate identically to those described above, except that they also provide buffering and line control management. Many dumb terminals allow some form of basic configuration and have dip switches you can set to change the display set-up. This type of terminal also may have some error detection capability but usually will not have control capabilities for retry. It might also have serial printer support to dump the screen to a printer for a hard copy.

Smart Terminals

Smart terminals contain intelligence in the form of a microprocessor and memory. The terminal design can be general or specific, depending on the application it is intended to handle. Examples of specific designs include airline terminals and automatic teller machines. Smart terminals are sometimes referred to as page-mode terminals because they hold pages in memory and transfer the complete page rather than send bytes one at a time to the terminal controller lines.

Probably the most popular smart terminals in use today are the VT family of terminals from Digital Equipment and the IBM 3170 series of terminals. The standard smart terminal can be either asynchronous or synchronous. DEC terminals operate asynchronously, while the IBM 3170s employ synchronous operation.

Almost all smart terminals are microprocessor-based and have extensive programming in read only memory (ROM). This code contains diagnostic programs that monitor and test activities such as character generation, memory, framing and deframing of the transport data and extensive error detection.

Smart terminals provide pixel addressability, which is the ability to move a text or graphics character to a specific location on the display. They also provide a protected field and a field tab capability. A protected field is an area of the display that cannot be modified by the user. Field tab capability enables the cursor to tab to the next unprotected field on the screen. Most smart terminals support both serial and parallel printers. Some of the more sophisticated terminals, such as the Tektronix Inc. color display system, provide extensive color display configuration capabilities.

Terminal Emulation Using PCs

PCs are used as both standalone peer devices acting as nodes in a communications network and as emulation devices for smart terminals. The PC has become valuable in environments where both the personal computer and a host-connected terminal are required. Use of the PC in this environment provides a more efficient method for accessing and processing information than a dumb or smart terminal because it can assume some of the processing activity that otherwise would be performed by the host, including screen formatting and data manipulation.

Computer systems such as those from Digital Equipment and Hewlett-Packard can often communicate directly with PCs using software control. However, because the PC performs data communications and data processing activities somewhat differently than a dumb or smart terminal, it often will require an add-on board for terminal emulation. This is especially true for IBM host computer connectivity because of the way an IBM computer normally communicates with its terminals.

Many add-on boards are manufactured for PC-to-host connectivity. One example is the IRMA board from Digital Communications Associates Inc., which is designed for IBM terminal emulation. Many other communications equipment manufacturers also produce boards to enable the personal computer to act as either an asynchronous or synchronous terminal in a large computer environment.

A PC emulating a terminal provides many more functions than a dumb or smart terminal, including the capability to communicate with the host as a native device, download files to its own disk storage devices and operate as a standalone computer to process data. Use of the PC as a terminal enables data processing functions to be distributed to remote sites where they can provide the most benefit. Such functions were once available only on the host computer. Today, in many cases, the host computer site is downsized because the processing power required to support large networks can be shifted to remote PCs.

REMOTE AND NETWORK JOB ENTRY TERMINALS

Remote and network job entry (RNJE) terminals are no longer considered terminals, but rather complete processing systems. RNJE has evolved from a pre-PC period when it represented the only method for remote data capture and printing to a current environment in which it is used for remote ancillary functions such as high-speed printing and terminal access. The role of the RNJE terminal has changed from a remote batch input/output device to one of remote processing capable of supporting the processing needs of the remote sites and then transmitting or receiving the processed information to or from the host computer.

Generally speaking, the RNJE processor provides limited capabilities for independent processing because of its restricted logic and memory. It is typically used as a pathway to a remote host computer for multiple terminals or printers. The RNJE terminal environment consists of several components and is somewhat expensive in comparison to the asynchronous or synchronous terminal, ranging from $20,000 to $75,000.

RNJE terminals are designed primarily for high-speed synchronous data transfer (9600 bps or greater). They are usually connected via synchronous dedicated links and full-duplex modems. Components of RNJE terminals include the processor (which is usually a minicomputer such as the IBM 5200-8200), a control console that establishes the linkages with the host and supervises the data transfer operations, and a number of attached I/O devices such as readers, data entry terminals, disk drives for local storage, tape drives and printers.

MULTIUSER WORKSTATIONS

The multiuser workstation is an advancement on the data entry workstation concept that has been available for quite some time. It offers a concurrent-window, multiple-access environment so that users can view and access multiple environments such as PC-DOS, UNIX and ASCII terminal emulation.

This type of system consists of a minicomputer or microcomputer with a reduced instruction set computer (RISC) processor, extensive memory and I/O capabilities. It is normally designed to use an operating system that has multitasking capabilities, such as UNIX. The system supports a number of semi-intelligent terminals and the processor provides communications links for each of the terminals on request in order to interface with other systems. Most of these systems provide secondary storage disks and tapes as well as printing capabilities for each of the users. Network control is provided for links to outside networks. Manufacturers of multiuser workstations include Sun Microsystems, Hewlett-Packard, Motorola Inc. and IBM.

Multiuser workstations are used extensively in engineering environments. They provide high-processing throughput and are ideal for the CPU-intensive activities required for engineering, design, high-definition graphics and computer aided design (CAD).

Many manufacturers refer to multiuser workstation environments as client-server or terminal-server environments. They can also be considered local area networks; for example, the Sun Microsystems terminal-server environment uses the Ethernet LAN access method for communications between each of the terminals.

GATEWAYS AND BRIDGES

Often, the mechanisms involved in communications between dissimilar devices requires extensive CPU capabilities because of the differences in packet sizes, character sets, protocol interfaces, data security and data formats. Gateways and bridges are intelligent devices used to permit internetwork communications between similar and dissimilar networks (multivendor networks). These devices relieve the various user nodes on the network of interface responsibilities. Gateways and bridges perform the same basic function, that of providing access to other networks and nodes. However, gateways and bridges each have different responsibilities.

Gateways

A gateway connects dissimilar networks (see Figure 9.10). Gateways provide the following services:

- Character code sets (ASCII to EBCDIC) and protocol conversion from one network format to another (e.g., an IBM SNA network to a DECnet network).

- Segmentation (breaking the frame into smaller pieces) and reassembly of frames (putting the pieces back together) when traveling from one network to another.

- Secured access between networks (password validation).

- Assistance in providing dynamic routing to internetwork nodes through an intermediate network. Dynamic routing means that the gateway provides the speediest possible path for the data.

- Expedited data services and resequencing services, depending on the intelligence of the gateway. Expedited data services allow priority transfer and resequencing services to ensure that packets are delivered in the same order they were sent.

Bridges

Bridges connect similar networks such as two DECnet networks or two IBM Token-Ring networks. Depending on their level of intelligence, they also may provide many of the services that gateways provide, such as security, segmentation and reassembly, and expedited data services. Figure 9.11 illustrates a multilevel bridge connecting multiple Ethernet LANs.

Typically, bridges are used to connect two LANs because LANs operate more efficiently when their nodes are limited to a small geographical area. The bridge permits workstations on a LAN to communicate with each other over a wider area, and at the same time enables the bridged LANs to maintain a higher level of performance.

A typical example of a bridge in use might be in a company that has multiple local area networks. The reason it uses multiple LANs is because each department is responsible for its own data and processing and the use of a LAN allows members of each of the departments to share common data. Bridges are employed between departments such as purchasing and accounts receivables, because of the departments' need to share corporate data occasionally.

CASE STUDY (CONTINUED)

Selecting the required communications equipment was difficult for the bank because it wanted to make sure that the acquired hardware would be upgradable and have a life of at least three years. The bank's planning team established a set of guidelines for purchasing or leasing hardware that specified that all branch components would be standard from the same vendor. They also wanted local support from the vendor or distributor, and all hardware had to be field upgradable.

For each branch, the planning committee selected medialess PCs for the teller workstations. This will provide a degree of intelligence and will assist in improving transaction response time. Each of the workstations will be connected to a branch local area network controlled by an administration PC with disk storage. This, as well as other administration workstations used for other branch activities, will be connected through a dedicated link back to a service center. If multiple ATM machines are installed at the branch, they will share a dedicated line using a time-division multiplexer.

The service center does not use a multiplexer because of the small size of the network and the expense associated with multiplexers. However, a front-end processor is used to handle all of the branch links as well as the high-speed link to the other service centers. The front-end processor will be configured to handle 50 dedicated links and up to 10 directly attached terminal controllers. This will provide support for the programming staff, which will use smart terminals for all online activities.

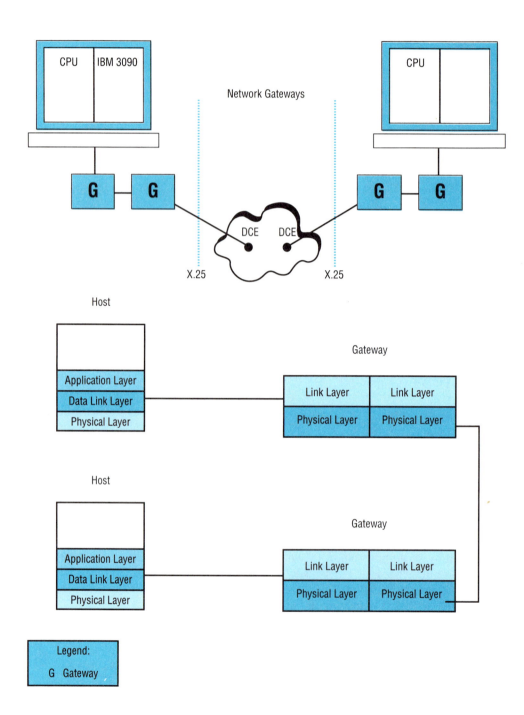

Figure 9.10   Example of a Gateway Connection

Data Communications Hardware

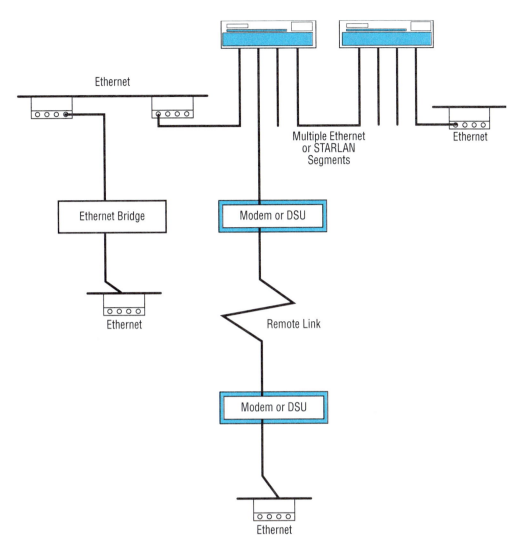

Figure 9.11   Ethernet Bridge Connecting Multiple LANs

REVIEW QUESTIONS

1. What activity of the host computer is relieved by the communications processor?
2. Name three major functions of the FEP.
3. True or false: FDM stands for frequency-directing modulation.
4. True or false: Multiplexers provide four different techniques for the transfer of data.
5. True or false: STDM is the most current multiplexing scheme.
6. Wave-division multiplexing is used with what medium?

7. True or false: Network controllers provide a focal point for monitoring the communications network.

8. True or false: The terminal controller requires software to function properly.

9. True or false: Smart and dumb are two classifications for terminal types.

10. True or false: Remote job entry systems are normally used for batch data transfer activities.

CHAPTER

10

Communications Using Modems

INTRODUCTION

The word "modem" is a contraction of modulator-demodulator. Modems attach to computers, terminals, terminal controllers, multiplexers or communications processors. They convert (modulate) binary digital signals into analog signals (electrical signals representing ones and zeros). The converted signals then can be sent across a telephone network using standard analog telephone lines. A paired modem on the other end of the link reconverts the analog signals into digital signals for input into a device at the receiving side.

Early in the evolution of the modem, users discovered that not all modems are created equal. If an attempt was made to connect modems built to the same standards from different manufacturers, they often would not work together. Today, because CCITT standards are very specific, modems from different manufacturers that conform to a specific CCITT standard will interface properly.

All public telephone operating companies follow the same rules regarding the connection of modems to their networks. These rules were devised by the old North American Bell system and are now covered by international CCITT V series standards for signal strength, modulation technique, interfaces, bit rate and error correction. These standards govern many types of modem connections to the various worldwide telephone networks.

Unlike computers that transfer bytes in a parallel manner (i.e., eight bits sent over eight wires or channels at the same time), most modems operate in a serial manner (one bit after the other over a single channel). The majority of modems available for use in the world today are of the serial type because of timing problems associated with parallel transmission. A special class of parallel modems has been defined in the old Bell standard; however, due to propagation delay that can vary the bit times from one channel to another, they are not generally available and are considered experimental. Modems are manufactured by many companies, including Racal-Vadac, Codex, IBM, Hayes Microcomputer Products Inc. and Everex Systems Inc.

MODEM HISTORY AND DEVELOPMENT

Originally, AT&T, the worldwide telephone companies and the regional Bell operating companies referred to modems as datasets or data termination equipment (DTE) devices. Customers who wanted to use the public telephone network for data communications were required to use equipment provided by those telephone companies.

The telephone carriers required customers to use a dataset supplied by a telephone or telecommunications company, as well as a direct access arrangement (DAA) device. This device was an external registered protective circuitry device installed between the dataset and the line. Its function was to protect the telephone companies' lines and central office equipment from high-voltage surges, out-of-bandwidth frequencies and high signal levels. In other words, it kept the dataset from putting out voltages high enough to cause the lines to catch fire.

While control of the attachment of datasets to the telephone network was and still is necessary, it was also construed as a monopolistic practice because the telephone companies would not allow datasets manufactured by anyone other than themselves to be used. Due to activities started by various modem manufacturers that ultimately led to a supreme court ruling in 1968, restrictions on the use of non-Bell attachments were lifted. DAA devices are no longer required because their function has been incorporated into the various modems now available. Internationally, many telephone companies outside North America still require customers to lease or purchase modems from them rather than from an independent source.

MODEM STANDARDS

Bell Standards

AT&T set the *de facto* standards for modems, and many of those standards are still valid in North America. Most Bell standards have a compatible CCITT V standard that is used worldwide, while some Bell standards have become obsolete. Currently, most modems installed in North America and Europe conform to the V series standards.

CCITT V Standards

The CCITT is the major international organization responsible for modem standards. Many of those standards have replaced the Bell standards. In many cases, CCITT and Bell standards are compatible or identical. Because modem technology has advanced rapidly since the Bell standards were developed, many CCITT standards do not have a Bell counterpart.

The CCITT is also responsible for many other standards, including modem interface standards. These are electrical and mechanical standards for the connection of modems (DCE) to terminal equipment (DTE); the CCITT V.34 and V.21bis standards are good examples. The V.24 interface standard (similar to EIA-232) and the V.28 standard are also commonly used. A newer class of standards is emerging from the CCITT for modem error correction and data compression and currently consists of V.42 and V.42bis. The suffix "bis" or "ter" following a standard means that the standard has an authorized variation.

Table 10.1 lists the standards for most CCITT V series modems. Where applicable, corresponding Bell standards have been included.

The following V recommendations are some of the more important standards that apply to modems and data transmission:

V.2 — Specification of power levels for data transmission over telephone lines

V.5 — Specification of synchronous data signaling rates over the switched network

V.6 — Specification of synchronous data signaling rates over leased lines

V.7 — Definition of other key terms used in the V series recommendations

V.10 — Description of an unbalanced physical-level interchange circuit

V.11 — Description of a balanced physical-level interchange circuit

V.24 — Definition of the interchange circuit pins between DTE and DCE

V.28 — Description of unbalanced interchange circuits operating below 20 Kbps

For more information on these standards, refer to Appendix A.

CCITT Standard	Normal Data Rate	Fall-back Rate	Circuit Supported 2-wire	Circuit Supported 4-wire	Modulation Method	Sync/Async	Bell Version
V.21	300	—	Duplex	—	FSK	Async	-103
V.21ter	300	—	Duplex	—	FSK	Async	-212A
V.22	1200	—	Duplex	—	PSK	Sync/Async	212A
V.22bis	2400	1200	Duplex	—	QAM/DPSK	Sync/Async	None
V.23	1200	600	Half	Duplex	FSK	Async	*202
V.26	2400	—	—	Duplex	DPSK	Sync	201
V.26bis	2400	1200	Half	Duplex	DPSK	Sync	
V.26ter	2400			Duplex	(TCM or QAM)	Sync	
V.27	4800	—		Duplex	DPSK	Sync	-208
V.27bis	4800	2400		Duplex	DPSK	Sync	
V.27ter	4800	2400	Half		QAM	Sync	
V.29	9600	4800**	—	Duplex	QAM	Sync	-209
V.32	9600	4800**	Duplex	—	TCM/QAM	Sync	None
V.33	14400	12200	—	Duplex	TCM/QAM	Sync	None
V.35	48000		Duplex				
V.36	48/56/64/72 kbps						
V.37	72 kbps		Duplex				

* Some compatibility
— Similar not compatible
** Additional fall-back speed of 2400 bps

Table 10.1   CCITT Modem Standards

MODEM INTERNALS

Modems are designed to transmit as well as to receive data; therefore, they must contain circuits to handle both activities. Two primary circuits are called the transmitter/modulator circuit, which manages the output activities, and the receiver/demodulator circuit, which controls the line input (see Figure 10.1).

The transmitter/modulator circuit is responsible for converting the digital bits originating from the terminal into electrical signals compatible with the analog transmission facility. This circuit consists of several components. The data encoder is used in conjunction with transmitter timing to determine the modulation changes required (i.e., dibits, tribits, etc.), depending on the modulation technique employed by the modem. The transmitter control is used to control the on/off cycle of the carrier and the request-to-send/clear-to-send delay times needed to keep the terminal in synchronization.

The transmit timing source is a component used to output a transmit clock (TC) signal for synchronous modems only. It provides the bit clocking signal for the terminal if the terminal does not contain a clocking source of its own. All modems must contain a modulator, which changes the carrier waveform using one of the CCITT or Bell modulation standards to represent data as determined by the data encoder.

Modems also contain a band-limiting filter that shapes the frequency spectrum and ensures that all signals are placed on the correct frequencies within the analog spectrum generated by the transmitter/modulator. A line amplifier also may be found in some modems, which allows the output signal to be adjusted for more or less strength. Most modems contain a transformer that provides a connection between the modem and the line; it is used for both the transmit component and the receive component.

On some modems, a test generator may be incorporated to generate a pseudo-random data pattern for diagnosis when in the test mode. This pattern is used to validate the modem's integrity.

The receiver/demodulator circuit accepts analog signals from the communications link and converts them back to their original digital format. After conversion, the formatted digital information is transferred to the terminal or computer via an interface cable for processing. The receiver comprises several components. A data decoder is used in

Transmitter	Receiver
Data Encoder	Demodulator
Modulator	Data Decoder
Transmit Clock	Clock and Phasing
Transmitter Control	Pattern Checker
Filter and Amplifier	Filter and Equalizer
Transformer	Amplifier
Test Generator	Transformer

Figure 10.1   Modem Internals

conjunction with the demodulator to format the received data into serial digital form. The modem's receive circuit may also contain clock and phasing circuits that generate a receive clock signal from the demodulated signal for output on the V.24/EIA-232 interface to the terminal. The modem receive circuit also contains a demodulator that extracts the part of the spectrum signal containing information as it is received from the telephone link.

Most modems also contain an equalizer that compensates for channel distortion allowing higher data rates and better performance because the data signal is cleaner and requires less error handling. Another component is the AGC amplifier, which provides automatic gain control of the incoming signal. The AGC amplifier allows the modem to compensate for amplitude variations in the telephone line; this ensures that the signal strength stays constant. AGC has been used in television for quite some time to limit the strength of the signal so as to better manage and convert it to sound and images. A band-limiting filter may be included to shape the frequency spectrum of the analog signal received from the telephone line. It eliminates any extraneous frequencies that are outside the bandwidth of the analog data stream.

Finally, if the modem incorporates a test generator, it will also have a pattern checker. This is used to validate the received pseudo-random data pattern from the pattern generator for errors when the modem is placed in the test mode.

TRANSMISSION METHODS

Modems use one of two transmission methods for transporting data across a communications link: asynchronous and synchronous. Modems are primarily designed to support one or the other method; however, some modems can be configured to support either type of transmission. Each method is used with specific network architectures and transmission protocols.

Asynchronous Modems

Asynchronous modems are usually low-speed devices (50 bps up to 2400 bps) and are normally less expensive than synchronous modems. Because of their low costs, they generally offer fewer features than synchronous modems. But this is rapidly changing because of the popularity of the personal computer and the market it represents for low-speed modems.

The asynchronous modem is used primarily for low-speed start/stop, character-oriented transmission where 10 or 11 bits are sent at a time. Some of the more expensive modems can transmit and receive asynchronous data at rates up to 16,600 bps by using error detection and correction logic and bit compression. Asynchronous modems are supported by standards from the American National Standards Institute (ANSI) and the CCITT.

With asynchronous transmission, no clocking or timing signals are required by the transmitting or receiving modem because only a single character is transported at a time. Bit counts are used in place of timing circuits to delineate one character from another. Every character sent consists of a start bit (0 bit), seven or eight data bits, a parity bit and a stop bit (1). When the line is idle and no data is being transmitted, the modems will exchange one bits. Buffering and blocking activities are a function of the DTE; therefore, the modem usually receives a steady stream of bits for transport and rarely has to wait for the terminal.

Synchronous Modems

Synchronous modems are high-speed devices with speeds up to 64 Kbps. Synchronous transmission implies the use of clocks to time the data bits being sent and received. Clocking is derived both from the incoming bit rate and from a modem or terminal clocking source. Clocking is required to ensure synchronization between the DTE (terminal) and the DCE (modem). The clocking signal is a digital square wave exchanged between the modem and the terminal at the same rate as the transmission bit rate of the modem.

Two clocking sources may be used: the internal clock signal and the external clock signal. The internal clock signal is generated in the modem and provides the terminal with transmit signal timing information (via pins 15 and 17 in the EIA-232 interface cable). The external clock is a timing signal sent from the terminal that provides signal element timing information to the modem (transmit clock) via pin 24 of the RS-232 interface.

A third type of timing option is referred to as slave or loop timing. Slave timing is derived by taking clocking information from the timing recovery circuit in the demodulator and passing it to the modulator. It also passes the clocking information to the DTE's transmitting circuits and to all other devices requiring timing. This type of timing is vulnerable to line impairments such as phase hits and phase jitter, which were described in Chapter 8. One case in which it might be employed is when a single clocking source for the entire network is required to ensure that the bps rate is exactly the same in both directions of the link, such as with statistical multiplexers.

Synchronous modem transmission is used primarily for high-speed data transmission. Data rates are normally greater than 2400 bps and can exceed 56 Kbps. Telephone carrier clocking signals derived from the telephone carrier's master clock may be used to synchronize the receiver with the distant transmitter and to provide the clocking signals to the terminal. Additional error checking and correction abilities may be provided with modems using synchronous transmission.

Synchronous modems are usually more expensive than asynchronous modems. In many cases, asynchronous modems operating at speeds higher that 1200 bps are really operating in a synchronous mode (i.e., an asynchronous and synchronous converter is incorporated into the modem).

OPERATIONAL MODES AND OPTIONAL FEATURES

A number of different types of modems are available for a particular specification: In other words, not all 2400-bps modems are identical. The following options are either software-configured in microprocessor-based modems or strap-configurable. (Straps or jumpers within the modem have to be manually changed.)

The leased-line modem may be configured by a technical user or the data communications support group to use a continuous carrier. With this option, the modem will transmit a carrier 100 percent of the time regardless of the state of the terminal request-to-send. A modem configured with continuous carrier may also be positioned with switched request-to-send. In this case, the RTS-CTS handshake is provided to the DTE for timing purposes.

The switched noncontinuous carrier option turns the carrier on or off in accordance with the request-to-send signal. This option must be used for remote locations in a multipoint environment. Some half-duplex modems provide a low-speed reverse channel for the transfer of control information. A reverse channel provides a very low-speed circuit, which is a benefit in that the line does not have to be turned around using valuable transmission time. The Bell Series 202 modems have such a reverse channel, allowing up to 50 bits per second to be sent or a reverse channel tone for circuit assurance.

Dial-up modems do not usually have carrier options. Full-duplex modems provide continuous carriers in both directions, and half-duplex modems provide switched carriers.

Some modem manufacturers provide additional options for customizing the modem for a specific application. The request-to-send control option can be set either to be controlled by the terminal or to function as constant carrier output. The clear-to-send delay times can be varied depending on the use of the modem as a master or slave device. A two-wire or four-wire option permits the user to configure the modem for either two-wire or four-wire operations. If the data set ready option is provided, it can be set to indicate that the modem is off-hook in the dial-up mode.

Another option allows the user to adjust the carrier detect level. Analog pre-equalization permits a user to configure the modem based on the use of conditioned or unconditioned lines. This option would normally be operating when conditioning is present on the line. Private line disconnect/line current disconnect is an option that allows the modem to disconnect (turn off) when it detects no line current for a specified period of time. Another option enables the user to increase or decrease the transmit output level.

The one-second holdover option permits the receiving modem to maintain timing during periods of momentary dropouts not exceeding one second. This option is used with modems having a continuous carrier from a distant transmitter and cannot be used by a multipoint master station.

An additional option for dial-up modems is the send space disconnect. This option permits a modem at the other end of the connection to disconnect from the line while in an unattended state by sending approximately three seconds of space signals. Also, receive space disconnect permits the dial-up modem to disconnect from the line in response to receiving approximately two seconds of space signals.

Optional line-testing capabilities are provided in some modems depending on their cost and the manufacturer. These tests may include loopback tests, frequency tests and power level tests. Several manufacturers offer modems with switches or intelligence that enable them to handle different data speeds. Another option, known as auto-speed sensing, enables the modem to sense the incoming speed of the line and change its own receiving speed. Several modem manufacturers provide modems that can automatically dial a telephone number and automatically answer incoming calls.

While computer system security is primarily a software problem, line access security is also a major concern. Restricted access to the modem is often difficult to implement, but it is the first line of defense against unauthorized system access. One optional feature available for modems from several manufacturers is intelligence programmed to validate the user on the incoming line. One method stores the telephone numbers of all authorized users and calls them back after validation using the stored numbers. Modems with this feature are referred to as call-back modems.

Some leased-line modems contain logic for dial-up back-up capabilities. This feature allows the modem to automatically dial a number stored within the modem's memory and is used for reconnection of a failed leased circuit.

TYPES OF MODEMS

Types of asynchronous or synchronous modems include external or standalone, integrated, line drivers and modem eliminators. These can be divided into two major classes, dial-up (switched-line) and dedicated (leased line). DSUs and CSUs are the digital counterparts to analog modems.

Switched-line or dial-up modems are generally considered to be low-speed modems supporting speeds of up to 22,000 Kbps. They may operate using either the asynchronous or synchronous transmission method. The dial-up modem generally provides for the attachment of a telephone handset for call placement and a switch for voice or data. Many types of switched-line modems are available and comply with either Bell or CCITT standards.

Dedicated or leased-line modems operate over leased lines that are in place full time. They operate at speeds of up to 64 Kbps in a synchronous mode. This class of modem provides an extensive array of options, including loopback testing and in many cases data compression. Like the switched modem, this type may have a handset attached for voice communications. Many dedicated modems require C- and D-level conditioning, described in Chapter 8, to operate correctly.

The following sections describe some of the many different types of switched-line and dedicated modems.

Acoustical Couplers

The acoustical coupler is rarely used today, having been replaced by the integrated modem, but some equipment still requires them. These devices allow you to position a standard telephone handset transmitter and receiver into a box with an ear and mouth piece after you have dialed up the computer and have received a carrier tone. They are normally used with some of the older portable computers or terminals such as the Texas Instruments Silent 700. They often are used in a low-speed environment and are limited to 300 bps. Acoustical couplers are designed to use voice-grade dial-up lines only and are normally used asynchronously.

Standalone Modems

Standalone modems, or external modems (as opposed to an internal modem such as those that fit into a PC), are self-contained devices with a standard telephone and the line attached to it. The computer or terminal device is attached on the other side of the line using an interface cable such as the EIA-232. This type of modem is primarily used with computers other than the PC.

The standalone modem supports bit speeds of 300 to 4800 bps (asynchronous) and 1200 to 64 Kbps (synchronous). No distance limitation exists for this type of modem. They normally support half- or full-duplex transmission and may provide internal or external clocking for synchronous transmission. Standalone modems support both switched (voice grade) and dedicated lines.

Integrated Modems

A dial-up or private-line integrated modem is built into the terminal or computer. It may be either part of the communications controller or an expansion board that plugs into a PC card slot. The Hayes model 2400 Smart Modem is an example of an integrated modem used in microcomputers. The integrated modem can be asynchronous or synchronous and can support speeds from 300 bps to 64 Kbps. Integrated modems can operate using either switched or dedicated lines and may have auto-answer/auto-dial capabilities. They often can be provided in customized configurations for synchronized networkwide activities.

Limited-Distance Modems

Short-haul or limited-distance modems (LDMs) are another class of standalone modem that are advisable or necessary when distances between devices requiring interfacing exceed the allowable cable lengths supported by EIA-232-D and other interface cable standards. Normally, an LDM is used in large computer environments where distances exceed 500 feet but are less than several miles, depending on the type of wire being used. Generally, private lines that pass through a central office are not suitable for an LDM device because they do not support the wider bandwidth that short-haul modems require. This dictates that most LDM devices be connected using private metallic twisted-pair wiring. Characteristics of the LDM include 1200 to 19.2-Kbps rates, a maximum of 50 miles distance (speed dependent), half- or full-duplex operation, internal and external clocking, point-to-point or multidrop, and loopback testing.

Line Drivers

Line drivers are not really modems in the classic sense, but rather are considered to be interface converters. They do, however, perform most functions of a standard modem. One area in which they differ is the modulation techniques they use to drive the data across the line. Line drivers convert the digital bits received from the interface cable into a low-voltage, low-impedance signal that is better suited to the twisted-pair media being used.

The characteristics of the binary signal remain unchanged, making the line driver insensitive to the code set or protocol. The principal difference is that they do not normally use the telephone network, requiring dedicated twisted-pair metallic lines. Characteristics of the line driver are a 20-mile distance limitation, half- or full-duplex capability, internal and external clocking, point-to-point or multidrop operation, and dedicated metallic lines only (no loading coils). Line drivers are typically used in factories or office buildings because the wiring is usually easy to install and distances are limited.

Fiber-Optic Modems

Fiber-optic modems are also referred to as fiber-optic drivers. They provide the same capabilities as standard line drivers plus the added benefits associated with fiber-optic technology. Fiber-optic modems usually provide full-duplex high-speed links. These links are plug-compatible V.24, EIA-232-D or RS-422 links that support speeds of up to 50 Mbps and of distances up to 10 km. Another capability of fiber-optic drivers is the provision of asynchronous or synchronous transmission (if synchronous, they will provide clocking signals). In addition, the error rate is less than 10^9 or better at speeds up to 20 Mbps.

The fiber-optic driver is in a constant state of change due to the rapid advancement of fiber-optic technology. At the present time, many fiber-optic drivers operate as direct replacements for devices used with conventional transmission, offering little additional benefit. With the advent of new high-speed fiber protocols and curbside fiber, the fiber-optic driver is quickly maturing and more benefits are being realized.

Modem Eliminators

Modem eliminators are not considered modems at all but interface blocks. A modem eliminator allows hard-wire attachment of computers or terminals to terminal controllers or communications processors over greater distances than allowed in a direct connection using coaxial cable.

The interface blocks can be considered EIA-232-D interface connectors configured for crossover wiring. The transmit and receive leads (pins 2 and 3) and the clear-to-send and request-to-send leads are crossed from one side to the other. For synchronous transmission, additional crossovers are required for pins 15, 17 and 24.

Modem Sharing or Pooling Devices

These devices are also referred to as line splitters. They can be viewed as bridging units that allow several inputs to share a single output. Their primary purpose is to reduce the need for multiple modems at the remote location.

Split-Stream Modems

Split-stream modems, also referred to as multiplexing modems, perform many of the same functions as a multiplexer on a much simpler level. They can connect to multiple DTEs and multiplex and demultiplex the signals going to and coming from each DTE (see Figure 10.2).

Extended Circuit/Tail Circuit Modems

Tail-circuit modems are used to capture and extend one channel of a multiplexing modem. They may be used in cases such as multiplexing four channels from one city to another. As an example, two modems having four channels, each with multiplexing capabilities, can be located in different cities. Via the use of tail-circuit modems at each location, any one of the four channels can be extended to other locations. The end points can be in the local area or in a different city (see Figure 10.3).

An extended modem must be able to pass through some of the EIA-232/V.24 standard control signals, including request-to-send, carrier detect, data-terminal-ready, data-set-ready and the various timing circuits in a synchronous environment. These circuits are used to control tail-circuit configurations, allowing the local terminal full control of the remote modem.

Also available are tail-circuit adapters, which are used to perform the null modem function of reversing the data leads and crossing the control signals as required to attach two modems together. Each modem must be able to transfer or cross the send and receive clocks as well as buffer data for reclocking when necessary.

DIGITAL SERVICE UNITS AND CHANNEL SERVICE UNITS

DSUs and CSUs provide a digital connection for the computer or front-end processor communications port to the telephone company's digital telephone network. The DSU and CSU are combined into one DCE-type device but originally consisted of two independent devices provided by the carriers.

At the beginning of North American AT&T digital service in 1962, the local Bell telephone companies provided user sites with a device referred to as network channel

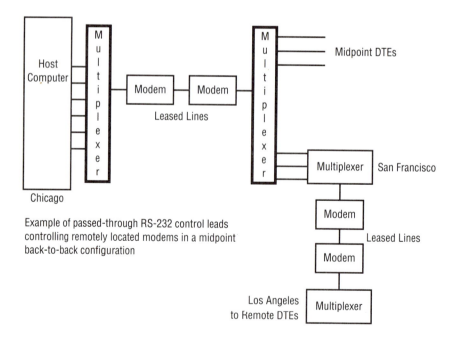

Figure 10.2 Split-Stream Modems

terminating equipment (NCTE). The NCTE provided impedance matching, loopback testing and diagnostics. The NCTE connected to a digital service unit supplied by AT&T that provided the digital line interface to the terminal or computer.

Local telephone companies in the U.S. are no longer allowed to provide NCTE devices. NCTE devices are now called CSUs and are normally combined with DSUs.

The DSU connects to the DTE using one of several interfaces, the most common of which are the EIA-232-D and the CCITT V.35 interfaces. The CSU attaches to a DDS link over four wires using a bipolar digital signal. DSUs and CSUs are designed to support bit speeds of up to 64 Kbps and interface to T1 links.

DIAGNOSTICS AND TESTING

When a network experiences a failure, the first step in resolving the problem is to isolate and identify it. A series of diagnostic tests are usually provided as built-in functions in most modems to identify interface, line and transmission problems. These tests can be invoked by the user to ensure the quality of the modem's operations. If the modem is operational, additional testing services may be provided by the various Bell operating companies or AT&T to determine the operational status of the telephone company equipment and hook-ups.

Some modems have a self-test capability that tests all clock, transmitter and receive circuits in the modem. Additional testing circuits may perform noise and frequency checks. Some of the more intelligent modems have tests to determine if noise levels (signal-to-noise ratios) on the line are within telephone company specifications. They also may check that the modems are using the frequency properly.

Loopback tests are normally provided as part of the modem's diagnostics. The local analog loopback test function tests the local terminal or computer, connecting cable and local modem; it does not test the interface to the telephone lines (see Figure 10.4). The remote analog loopback test allows the DCE to test the local digital cable, its own digital and analog circuits, the telephone circuits, the telephone interface to the remote modem and the analog circuit of the remote modem. The local digital loopback test allows the

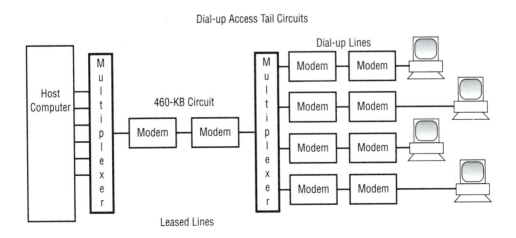

Figure 10.3   Modems Connected Via an Extended-Tail Circuit

DCE to test itself, the interface cable and the digital circuits of the local modem. The remote digital loopback provides the same functions as the remote analog loopback but also tests the remote modem's digital circuitry (see Figure 10.5).

ERROR CORRECTION

A select class of modems provide error correction. These modems are microprocessor-based and have sophisticated logic, buffers and memory management. Error detection and correction are usually accomplished using an error-correcting protocol provided by the modem manufacturer, such as the Codex 2270/2280 error-correcting data modem or the Microcom Inc. error-correcting modem using the Microcom Networking Protocol (MNP). MNP is a proprietary protocol that Microcom licenses to other modem manufacturers. A protocol defines the rules for handshaking between two computers, two networks or from end to end (see Chapter 15). MNP supports computer-to-computer handshaking.

The MNP logic included in the modem supplements the protocol provided by each computer in the point-to-point link. If you were to look at data communications as a hierarchical function, MNP would be placed at the physical layer, which is transparent to other protocols at higher layers. MNP provides up to 11 classes of error correction that offer a 70 percent to more than 200 percent increase in data transmission efficiency. A key feature of MNP protocol is that it is transparent to communications hardware and software activity at the host and remote locations. It provides increased throughput using real-time adaptive data compression techniques and incurs no overhead.

Another method of providing error correction is to include a vendor-supplied error controller at each end of the link between the DCE and DTE devices. This type of device uses MNP or CRC for error-correction. The CCITT is reviewing error correction and will soon finalize its own V.42 error-correction standard.

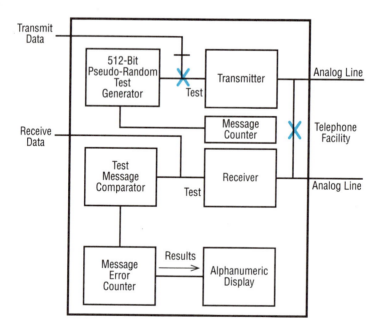

Figure 10.4 Analog Loopback Self Test

Communications Using Modems

INTERFACES

When interfacing modems to the telephone network, it is important to note that most central offices require an operating signal strength level about 12 dBm. Normal line loss between the customer's site and the telephone central office is usually 3 to 6 dBm. The signal level of the modem must be high enough to maintain a good carrier with the central office. Many types of data jacks that plug into the modem are certified for use with the public switched telephone network, as well as for dedicated line use. The following sections describe those most commonly used in North America. Many countries have established their own standards for data jacks.

Permissive Connections

This data jack permits a fixed level of transmission over switched public network facilities. It is designed to limit the line signal strength from the subscriber's site to the central office to no more than 9 dBm. The permissive connection does not guarantee the signal level at the central office, nor does it guarantee line quality. Two-wire circuits use a six-pin modular jack referred to as RJ-11.

Programmable Connections

Programmable connections installed at customers' sites provide a means of adjusting the signal level that is sent from the modem to the central office over switched facilities. This type of connection allows for a maximum signal level to be transmitted, and modems requiring this type of connector must be specified by the equipment vendor. The "programmable arrangement" data jack uses a resister to adjust the signal level. The fixed loss loop arrangement output signal level is attenuated to a signal strength of 4 dBm. The local telephone company

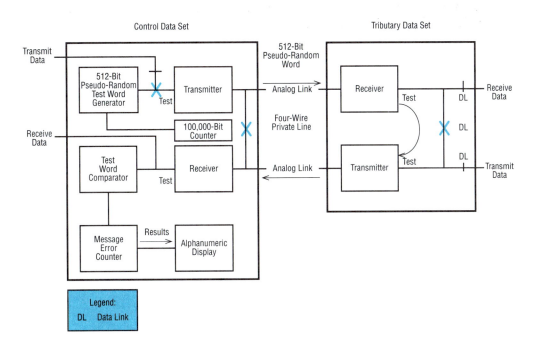

Figure 10.5 Remote Digital Loopback Test

balances the output of the data jack to the signal level received at the locally attached central office. These connections are known as RJ-41 and RJ-45 data jacks.

Private-Line Interfaces

Modems using private-line facilities require a network termination interface (NTI) device. Each country providing leased-line capabilities specifies the terminating devices permitted for use with its telephone network.

CASE STUDY (CONTINUED)

The Bank of Scotts Valley uses both dedicated-line modems and dial-up modems for its branch operations. The connection of each branch's teller network back to its service center necessitates the use of 19.2-Kbps dedicated-line modems employing both C level and D level conditioning. The ATM network also uses a dedicated-line modem for its communications. But because it requires very little data transfer, line speeds are limited to 2400 bps. If the primary link fails, the ATM will instruct a standby dial-up modem to establish a new connection using auto-dial capabilities.

The bank has decided not to use digital links between the service centers and their branches because of the low initial traffic requirements and the expense for digital transmission lines. The bank's data communications planning group also intend to install modem-pooling equipment at each of the service centers because traffic is light enough to use this type of modem. As the communications volume grows, the bank will install additional modems to manage the traffic.

As part of the overall communications system, the bank wants to provide several dial-up links that will include 1200-, 2400- and 4800-bps asynchronous lines. At the present time, these dial-up lines are available to the programming staff and for back-up connectivity to the branches should a primary link fail.

Communications between the front-end processors located at each service center is handled by T1 digital service units.

REVIEW QUESTIONS

1. Modems provide what basic function?
2. True or false: The two classes of modems found in use today are asynchronous and synchronous.
3. Why does synchronous data transmission require a clock?
4. Describe auto-dial and auto-answer.
5. What CCITT-type modem would be used in high-speed data communications over full-duplex lines?
6. True or false: Standard modems do not have a distance limitation.
7. True or false: Some modems are limited to half duplex only.
8. True or false: Modem eliminators are not really modems at all.
9. True or false: Security is a function of the computer, not the modem.
10. True or false: Auto-answer will automatically make a call for the user.
11. What are the four loopback tests available for testing lines and modems?
12. Name two diagnostics available with most modems.

CHAPTER 11

Hardware and Logical Interfaces

INTRODUCTION

An interface connects intelligent devices together and provides a means by which they can communicate with each other. Before the development of standards that govern the interconnection of electronic or electrical devices, it was often impossible to connect certain types of equipment together. This was primarily because manufacturers defined their own interfaces and connections, which were often incompatible with other manufacturers' equipment.

When data communications was in its infancy, the typical interface (the cable) for terminals and dataset connections often used a proprietary wiring method. Often, a 20-milliampere current loop wire or other similar low-level wiring technique was used as the interface. Bit rates were limited, and little or no flow control was provided. This permitted equipment interfaces to be quite simple, but also created the potential for transmission errors because the modem could lose its carrier and did not have the ability to inform the terminal or computer to stop sending data.

The rapid growth of data communications and the need for reliable, higher-speed devices dictated that a new type of interface be designed. Separate circuits were needed for control and timing activities to create a higher degree of efficiency. These circuits were developed to transport information between the terminal and modem, taking into account timing, status conditions and carrier availability. Data communications networks consist of many hardware components that require physical and electrical interfaces at different points in the network. Several different types of interfaces were developed during the 1960s to satisfy those requirements. These interfaces have since evolved into standards used throughout the world. The main standards in use today originate from the EIA, ANSI and the CCITT.

This chapter discusses several standard electrical and physical interfaces, including the EIA-232-D and the V.24 low-speed interfaces and the RS-449, X.21 and V.35 high-speed interfaces.

INTERFACE RESPONSIBILITIES

Each node in a network consists of one or more intelligent processors, such as computers, and one or more modems or digital service units used for the actual transfer activity. For communications to occur between any two nodes on a network, certain activities must occur between the modems or DSUs at each end of the link, as well as between the computer and modem or DSU at each of the nodes. A DTE-to-DCE interface provides a physical and electrical connection for the computer to the modem or DSU and communications line. (DTE refers to a computer or other intelligent device that creates or processes data for transmission across a network; DCE is used to describe a modem or other type of transmission equipment that actually performs the data communications.)

The interface must accomplish four primary functions for communications to take place successfully:

- Data bits must be transferred between the computer and the modem.

- Control signals must be transferred between the DCE and DTE to ensure that both devices are ready.

- The transfer of timing signals between the DCE and DTE must occur to ensure synchronization between both devices.

- Electrical grounds must be present.

TYPES OF INTERFACES

The use of specific interfaces depends on the specific environment that they will be required to support, such as low- or high-speed communications, serial or parallel communications, analog or digital communications, or combinations thereof.

EIA-232-D Interface

The EIA-232-D is perhaps the most common interface in use between modems and computers around the world today. It has been a standard connectivity method for many years. Developed by Bell Laboratories, the EIA-232-D interface is used for most low- and medium-speed communications links. Outside of North America, it is referred to as the CCITT V.24 interface. The interface may be used in a variety of ways; therefore, how the EIA-232-D is used will determine which signals and connector pins are incorporated.

Typical uses of the EIA-232-D interface include:

- Modem-to-computer connections

- Storage device, tape drive and disk drive connections to the computer

- Connections between two microcomputers

- Connection of printers and plotters

The EIA-232-D interface supports half- or full-duplex transmission over dial-up or leased telephone links either asynchronously or synchronously.

The EIA-232-D interface uses a 25-pin connector referred to as the DB25 connector, which supports up to 20 concurrent signals (see Figure 11.1). It may also use a 15- or

9-pin connector because many interfaces require less than 20 circuit signals. Not all EIA-232-D interfaces are wired the same; wiring specifically depends on the devices, the transmission mode and the computer or modem configuration. The CCITT V.24 and EIA-232-D specifications are identical except for pin usage descriptions. The most commonly used signals and pins are illustrated in Figure 11.2.

EIA-232-D is certified to support a maximum length of 50 feet. EIA-232-D signals are capable of going farther than 50 feet; however, this limit is established by the CCITT and EIA to reduce error rates and ensure integrity. The maximum bit rate supported is 20 kilobits per second, but this depends greatly on the distance the data must travel. Typical voltage levels are -3 volts to +25 volts, with a nominal operating voltage of 12 volts. Table 11.1 lists the comparable V.24 circuit functions and pin designations.

EIA-232-D Signal Sequence Phases

Link Activation Phase. This phase creates the connection between the DCE and the DTE, generally at the time the carrier is being established. The following activities normally take place in a standard modem/terminal interface sequence:

- Data terminal ready — (terminal) indicates to the modem that it is ready
- Data set ready — (modem) informs the terminal that it is ready
- Request to send — (terminal) issues an RTS to the modem
- Clear to send — (modem) responds with a clear-to-send to the terminal
- Carrier detect — (modem) informs the terminal it has a carrier

The following additional signal is used for dial-up lines:

- Ring indicator — (modem) indicates to the terminal that a call is incoming

Data Transfer Phase. This phase involves the actual data transfer and acknowledgment between the modem and the computer. This phase includes the following signals:

- Request to send — (terminal) must be on for it to send
- Clear to send — (modem) must be on to receive from the terminal
- Transmit data — (terminal) indicates that data is being transferred
- Receive data — (modem) indicates data is being transferred

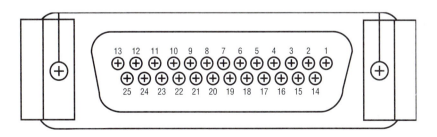

Figure 11.1   EIA-232-D V.24 Connector

- Dataset ready — (modem) informs the terminal that it is alive and well

Link Deactivation Phase. Link deactivation involves the orderly termination of the data link between the modems and terminals. The following signals are required:

- Data terminal ready — Issued by the terminal
- Dataset ready — Issued by the modem
- Received data — Issued by the modem
- Carrier detect — Issued by the modem
- Transmit data — Issued by the terminal

RS-449 Interface

The EIA interface RS-449 was developed as an eventual replacement for EIA-232-D. However, it appears to be slow in catching on, despite the U.S. government's requirement that it be available on all newly purchased equipment. It is important to note that adapting a new interface standard requires a reengineering of the hardware components to support the new interface. This is often both expensive and time-consuming. It may be necessary to support the old interface as well.

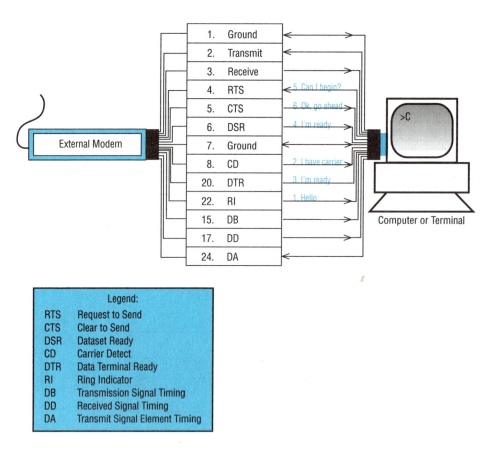

Figure 11.2 Modem-to-Computer or Terminal Handshaking

Hardware and Logical Interfaces

The RS-449 interface is a mechanical interface supported by two different electrical standards. This differs from the EIA-232-D, which is both a mechanical and an electrical standard. The electrical standards are referred to as RS-422-A and RS-423-A. These standards are also referred to as the CCITT V.10 and V.11 interfaces, or the X.26 and X.27 interfaces. While the RS-449 standard was designed to replace the EIA-232-D standard, it incorporates many of the EIA-232-D circuits in order to maintain compatibility.

The RS-422-A electrical standard applies to higher-speed native RS-449 usage and utilizes different circuits and different voltage levels than the RS-423-A electrical standard. The RS-423-A electrical standard is used for interfacing EIA-232-D devices to RS-449 interface device signals and provides compatible electrical signal strength and circuits.

The RS-449 interface uses a 37-pin connector or a secondary 9-pin connector when only basic functions are required. This interface provides much better noise and crosstalk isolation and, when used with the RS-422 electrical standard, provides balanced transmission between each end. The RS-449 interface is functionally equivalent to the CCITT V.10/X.26 and V.11/X.27 standards. RS-449 supports a data bit rate in excess of two megabits per second.

Circuit Function	Pin	CCITT/V.24 Designation
Protective Ground	A	101/AA
Signal to Ground	B	102/AB
Request to Send	C	105/CA
Clear to Send	D	106/CB
Data Set Ready	E	107/CC
Carrier Detect	F	109/CF
Test Mode	K	142/
RX Data A (Received Data)	R*	104/BB
RX Data B (Received Data)	T*	104/BB
RX Clock A (Received Timing)	V*	115/DD
RX Clock B (Received Timing)	X*	115/DD
TX Clock A (Transmit Clock)	Y*	114/DB
TX Clock B (Transmit Clock)	AA/a*	114/DB
TX Data A (Transmit Data)	P*	103/BA
TX Data B (Transmit Data)	S*	103/BA
External Clock A	U*	113/DA
External Clock B	W*	113/DA
Remote Loopback (Test)	BB/b	140/CG
LL Loopback	J	141/
RT Loopback	EE/f	126/
Test Pattern	L	125/CE

* Balanced Pairs

Table 11.1 V.24 Interface Circuit Functions

Introduction to Data Communications: A Practical Approach

A maximum of 31 circuits are available, and the interface cable length can be extended to 200 feet. When RS-449 is operating with the RS-422 electrical standard, it provides additional interface control and loopback control functions over the EIA-232-D interface. Figure 11.3 shows the pin assignments for the RS-449 interface. Table 11.2 provides a comparison between the EIA-232-D, V.24 and RS-449 interfaces.

CCITT X.21 Interface

X.21 is a CCITT standard released in 1976 that defines the interfaces for public circuit-switched data networks. This interface provides functions between the modem and terminal using a 15-pin connector. When X.21 was released, the CCITT intended to make it a universal synchronous interface. With the advent of very high-speed communications devices, X.21 is now considered an interim interface until a newer standard replaces it.

The design of X.21 was based on minimizing the number of physical circuits while adding to the interface's functions. The interface uses the data circuits for control when they are temporarily idle and relies on the intelligence that must be built into the modem and the computer.

X.21 supports balanced and unbalanced configurations and consists of circuits for signal ground, common return, transmit, receive, bit timing and byte timing. Control functions use transmit and receive circuits when no data is present.

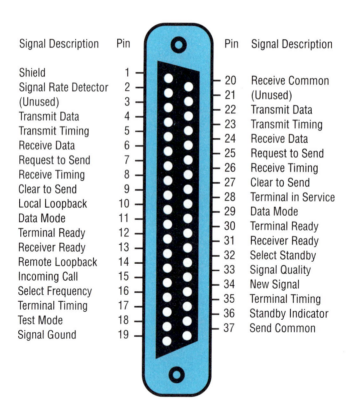

Figure 11.3 RS-449 Pin Assignments

CCITT V.35 Interface

The CCITT V.35 interface is used to interface DTE devices to DSU/CSUs (digital modems) on wideband circuits. Where the V.24 interface is used for speeds below 20 Kbps, the CCITT V.35 interface establishes the standard for speeds above 20 Kbps. This standard specifies an interface cable that uses a balanced twisted-pair arrangement with characteristic impedance of around 100 ohms. Differential voltage across the transmitter pair is 0.55 volts.

The V.35 interface uses a 34-pin connector designated as ISO 2593 and consists of balanced pairs for reduced noise, crosstalk control, data transmit and receive, and timing circuits. Its operational range is up to 48 Kbps, and it is used primarily with wideband analog transmission facilities and synchronous terminal communications (see Figure 11.4).

ES-449		EIA-232-D		CCiTT V.24	
SG	Signal Ground	AB	Signal Ground	102	Signal Ground
SC	Send Common			102A	DTE Common
RC	Receive Common			102B	DCE Common
IS	Terminal in Service				
IC	Incoming Call	CE	Ring Indicator	125	Calling Indicator
TR	Terminal Ready	CD	Data Terminal Ready	108/2	Data Terminal Read
DM	Data Mode	CC	Dataset Ready	107	Dataset Ready
SD	Send Data	BA	Transmit Data	103	Transmitted Data
RD	Receive Data	BB	Receive Data	104	Received Data
TT	Terminal Timing	DA	Transmit Timing (DTE)	113	Transmit Signal Element Timing (DTE Source)
ST	Send Timing	DB	Transmit Timing (DCE)	114	Transmit Signal Element Timing (DCE Source)
RT	Receive Timing	DD	Receive Timing	115	Receive Signal Element Timing (DCE Source)
RS	Request to Send	CA	Request to Send	105	Request to Send
CS	Clear to Send	CB	Clear to Send	108	Ready to Send
RR	Receive Ready	CF	Received Line Signal Detector	109	Data Channel Receive
SQ	Signal Quality			110	Signal Detector
NS	New Signal	CG	Signal Quality Detector	128	Select Transmit Frequency
SF	Select Frequency	CH	Rate Selector (DTE)	111	Rate Selector (DTE)
SI	Signaling Rate Indicator	CI	Rate Selector (DCE)	112	Rate Selector (DCE)
SSD	Secondary Send Data	SBA	Secondary Transmit Data	118	Reverse Channel Transmit
SRD	Secondary Receive Data	SBB	Secondary Receive Data	119	Reverse Channel Receive
SRS	Secondary Request to Send	SGA	Secondary Request to Send	120	Reverse Transmit LINE Signal
SCS	Secondary Clear to Send	SCB	Secondary Clear to Send	121	Reverse Channel READ
SRR	Secondary Receive Ready	SCF	Secondary Line Signal Detector	122	Reverse Receive LINE Signal
LL	Local Loopback			141	Local Loopback
RL	Remote Loopback			140	Remote Loopback
TM	Test Mode			142	Test Indicator
SS	Select Standby			118	Select Standby
SB	Standby Indicator			117	Standby Indicator

Table 11.2 RS-449, EIA-232-D and CCITT V.24 Interface Equivalency

Centronics Parallel Interface

The Centronics 100 interface cable is used primarily for printer connections, but it also may be used for data communications. It consists of a pair of 32-pin connectors carrying 15 pairs of signal wires. The interface cable is made up of braided shielded twisted pairs and can have a maximum length of 25 feet. The Centronics interface is used for the connection of parallel devices and supports bit rates up to 50 Kbps having either positive or negative logic. Its nominal voltage levels are 0 to +5 Volts DC (VDC), and it uses Amphenol industrial connectors 57-40360 and 57-30360. Figure 11.5 illustrates the Centronics interface connector. Table 11.3 describes the Centronics interface pin assignments and functions.

Dataproducts Printer Interface

The Dataproducts interface cable is almost identical to the Centronics interface cable except that it consists of a pair of 100-pin connectors carrying 14 pairs of signals. It is made up of braided shielded twisted pairs and can have a maximum length of 25 feet. This cable is also used primarily for the connection of parallel devices. The interface uses the equivalent of a Winchester MRA 50 S D5J connector. It supports bit rates of up to 50 Kbps with either positive or negative logic. The nominal voltage levels are 0 to +5VDC and Amphenol Connectors 57-40360 and 57-30360 are used. Table 11.4 shows the pin assignments and functions of the Dataproducts interface.

IEEE-488 Interface

The IEEE-488 bus standard defines the digital interface for programmable devices and test instrumentation connected to a computer. This interface is an internationally accepted connection method that defines the connection of no more than 15 devices at maximum distances of 60 feet. The maximum bit rate cannot exceed 1 Mbps; actual speed depends on the length of the bus. This interface transmits and receives data in a byte-serial, bit-parallel manner between system components.

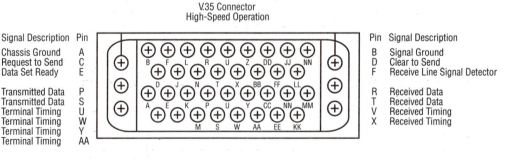

Figure 11.4 V.35 Pin Assignments

Hardware and Logical Interfaces

Signal Name	Pin Number*	Source	Description
Data Strobe	1, 19	Host	1.0 µsec pulse (minimum) used to clock data from the processor to the printer.
Data 1	2, 20	Host	
Data 2	3, 21	Host	
Data 3	4, 22	Host	Data 1 - Data 8: Input data levels. A high represents ONE, a low represents ZERO.
Data 4	5, 23	Host	
Data 5	6, 24	Host	
Data 6	7, 25	Host	
Data 7	8, 26	Host	
Data 8	9, 27	Host	
ACK	10, 28		Acknowledge pulse indicates input of a character into memory or the end of a functional operation.
BUSY	11, 29		Indicates that the printer cannot receive data.
FAULT	32		After initialization this signal is always high.
PE	12		This signal is always ZERO.
SELECT	13		Printer selected; remains at ONE after warmup indicating online and no-fault condition.
+0V	14, 16, 35		Signal ground.
Chassis ground	17		Chassis ground.
FAULT	32		After initialization this signal is always high.

The following pins are not used: 15, 18, 30, 31, 33, 34, 36.
*Second pin of pair is the twisted signal return (+0V).

Table 11.3 Centronics Interface Pin Assignments

Signal Name	Pin Number*	Source	Description
Data 1	B, D	Host	Data 1 - Data 8:
Data 2	F, J	Host	Input data levels.
Data 3	L, N	Host	A high represents ONE,
Data 4	R, T	Host	a low represents ZERO.
Data 5	V, X	Host	
Data 6	Z, b	Host	
Data 7	n, k	Host	
Data 8**	d, f, or p, s	Host Host	
DATA STROBE	j, m	Host	A 0.5 μsec pulse (minimum) used to clock data from the processor to the printer logic.
DEMAND	E, C	3700	Indicates that the controller is capable of receiving a character.
READY	CC, EE	3700	Indicates that the controller has powered up successfully.
ONLINE	y, AA	3700	After warmup, this signal is ONE, unless the print file is full.
Interface connect	x	3700	Pins x and v provide electrical continuity only.
Verify	v	3700	

The following pins are not used: A, H, K, M, P, S, U, W, Y, BB, DD, FF, HH, a, c, e, h, r, t, u, w, and z.
*Second pin of the pair is the twisted signal return (+0V).
**Either d, f or p, s may be used for the eighth bit; if VFU is to be used, p, s must be selected. This option is selected through the Interface Setup, Parallel Settings, Interface, and Dataproducts menu dialogues.

Table 11.4 Dataproducts Interface Pin Assignments

Hardware and Logical Interfaces

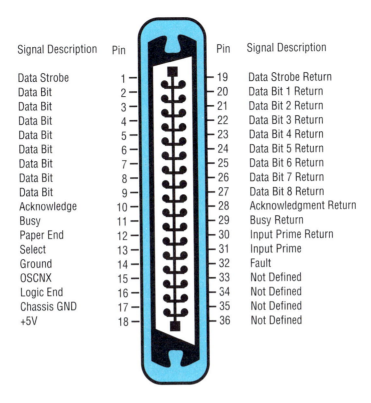

Figure 11.5 Centronics Interface Connector

REVIEW QUESTIONS

1. What CCITT interface is considered to be the industry standard for DCE-to-DTE connections?

2. What is the bit rate for the RS-449 interface?

3. How many connector pins does the EIA-232-D interface have?

4. What interface uses balanced pairs?

5. What is the V.24 interface equivalent to?

6. What are the distance and speed limitations for the EIA-232-D interface?

7. Name the three phases of activities associated with EIA-232-D?

8. Why is the RS-449 interface better suited to high-speed data communications than the EIA-232-D interface?

9. Name the four signal types that are used for the transfer of information between DTE and DCE equipment.

10. What is CCITT V.35?

Part V

Standards, Network Architectures, Topologies and Protocols

CHAPTER
12

Regulatory Agencies and Standards

THE NEED FOR STANDARDS

A major issue facing the data communications industry and the user community today is worldwide compatibility. Buyers and users of data communications and computer equipment would like equipment from different vendors to be compatible because of their need for global communications. Requirements dictate that all nodes in a network be able to communicate with each other, regardless of who manufactured the products.

In North America and in several other countries, users can select data communications products from a variety of vendors. By choosing products manufactured to the same specification, users can achieve interoperability within and among networks. Unfortunately, this is not the case worldwide, because of the different interface standards or software protocols permitted by some telecommunications authorities and licensed manufacturers.

In the early 1970s, users and vendors began to realize that standards were needed for hardware and software interfaces. Until that point, almost every manufacturer built equipment according to its own specifications.

In 1976, the ISO (International Standards Organization) was established to address the worldwide compatibility issue and develop international standards. Over the years, several additional international and national standards organizations were formed to address various areas of concern, such as software and language compatibility, hardware electrical interfaces, media compatibility, communications signal compatibility and formatting.

Software and Language Compatibility

A major area of importance to the international standards groups is software and programming language compatibility. Software compatibility is required to ensure that control information transported over the network can be understood by each node in the network. This control information consists of addressing, acknowledgment and network routing. Language compatibility enables users to move software from one type of computer to another. An example is the UNIX operating system developed by AT&T Bell Laboratories. UNIX is rapidly becoming a supported operating system on most computers today. The term "supported operating system" means that a specific computer vendor has adopted UNIX for use on its computers and ensures interoperability at some level with other manufacturers' UNIX adaptations.

Hardware Electrical Interfaces

Electrical and cable interfaces also necessitated the attention of the standards organizations. Standardizing electrical and cable interfaces ensures that equipment manufactured by different vendors can communicate using the same specifications. These specifications include the designation of maximum voltages for electrical signals, nominal operating voltages, binary encoding standards and designation of control information.

Media Compatibility

As early as 1964, media compatibility became a major issue, evidenced by problems such as the differences in widths of the magnetic computer tapes used by IBM and Honeywell Inc. Tape media compatibility relates to tape width, reel and hub sizes, recording densities and certification. Another media compatibility concern is disk media interoperability between different types of drives.

Communications Signal Compatibility

Worldwide standards are essential when it comes to communications signal compatibility. Since 1911, standards have existed for ensuring that telephone and communications networks located around the world are able to communicate with each other. The standards for communications signal compatibility include the specification of wire type, voltage levels, carrier frequencies and bandwidth.

Format Standards

Another area of emerging data communications standards is formatting. Standards are required because not all screens are alike in format, nor are all electronic mail messages the same. In addition, standards are needed so that both images and text can be understood by different brands of equipment.

While it appears that major headway is being made to address and rectify the issue of incompatibility, different standards still exist. In many cases, however, the standards can be interfaced by incorporating bridges and gateways. Such adjuncts that mitigate compatibility problems most likely will remain active for quite some time.

INTERNATIONAL STANDARDS ORGANIZATIONS

International standards organizations are voluntary organizations consisting of representatives from the United Nations' member countries. These organizations accept input from members and develop recommendations based on common needs and requirements. While the standards that these organizations develop do not bind the manufacturers to compliance, they do set forth a worldwide recommendation.

International Telecommunications Union (ITU)

The ITU is an international agency of the United Nations established to assist in creating international standards for communications, data processing and data communications. Its main area of focus is equipment compatibility and transborder data communications. The ITU has four standards committees: the General Secretariat, the International Frequency Registration Board (IFRB), the Consultative Committee for International Radio (CCIR) and the CCITT.

The General Secretariat is responsible for the administration of the Union's headquarters. The IFRB is responsible for ensuring technical cooperation between member countries on radio frequency assignments. It is also responsible for standards dealing with the use of the frequency spectrum and the positions of satellites. The CCIR is responsible for the standards concerning radio communications. The CCITT is responsible for developing telephone and data communications standards among participating agencies. The CCITT is accountable for the X series of standards for public data networks and the V series of hardware and electrical interface standards. See Appendix A for a list of CCITT standards.

International Standards Organization (ISO)

The ISO is a voluntary international group chartered in 1946 to achieve worldwide agreement on international standards. Its members are representatives from national standards bodies and interested nonvoting organizations. The main responsibilities of the ISO are:

- Interfacing with national organizations such as ANSI for distribution of proposed standards for worldwide review
- Interfacing with other international organizations such as the CCITT to decide standards that affect data communications networks
- Assisting the CCITT in defining the X and V series interface standards
- Defining worldwide standards for procedures, parameters and formats for data transfer

The ISO comprises groups whose responsibilities include the development of standards over a wide area of technical issues. A standard generally takes seven steps to reach maturity and requires a time frame of approximately four years. These seven development steps are listed below:

1. Creation of the draft proposal
2. Review by the membership
3. Modification of the draft proposal
4. Submission of the second draft
5. Review by the membership
6. Final draft submission
7. Acceptance as a standard

EUROPEAN STANDARDS ORGANIZATIONS

European Computer Machinery Association (ECMA)

In 1961, the ECMA was formed to promote the development of international standards. It has 15 voting members and seven nonvoting members who manufacture data processing and communications equipment in Europe. The ECMA oversees a set of technical committees that make recommendations to the CCITT regarding data communications equipment.

European Conference of Posts and Telecommunications Administrations (CEPT)

Founded in 1969, this organization's charter is to promote cooperation between post, telephone and telecommunications providers within Europe. Membership is open to the administrations of European countries that belong to the Universal Postal Union or the ITU. As of 1989, 26 countries were members.

NORTH AMERICAN STANDARDS ORGANIZATIONS

North American standards organizations include manufacturers and users of data processing and data communications equipment and services. A major goal of these organizations is to develop national standards that eventually will be adopted as worldwide standards. Many of those standards have been adopted by the ITU and its member organizations.

American National Standards Institute (ANSI)

ANSI is a volunteer organization comprising equipment manufacturers and users of data processing equipment and services. ANSI publishes national standards but does not develop them. Its responsibility is to submit to the International Telecommunications Union committees proposed standards and suggested changes from its members.

Electronics Industries Association (EIA)

The EIA is a trade association of American equipment manufacturers responsible for hardware and electrical interface standards used around the world for modem and communications equipment. See Appendix A for a list of EIA standards.

Institute of Electrical and Electronics Engineers (IEEE)

The IEEE is the world's largest professional society, with a membership that exceeds 200,000 people. The IEEE is an international organization that was founded in the U.S. The IEEE works closely with ANSI to develop many types of standards in the areas of communications and information processing. Among the types of standards the IEEE is responsible for are LAN standards. See Appendix A for a list of IEEE standards.

U.S. National Bureau of Standards (NBS)

The U.S. NBS is a federal agency responsible for many areas of standards development. Many American states have adopted NBS standards in the absence of local testing facilities.

U.S. Federal Communications Commission (FCC)

The FCC is responsible for rules, regulations and standards pertaining to telephone equipment and radio frequency transmission, as well as for establishing radiation emission standards. The FCC works closely with the international CCIR and the IFRB as well as ANSI to ensure that standards are compatible worldwide.

Corporation for Open Systems (COS)

In 1984, when COS was formed, it had a membership of more than 20 manufacturers of computers and semiconductors. COS was created to make some order out of the multitude of existing standards. It accomplishes this primarily by providing a certification service for companies that want to have their products certified as ISO compliant.

Figure 12.1 illustrates the major standards organizations and how they relate to each other.

DE FACTO STANDARD SETTERS

A *de facto* standard is a procedure or method that at one time was a specific manufacturer's method of building a product or specifying its connectivity. Over time, this method becomes an unwritten standard (*de facto*) because the product is seen as an advantageous means of achieving connectivity among different vendors' equipment. Due to widespread use of these methods, they became the standards by which one manufacturer's equipment becomes compatible with another.

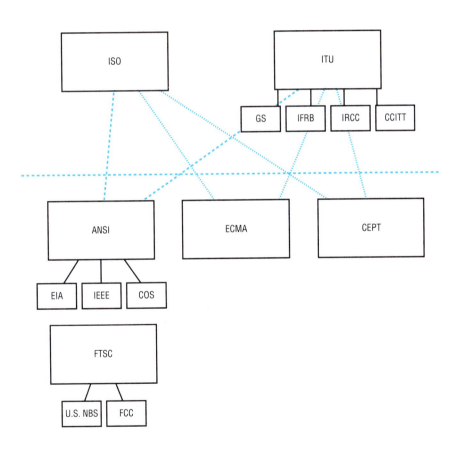

Figure 12.1 International, European and North American Standards Organizations

IBM

IBM has been instrumental in establishing many of the standards in existence today. Examples are the ASCII and EBCDIC code sets. These code sets are in use around the world and have become both ANSI and ISO standards. Another IBM standard is the Binary Synchronous Communications protocol. This early protocol is widely used as a handshaking technique to connect with IBM communications equipment. SDLC, which is the foundation for another protocol supported by the ISO and the CCITT is another standard that originated with IBM. Finally, IBM developed the Systems Network Architecture, a set of standards for connectivity among IBM wide area and local area networks.

AT&T Bell Laboratories

AT&T Bell Laboratories has been responsible for many different standards. Among them are modem standards, telephone network interface standards, the original RS-232 standard and the UNIX operating system, which is becoming an open operating system standard and has been implemented by a large number of computer manufacturers.

Digital Equipment

Digital Equipment, a major computer, software and communications product manufacturer, has played a role in the creation of many standards as well. Its primary contribution was in the development of ASCII terminal standards and the Ethernet LAN standards, which were jointly developed with Intel Corp. and Xerox Corp.

CASE STUDY (CONTINUED)

At some point in the future, the Bank of Scotts Valley will require internetworking capabilities to permit customers such as other banks to access certain types of data. The bank's planners believe that internetwork communications will necessitate an open systems approach because they want to be able to communicate with non-IBM banking networks. Despite this need, they have selected IBM as their principal vendor because of IBM's ability to provide the required hardware and a wide variety of banking software. IBM also meets the bank's requirements for 24-hour support, which can be provided locally.

The planners believe that any internetwork connectivity required in the near term can be satisfied using one of the many available bridges, gateways and protocol converters that attach to IBM equipment. The major requirement is that all communications equipment support international standards, and IBM can provide hardware and software interfaces that conform to those standards. A system that provides compatibility with other networks using international standards is important to the bank because, at some point, it may want to open a branch in another country.

Another reason the bank wants its data communications activities to conform to international standards is that it will have to exchange information frequently with other local banks and federal agencies. When requested to do so, the bank will exchange information with the U.S. Internal Revenue Service, Social Security Administration and Federal Reserve Bank.

REVIEW QUESTIONS

1. Name the two CCITT standard interfaces most commonly used today.
2. What is the CCITT responsible for?
3. Why was the International Telecommunications Union created?
4. What major contribution has the IEEE made to data communications?
5. To what activity do the X.21, X.25 and X.29 standards apply?
6. What are the two main standards organizations in the world today?
7. Name two organizations responsible for *de facto* standards.
8. Name a standard that ANSI developed.
9. What does the EIA do?
10. Why are standards necessary?

CHAPTER 13

Network Configurations, Network Design and Security

INTRODUCTION

The design of most networks incorporates a variety of different topologies. The word "topology" refers to the physical design and connectivity of a network. It is important to stress that networks should be designed to meet the needs of the network users, rather than based on a specific topology. Many network designers use basic topology concepts to form the basis of a design that meets the network user's criteria. In some cases, specific network topologies must be used to support the technology of the hardware. In LAN configurations, the star, bus and ring (loop) topologies are frequently used because of the way the networks must be wired and the components required.

The basic function of any network is to provide access paths by which an end user at one location can access end users at other locations. A node can be considered a computer, an intelligent terminal, an RJE terminal or a network switch. A topology can be defined as the physical arrangement of nodes and links to form a network, including the connectivity pattern of the network elements.

In the past, it was common to find large computer centers set up to support batch environments. Today, we see a combination of batch, online and distributed environments in use by many companies around the world. These networks are referred to as hybrid networks.

CENTRALIZED, DECENTRALIZED AND DISTRIBUTED NETWORKS

There are three basic types of communications networks: centralized, decentralized and distributed.

Centralized Networks

The centralized network is a self-contained entity that manages independent operations, such as those found with a computer system and its terminal network. The computer generally has primary/secondary relationships with each of its connected communications devices. This type of network requires dedicated hard-wired devices that operate using high-speed parallel transmission techniques. The hardware engineering of all components within the network provides native interfaces to other components.

Decentralized Networks

Decentralized organization implies some processing distribution function using a host processor to control a number of remotely located processors. The host processor can offload activities to other processors, but the host processor still retains control. The normal mode of data transfer is via serial links in a synchronous or asynchronous transmission environment. The host processor and communications processor can interface directly with a public communications network.

Distributed Networks

This type of network is generally considered to be a peer-to-peer network spread over a large area (see Figure 13.1). It usually consists of many different types of equipment, such as computers and communications processors. In distributed networks, all nodes in the network share responsibility for application processing. In many cases, this requires that data format conversion and extensive communications protocol handshaking occur in each node.

POINT-TO-POINT, MULTIPOINT AND PEER CONFIGURATIONS

Point-to-point, multipoint and peer-to-peer are terms that describe the methods of connectivity within a network.

Point-to-point configurations involve a primary station and a secondary station operating either in a contention mode or a controlled mode. Contention mode means that both points have equal status and must listen before attempting to transmit. This is illustrated by two computers exchanging data. Controlled mode means that both computers share in controlling the link.

In multipoint configurations, a primary station (the host computer) and multiple secondary stations (terminals, workstations or PCs) function in a selection or polled environment (see Figure 13.2). This requires a communications link configuration in which several terminals share access to the master on a single link. The secondary stations must have enough intelligence to recognize their addresses in a data or information packet sent from the host.

Peer-to-peer connectivity is used primarily within the IBM world and enables computers to establish a peer-level connection. No primary or secondary station is designated when the link is established. This was developed mainly to permit peer-level communications among IBM host computers running under the control of Systems Network Architecture and with non-IBM computers such as those of Digital Equipment and Tandem Computers. Prior to the development of peer-level connectivity, non-IBM computers that required connection to an IBM host were treated as if they were terminal controllers and their activities were restricted to that level.

Network Configurations, Network Design and Security

Some manufacturers have offered peer-to-peer communications for quite some time, using a connectivity procedure called asynchronous balanced communications mode. This allows the linked computers to treat each other as peer-level devices.

METHODS OF COMMUNICATING

Two distinct methods for communicating with each network node in point-to-point or multipoint configurations are selection and polling. Selection involves the primary computer sending an "I have something to send to you" packet that instructs the secondary computer to get ready to receive. The selection technique requires a controlling point

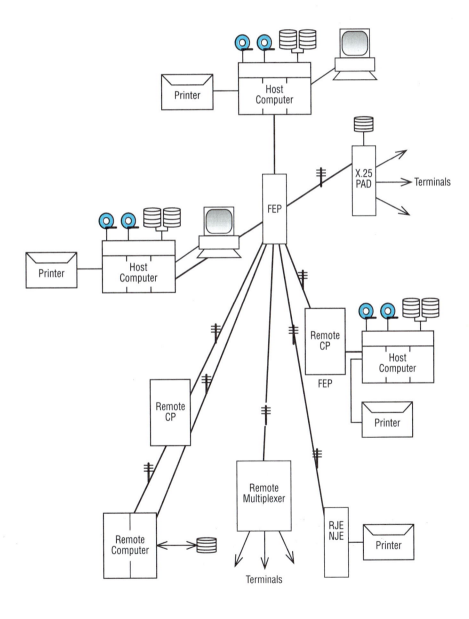

Figure 13.1 Distributed Network Environment

(primary station/secondary station environment) for network control. Another form of selection, broadcast selection, allows the primary computer to address all secondaries at the same time. This selection method is used for activities such as sending user start-up welcome messages and communicating network status to each terminal user.

Polling implies that the primary (master) station will ask each of the secondary stations if it has something to transfer by sending each of them a request. If a receiving terminal has traffic for the primary computer, it will return a positive response and the computer will establish a dialogue with the terminal.

There are two main methods of polling communications: list polling and hub polling. In list polling, the computer queries each secondary node to see if it has anything to send. It also can prioritize its request to the secondary stations so that some secondary stations can be accessed more frequently. In hub polling, the primary node polls only the first secondary device on the link. When that session is complete, the secondary device passes on the poll to the next secondary device on the line. Hub polling appears to be more efficient than list polling because of the reduction of message traffic between the primary node and each secondary node in the network.

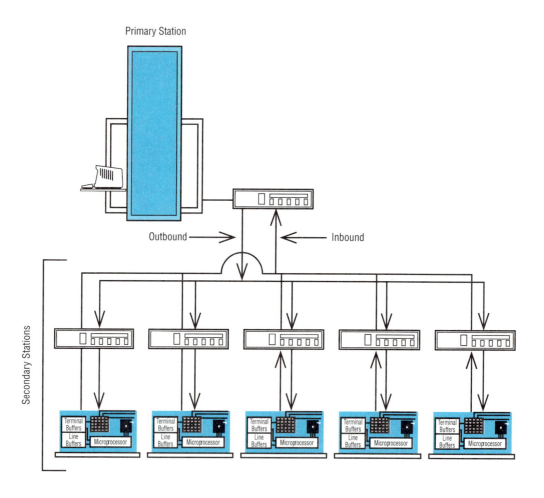

Figure 13.2 Multipoint Connection in a Controlled Environment

Network Configurations, Network Design and Security

Selection and polling can be either contention based or control based. Contention mode implies that each intelligent device (computer) monitors the link and contends for use of the link. It does this by sending a message to the other devices attached to the link indicating that it wants to use the link. This also may be referred to as a peer-to-peer or balanced arrangement. Peer-to-peer arrangements mean that each computer on the network operates within the network as a peer-level device. Controlled mode means that the network has a primary station, usually a host computer, and a number of secondary terminal stations. The primary node operates by alternately polling and selecting all secondary nodes in the network.

TYPES OF TOPOLOGIES

Star Topology

The star topology is used primarily for connecting communications devices that are considered local (dedicated hard-wired) to the host processor. If the star is organized in a centralized manner, it usually will be simple in design and have minimal software requirements (see Figure 13.3). Decentralized stars are more complex in both design and software.

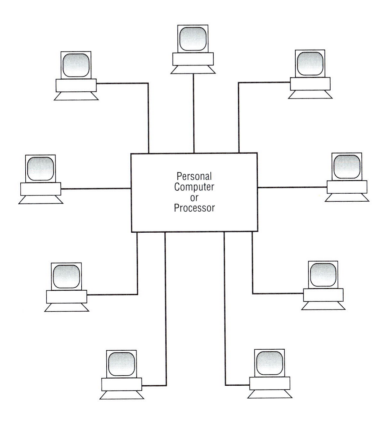

Figure 13.3 Centralized Star Topology

The centralized star topology permits easy routing because the central or hub node maintains the path to all other nodes in the star network. The intelligent central point easily controls access to and from the network nodes. The centralized star configuration also allows for a priority status mechanism to be used by any node when required.

The star usually has dedicated circuits to each of its nodes and will experience few problems. Any contention problems that do occur on the star network are normally resolved by the central node. The central node in the star topology must be very reliable because any failure at this node will bring down the entire network. The connection of each outer node to the central node is accomplished using a point-to-point line configuration. A failure at one of the end nodes would be considered an isolated failure. However, if the central node were to fail, the entire network would be down unless a redundant controller and links to each node were established.

The star topology implies the use of polling and selection techniques in a controlled (primary/secondary) communications environment. The star network is normally designed to support limited distances (usually within a mile), and bit transport performance is usually limited to less than three megabits per second. It is commonly used for the connection of terminals to a host computer. The star topology is also frequently used with local area networks either in a centralized or decentralized environment. An example of the star topology in a centralized environment is the StarLAN network developed by AT&T.

Ring Topology

The ring (loop) is another topology used for creating simple communications networks. It is principally used for connecting nodes in a LAN (generally within a five-mile radius), but it is not limited to the LAN environment (see Figure 13.4).

The ring topology permits an easy routing path because each node receives what is

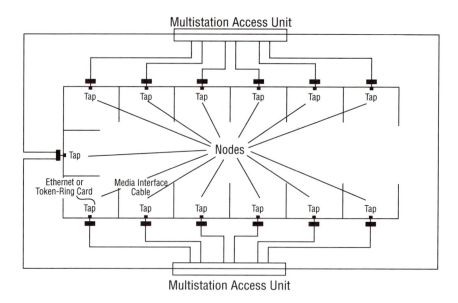

Figure 13.4   Token Ring LAN

transmitted and decides if the data or information packet is for itself. Rings can be implemented either as a one-way system or as a bidirectional system. Bidirectional systems are the preferred method; if a failure occurs within the ring at some point, the traffic can be routed in the other direction. Many LAN manufacturers use this type of topology for their products.

The ring topology uses broadcasting concepts in a controlled/contention environment. Each node operates in a controlled mode until one node wishes to use the ring. The node wishing to transmit then assumes the role of the primary station and broadcasts its data to a specifically addressed station. All stations on the network will receive the data transmitted. However, those stations not addressed will ignore the traffic. While this topology is typically used with local area networks, it can be used in other types of networks as well. Additional nodes can be easily connected to the network using current LAN technology.

Bus Topology

The bus topology requires a medium that allows traffic to flow in both directions at the same time. Unlike the star or ring topologies, nodes associated with a bus do no routing at all. This is primarily because the bus is a broadcast medium in which all nodes receive all transmissions (see Figure 13.5).

In many bus systems, all nodes contend with each other for use of the medium, which requires that all devices use a method for avoiding collisions. The lack of centralized control and routing makes the bus topology very reliable because it does not depend on a central node for routing and control. If a node failure occurs, it usually does not disrupt the network, and it is a simple task to add nodes to the network.

As with the ring topology, the bus topology uses the broadcast mode in a controlled environment. Each node operates in a contention mode until one node wishes to use the bus. It then assumes the role of the primary station and broadcasts the data to a specifically addressed station. All stations receive the data but ignore it if they are not the intended receivers.

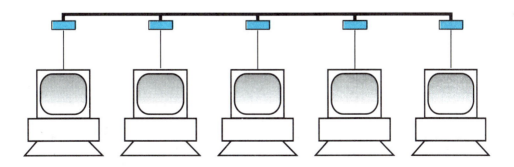

Figure 13.5 Ethernet Bus Network

Multipoint Bus Topology

The multipoint bus topology consists of a primary or master node and a number of secondary or slave nodes attached to the same media (see Figure 13.6). This topology operates in a highly controlled environment. The multipoint bus master polls or selects the node with which it wishes to communicate.

In a multipoint arrangement, the master invites each of the secondary nodes to send data in a predetermined rotation. No secondary can communicate with the master unless invited to do so. As explained earlier, two main methods of communication in a multipoint polling environment are list polling, where a specific device is polled using its unique address, and hub polling, a form of group pooling. The master can also use a selection technique, whereby the secondary node is informed that the master has something to send to it.

Two subcategories of multipoint communications are multipoint broadcast polling and conference multipoint polling. In multipoint broadcast polling, anything sent by the master

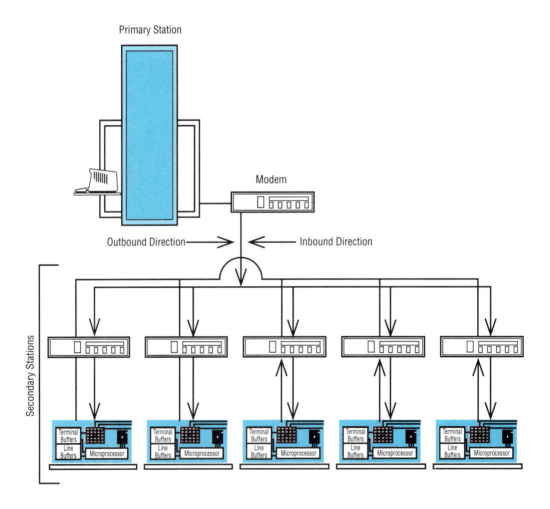

Figure 13.6   Multipoint Bus Network

is received by all remote stations and anything sent by a remote station is received only by the master. Remote nodes cannot communicate directly with each other. In conference multipoint polling, all stations can send directly to one another.

One major advantage of this topology is that it works well over long distances. Conversely, it can cause long delays because the master must check each secondary station continuously, regardless of the activity.

Tree Topology

The tree (hierarchical) topology is really just an extended star topology in which several stars are networked together. The tree topology is designed to support different types of configurations at the end of each tree and branch, making it a very flexible networking topology (see Figure 13.7).

The primary environment for the tree topology consists of clusters of end nodes at various remote locations. The tree's branches are connected using point-to-point lines. The tree topology allows centralized as well as decentralized networking, depending on the configuration of the nodes in the network. This topology uses a combination of controlled, contention, polling, selection and primary/secondary combinations.

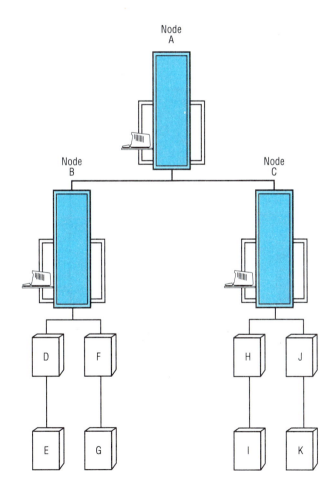

Figure 13.7 Tree Topology

Mesh Topology

The mesh topology is excellent for long-distance networking because it provides extensive back-up, rerouting and pass-through capabilities. Each node can communicate with any other node on the network and also can act as a pass-through node if necessary. This function is needed in the event of a line or node failure elsewhere in the network. The mesh topology is commonly used in large internetworking environments with stars, rings and buses attached to each node (see Figure 13.8).

The mesh topology is ideal for distributed networks because it allows for resource sharing and load balancing by making all nodes available via software control. Resource sharing allows user programs requiring resources on another node to be transparently switched to the other node. Load balancing permits a node to shift program activities to other nodes when its load factor exceeds a certain percentage. Resource-sharing and load-balancing software must be implemented in each node and require the exchange of control and status information.

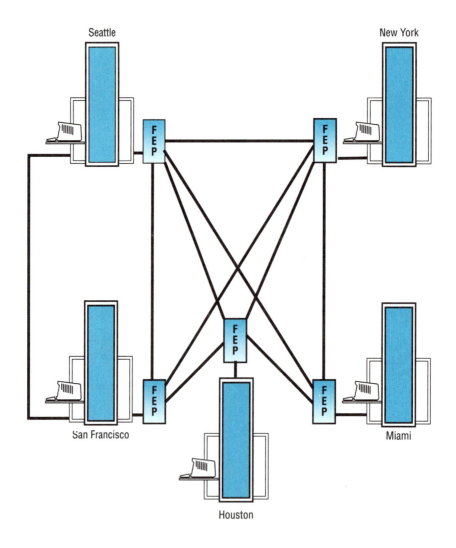

Figure 13.8 Mesh Topology

Network Configurations, Network Design and Security

The mesh topology is also used extensively in packet-switching networks supplied by value-added public data network vendors. With the mesh topology, PDN suppliers can utilize hardware and software resources so as to achieve the maximum benefit.

Mesh networks can be implemented using a variety of transmission methods that include DS-x links, fractional T1 links, back-up dial-up capabilities, and voiceband dedicated links. As the costs associated with network communications drop, the mesh topology appears to be one of the more feasible and cost-effective topologies available.

Mesh of Trees Topology

The mesh of trees is a hybrid organization combining both the mesh and tree topologies (see Figure 13.9). The internal network is actually a mesh and functions as previously described. The mesh of trees topology can be considered a distributed network system, allowing any of the end nodes access to the resources of any other node within the mesh via any available resource path. The end user is usually unaware of the actual route taken to make a connection to another node. The public switched dial-up network employs the mesh of trees topology.

NETWORK DESIGN AND SELECTION

Anyone involved with planning the implementation of a communications network must consider the overall design of the network, how it is to be implemented, and the ongoing growth and maintenance of the network. The following sections outline key elements to consider during the design phase.

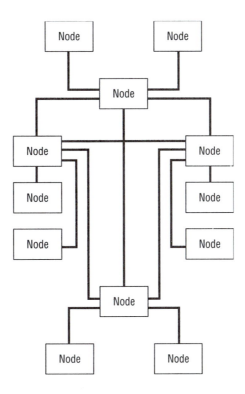

Figure 13.9 Mesh of Trees Topology

Computer/Terminal System Resources

The number of planned or required resources plays an important role in the design of the overall network and often determines the types of components that will be used. Another consideration is geographical location: Will the needed equipment be available for use in all the locations? It is also important to determine support policies before purchasing equipment because the availability of equipment does not always imply support from the vendor. System functions (point-to-point or multipoint operation) need to be explored because support may not be available from the telephone company network. It is important to determine what the data communications equipment requires prior to contracting for link services.

Customer or User Base

When designing a network, consider the number of end users as well as any planned expansion of the network. The location of the end users plays a major role in how the cables will be run, where the equipment is to be located and how link services will be provided. It is also important to understand the type of user (e.g., customer, employee, etc.) that the network will primarily serve. This is vital information for terminal or computer selection and for network configuration. There is a direct relationship between the type of user, the type of terminal or computer equipment, whether the network is interactive or transaction based, and response time.

Centralized and decentralized communications systems provide different levels of support and throughput. If the normal processing requirements are local, a distributed approach may provide the best operational environment. Data and access requirements also play an important role in response time.

Economic Considerations

Two basic premises for the implementation of data communications networks are that unlimited budgets do not exist and that growth is a contingency that must be planned for. It is important to forecast long-range requirements that include accurate, realistic costs. In most companies, growth is a problem because it can vary widely from year to year. To provide some degree of control, try to budget for equipment whose upgrade capabilities are built on a basic frame rather than on replacing equipment as growth becomes inevitable.

Carrier Considerations

To control costs, review public carrier and public network facilities. Do not assume that the telephone or network carrier will have all levels of service. Proper planning involves the consideration of communications link requirements. The availability of switched, dial-up, T1 and DS-x links, and their associated costs, plays a key role in determining whether private, public or dedicated transmission facilities will be employed. The most expensive aspect of any network activity is the monthly recurring line costs. The expenses associated with maintenance must also be considered.

Staffing for Maintenance and Administration

Staffing is another factor often overlooked in the planning of a communications network, yet it is important from both a budgeting and control standpoint. It may be a mandatory requirement for larger networks in order to monitor and maintain acceptable network performance.

The best-designed systems are as transparent to the end user as possible and are always designed with future needs in mind. It is crucial to isolate the end user from the physical network and not add another layer of complexity to online services. Without proper network planning, growth typically causes major disruptions to data communications activities and also can necessitate additional training programs for the end users. Bear in mind that the typical end user is not concerned with the communications network itself but with its ability to provide adequate access and processing capabilities.

NETWORK INTEGRITY

Network integrity is a key concern to network users and administrators. Integrity ensures that network configurations are well maintained and that only authorized users will have network access. In other words, maintaining the integrity of the network means that changes will not open the way for unauthorized access to network management resources. Network management resources include the communications control software, hardware access and configuration tools. Simply put, the addition of new nodes, the deletion of existing nodes and access to applications must be controlled from a central point to ensure that the network will not be corrupted.

Corruption can occur if management is not restricted to a limited number of people and an online management and tracking system is not in place. Online management and tracking allows central control of the network's access and configuration, provides visibility across the network and enables personnel to perform software maintenance. Online management should include access to information about all attached network hardware, their locations, any authorized applications the nodes have access to and all authorized users at each node or on the network.

NETWORK SECURITY

In today's internetworking environment, network security is a critical consideration because of the variety of access methods available. Several levels of security must be scrutinized if networks are to be made secure from internal as well as outside forces. To provide a safe and secure network, you must restrict access on the hardware, line and software levels.

Configuration and Control Software

System maintenance programs must be password protected to ensure that only authorized personnel have access to them. Passwords should be frequently changed as well as properly managed. Often, passwords for employees who leave the company are left on the system for an extended period of time. Procedures must be established and well managed so that security maintenance is performed on a regular basis.

User Access

User access security is of major importance, particularly with respect to dial-up access. Both the system software and application program must incorporate multiple levels of password protection. This can be accomplished by implementing multiple levels of security, including specific application access, read-only access, update access, timed access and multiple passwords.

Hardware Access

Hardware access security is difficult to implement other than on a key-lock basis or by tying user logon passwords to specific terminals. Another method of protecting hardware is to restrict the terminal or node to a specific set of applications. This requires that the security code be placed in communications control programs to validate logon identification.

Data Security

Data security is primarily a data processing problem, but it can cause concern in a data communications environment. Data transported in a nonencrypted format such as standard binary, ASCII or EBCDIC can be accessed via taps on the communications line. This type of intrusion can be protected against by using one of the many data compression or encryption security techniques available. These techniques operate by scrambling the bit patterns on the sending side and reassembling them on the receiving side. This type of security will work only if intelligence and memory are available at both ends of the link.

NETWORK BACKUP

In organizations that require a high percentage of network availability, communications links and hardware are possible failure points. Networks do fail, and network backup has always been a thorny issue because of the expenses associated with implementing and maintaining back-up systems. Knowledge of which back-up system (if any) is appropriate for your network and what your company's budget limitations are is mandatory. Occasional dial-up users probably would have no need for a back-up system; however, large, multinational corporations need to include back-up capabilities as an integral part of their operations. Several types of backup should be considered, including redundant communications links, standby communications processors and fault-tolerant processors. Redundancy means that alternate paths are available for the movement of data.

Communications Links

Several methods of backup can be used to guarantee that communications link failures do not bring the network down. The degree of backup required depends on the needs of the user. In a dedicated link environment, a second equivalent or lower-speed dedicated link can be employed as a standby. As an alternative, two links of equal bandwidth can be used so that one can take over priority traffic in the event of a line failure. A third possibility is to use modems that can fall back to a speed supported by the public switched network on dial-up links. Public switched networks such as British Telecom's Tymnet can also provide back-up link capabilities for either high-speed or low-speed environments.

For hard-wired networks such as local area networks, dual rings or buses are widely used. Satellites and private microwave network users should either duplicate the equipment at both ends of the link or have some number of dedicated back-up links available. You must exercise caution when considering back-up capabilities so that the costs of back-up links are justified. The creation of back-up capabilities can be a major expense and may not be warranted for some networks. A key consideration is what the potential loss will be if back-up capabilities do not exist and the network fails.

Hardware

Hardware components also fail and may require back-up capabilities. As with line costs, the cost of the back-up hardware must be evaluated against the amount of loss the company will experience if the hardware fails. The most common method for providing hardware backup is by having an identical component that can be used if the primary one fails. Because many modems and multiplexers are modular, spare boards may be all that are necessary. In some cases, a paired front-end processor arrangement is used with a line-switching capability. If one fails, the other one can assume all of the communications functions. In most cases, hardware failures are rare and can be kept to a minimum if time is allocated for preventive maintenance.

Network Configurations, Network Design and Security

CASE STUDY (CONTINUED)

When considering the topological makeup of the Bank of Scotts Valley's network, it was important for the network planning group to identify the overall network requirement for redundancy, security and backup. A review of these requirements helps to determine the overall network organization.

Within each of the branches, a double ring network is used for the connection of all administrative and teller workstations. The dual ring provides redundancy should the primary ring experience a failure. Each branch is connected using a star arrangement to its service center; the service center acts as the hub for the star. As described earlier, each branch is connected using a primary dedicated link, as well as a secondary back-up link.

The service centers are connected to one another using dual high-speed, point-to-point links. Additional redundancy is built into the service center connections because the bank uses the telephone company's network, which incorporates a mesh topology, so that service is 100 percent guaranteed. Figure 13.10 illustrates the types of topologies used by the Bank of Scotts Valley.

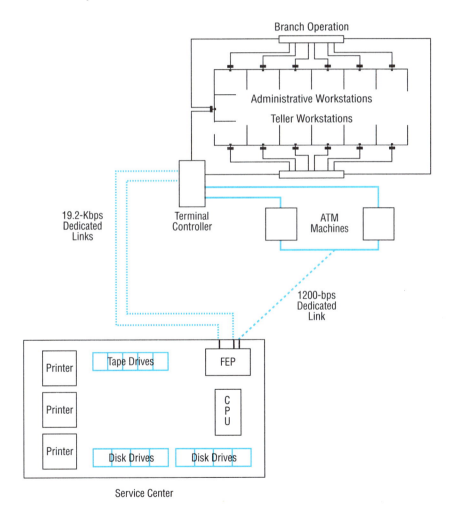

Figure 13.10 Connectivity at the Bank of Scotts Valley

REVIEW QUESTIONS

1. What are the two basic types of line connections used in network communications?
2. True or false: Multipoint topologies can only use dedicated links.
3. Name the six basic network topologies.
4. What are the two main modes of polling in a multipoint line configuration?
5. Define the differences between polling and selection.
6. True or false: The mesh topology offers one of the better methods for backup and redundancy.
7. Are economic considerations important in the design of a communications network?
8. Name some of the factors that must be considered when designing a communications network.
9. Would a local network require different design criteria than a remote network? Why?
10. Define distributed processing.

CHAPTER

14

Network Architectures

INTRODUCTION

A network architecture identifies communications products and services so that the various components can operate together. Defining and implementing a network architecture was a necessity for many vendors because their product lines could not communicate with each other, let alone with other vendors' products. Several manufacturers have developed proprietary network architectures to address this internal incompatibility problem, including IBM with its Systems Network Architecture and Digital Equipment with its DECnet architecture. It is important to note, however, that because they are proprietary, they cannot easily interface with one another.

Compatibility of processing techniques and transmission methods between different manufacturers historically has been a problem, and users have had to pay a large price for networking heterogeneous systems. Often, a company's technical support organization experiences great difficulty when attempting to link systems together that have dissimilar architectures. This was (and to some extent still is) due primarily to the reluctance of some manufacturers to address hardware and communications architectures other than their own.

To provide interconnection capabilities, many manufacturers have developed methods of interfacing their products with other vendors' systems. These interface methodologies generally provide a conversion activity using bridges or gateways (described in Chapter 9) to manage the different formats. These interfaces make communications between different networks possible. Although this works reasonably well, it is considered a closed systems approach to internetworking and can be costly because additional hardware and software must be acquired. Another problem with using bridges or gateways is that the conversion process may limit performance. Finally, conversion techniques are time-consuming to implement and to monitor.

A more functional approach to internetwork communications is an open systems architecture, which specifies communications using standard protocols. However, in the early stages of data communications growth, even if a manufacturer wanted to provide an open systems architecture, there was no agreement on what standards to implement. This was due, in part, to the multitude of incompatible national and international standards that existed. It was also due to some manufacturers' desires to sell their preferred networking solutions.

STANDARD ARCHITECTURES

When national and international standards groups began to take an interest in hardware and software compatibility, they reviewed various communications architectures. This review revealed that most hardware and software companies defined layers of functional responsibility for their networks. The functional responsibilities included electrical specifications, software handshaking and others. These layers of responsibility provided different levels of service to the data being transported. Many architectures have been defined, such as the Xerox Networking System (XNS), DECnet, the Advanced Research Projects Agency Network (ARPANET) and the U.S. Department of Defense Network (DDN). But two architectures, IBM's SNA (Systems Network Architecture) and the International Standards Organization's OSI model, have emerged as the major network architectures.

Both of these architectures segregate functions into layers (levels). These layers form a protocol stack in that each layer's functions can be modified or enhanced without affecting the other layers. Modification can take place as long as a layer's basic functions and its method of interfacing to other layers remain intact. A protocol, simply put, is a "handshake" that can be implemented in hardware components (e.g., the EIA-232 interface) or in software (e.g., one of the layers in the OSI model or SNA). Each of these layered protocols addresses a different networking function.

Today, due to the emergence of international communications architectures, manufacturers provide hardware and software designed to interface with other vendors' products using international standards. Digital Equipment, for example, has recently stated that its proprietary DECnet architecture soon will be fully compliant with the OSI model.

ELEMENTS OF LAYERED OPERATIONS

Network architectures are designed primarily to address the world of data communications; however, the top layers also support some data processing activities. These upper layers apply to the application process, the presentation format and the establishment of user sessions. The elements of a layered architecture consist of independent levels, each having specific responsibilities and functions. These functions include data transfer, flow control, segmentation and reassembly, sequence control, error detection and notification. Each layer of the architecture also has a specific responsibility for the data.

Data Transfer

This function allows the transfer of data from one node in the network to another using the transport services of more than one layer. Several data transport options exist, including normal or expedited data flow, packet sizing, segmentation and assembly.

Flow Control

Controlling the flow of packets throughout the network helps to reduce congestion and the degradation of network performance. Flow control is required because data traffic may at times be unpredictable, and congestion can occur when too many packets are placed on the network at the same time.

Segmentation and Reassembly

In large heterogeneous networks, it is often necessary to segment (take apart) the original packet and construct a number of smaller packets, because many networks do not have the same packet-sizing requirements. Specific layers of the communications architecture are responsible for this segmentation activity, as well as for the reassembly process on the receiving end.

Sequencing

One way to use the network efficiently is to keep all lines as active as possible. However, if multiple routes are available for moving the data to its destination, packets may arrive out of sequence. Packets segmented and sent across different routes take different amounts of time to arrive. To resolve this problem, each segmented packet is given an internal sequence number so that it can be reassembled in proper byte order by the receiver.

Error Detection

To provide guaranteed sequenced delivery of the data packets to their destinations, it is necessary to acknowledge receipt of the data back to the sender. It is equally important to inform the sender that one or more packets were received in error so that they can be resent. When several transmission and reception points exist within a large network environment, error detection and acknowledgment may be required within several of the operational layers of each node.

Notification

To maintain the data transfer activity, segmentation and reassembly, flow control and overall performance of the network, nodes must be able to communicate with each other. These communications use special management control packets and occur between network end points, internetwork gateway points and from node to node.

IBM SYSTEMS NETWORK ARCHITECTURE

In 1974, IBM developed SNA as a five-level architecture. SNA has evolved over a period of time into what is generally considered a seven-level architecture. (Some difference of opinion exists as to the actual number of levels.) SNA appears to closely follow the OSI model, but SNA does not map directly into the OSI model and many aspects of it are not compatible with OSI.

SNA consists of software and hardware interfaces that permit various types of IBM equipment and software to communicate with each other. The architecture consists of network nodes, physical units and logical units. Physical units manage the hardware and software needed for communications. Logical units manage the software for communications with end users. To understand how SNA functions, you need to understand the terms that IBM uses.

All physical devices in the network are identified as specific types of nodes. These represent strategic points in the network and consist of different types of hardware with specialized functions. A node can be a computer, communications processor, terminal controller, special processor or terminal. The types of nodes defined for an SNA network are described below.

Host Node. The CPU acts as the primary unit and is considered the host node. Each SNA network consists of one primary node and multiple secondary nodes that operate in a point-to-multipoint controlled mode.

CUCN. The CUCN (control unit communications node) controls the remote communications network to which it is attached. If this is a local node, the CUCN is a front-end processor such as the IBM 3745 communications processor. The CUCN also can be a remote device such as the IBM 3720 communications processor.

CCN. The CCN (cluster controller node) provides remote locations with access through the CUCNs to the host node for application services. It can be a programmable intelligent device and can support a wide variety of terminal devices. Typically, the IBM 3x74 is used as a CCN.

TN. The TN (terminal node) provides remote users with access to the host environment and its application programs.

Physical Units

All nodes in the SNA network can be classified as a physical unit (PU) type. A simple explanation of the physical unit concept is that it refers to a device that participates in controlling and routing network communications. Unique PU numbers are designated for different types of devices. PU types (illustrated in Figure 14.1) are as follows:

- PU Type 1 relates to non-SNA terminal devices. This PU type was a later addition to SNA and was implemented to recognize non-SNA/IBM devices and terminals.

- PU Type 2 devices are cluster or terminal controllers, such as IBM 3174, 3274 and 3276 types of controllers. PU Type 2.1 defines connectivity to IBM and non-IBM devices such as the IBM System/3x or the Tandem Nonstop system.

- PU Type 4 describes communications processors either remotely located or acting as front-end processors. It includes the IBM 3720, 3725 and 3745, as well as compatible processors from NCR and Amdahl Corp. running Network Control Program (NCP) software.

- PU Type 5 devices are host nodes such as the IBM System/370 family of computers and are responsible for managing one SNA domain.

Logical Units

Because end users are not identified within the SNA environment, a method was established for end-to-end communications called logical unit (LU) sessions. Logical units are the end-user terminals (e.g., CRTs and printers) or the originating application software located in the host. When an end user signs onto the SNA-controlled network, a pair of LUs are established at each end of the link, which creates a user session.

Systems Services Control Points

To establish a session between a user and an application process, all hardware must be identified, LUs must be established and software must be present to establish and maintain the communications session. The Systems Services Control Point (SSCP) is a system software program resident in the host processor designed to manage user-host communications. In some respects it can be likened to the software communications monitor described in Chapter 3.

Domains

A typical domain is an independent SNA network linked to other SNA networks. A domain consists of a controlling host processor containing the SSCP software and user nodes. A typical SNA network can consist of multiple domains running multiple SSCP software.

SNA now supports intelligent nodes connected for peer-to-peer communications. This is known as LU 6.2 communications. It enables intelligent devices to function on a peer-to-peer level without requiring host activity for communications support functions. LU 6.2 is commonly referred to as Advanced Program-to-Program Communication (APPC) or Low-Entry Networking (LEN). APPC software enables a variety of processors to communicate on a peer basis.

LU 6.2 supports interface functions at the application, session and presentation layers of the OSI model (described in a later section). Within SNA, the most important application-layer facilities supported by LU 6.2 are SNA Distribution Services (SNADS), Distributed Office Support System (DISOSS), Document Content Architecture (DCA) and Document Interchange Architecture (DIA). These application software systems support office automation and document handling/transfer services.

Many other companies that manufacture computers and data communications products have implemented SNA gateways and offer compatible equipment to provide interface capabilities for users of their products. Gateways are implemented using software and hardware to convert non-SNA data and communications formats into SNA-type formats.

Each layer of SNA's seven-layer architecture provides specific responsibilities (see Figure 14.2). Layer seven, the application/end-user layer, is responsible for end-user activities such as those provided by CICS (communications monitor), TSO (time sharing), CMS (conversational monitor) and IMS (database/data communications) software.

Layer six, the presentation services layer in SNA, offers functions provided by ACF/VTAM (Advanced Communications Facility/Virtual Telecommunications Access Method) communications software.

Layer five, the data flow control layer, and layer four, the transmission control layer, currently handle ACF/NCP (Advanced Communications Facility/Network Control Program) software functions.

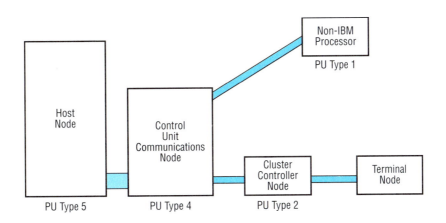

Figure 14.1 PU Types and Nodes

Layer three is the network/path control layer. In SNA, this layer is implemented in the front-end processor and remote communications processors in the form of NCP software.

Layer two, the data link control (DLC) layer, is implemented in SNA in the form of SDLC, which manages node-to-node communications.

Layer one provides the pathway for system and application programs to access the communications link. It is responsible for activating, maintaining and deactivating the physical links. The physical layer also defines the electrical and mechanical aspects of interfacing to a physical medium for transmitting data.

THE OSI MODEL

The ISO OSI reference model is a layered architecture comprising a series of international networking standards known as the X.200 standards (see Figure 14.3). These standards were developed over a period of six years and were completed in 1983. They are published as OSI guideline IS #7498, which defines a common set of rules that specify the way participating networks and nodes must interact to exchange information. Although this standard was designed primarily for interconnection of different networks internationally, manufacturers of data processing and data communications equipment around the world have implemented the OSI standards as the foundation for their communications architectures.

As with IBM's SNA, the OSI specifications are a set of layered standards that provide, via the layers' specifications, communications relationships between the different software modules that can operate within a network node. The intent of the layered approach is to define specific levels of service that can be negotiated between two end points or nodes in a network. The supporting software modules within each node provide an interface between the higher and lower layers to satisfy service requests.

Starting with the top layer on the sending side, each layer takes data and information received from a higher level, places it into a packet and provides a value-added service. This is then appended to the existing packet in the form of a header. Lower layers treat

Layer	Services
7	End User
6	NAU Services
5	Data Flow
4	Transport Control
3	Path Control
2	Data Link
1	Physical

Figure 14.2 SNA Layers

the header and data as a single entity referred to as a protocol data unit (PDU). Layers in the sending node negotiate levels of service with layers in the receiving node, establishing a common bond for communications. The receiving node takes the PDU, and then each subsequent layer strips off the header as it passes up the levels (see Figure 14.4).

Layer Seven: Application Control

This layer provides services that directly support user and application tasks, as well as overall system management. Network management, resource sharing and database management services reside within this layer. Functions of this layer include file transfer, interpretation of graphic formats and document processing. One activity that operates within layer seven is the X.400 electronic mail messaging service.

Layer Six: Presentation Control

This layer takes the transmitted data and translates it into a format that will enable it to be processed by the receiving system and displayed on terminal CRTs and printers. Functions of this layer include data formatting, code set conversion (e.g., ASCII to EBCDIC), text compression for higher throughput efficiency and encryption services.

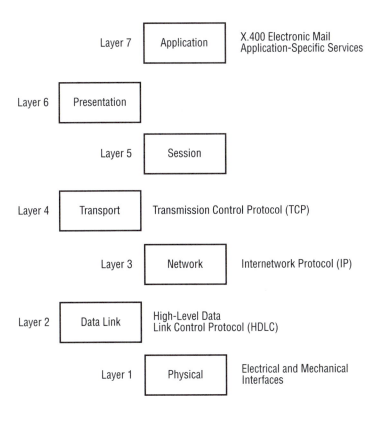

Figure 14.3 OSI Layers

Layer Five: Session Control

Layer five formats the data for transfer between end nodes of the network. This layer also provides session-to-session restart and recovery and is responsible for maintaining the end-to-end connection until a termination request is received from the user or the system.

Layer Four: Transport Control

Layer four is responsible for end-to-end integrity and control of a communications session between network nodes. It accepts data from the next higher layer (session layer) and passes it to the network layer. Two protocols have been developed to provide transport services: transmission control protocol (TCP), which is not an official OSI protocol, and the five levels of the OSI Transport Protocol (TP).

Layer Three: Network Control

The network layer addresses the messages and transports them to their destinations by setting up the required paths to various communications nodes within the network. The network layer is responsible for message routing, error detection and control of internodal traffic. The OSI Internetwork Protocol (IP) and other protocols provide services at this layer.

Layer Two: Data Link Control

The data link control layer establishes the communications link between devices over the physical channel. It is responsible for framing, error control, time-out levels and data formatting. It also maintains sequence control for frames on the communications link. OSI uses the HDLC protocol for these services.

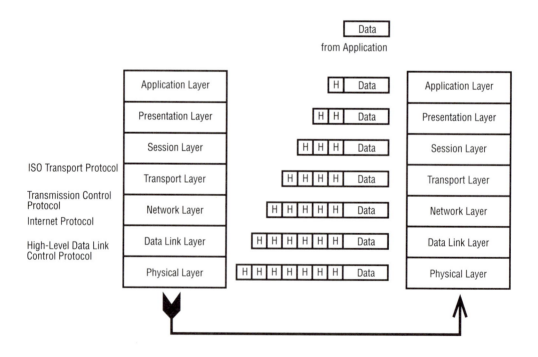

Figure 14.4 OSI Packet Construction

Layer One: Physical Control

Layer one is the physical link layer that defines the electrical and mechanical aspects of the interface to a physical medium for the transmission of data, as well as the initial setup. This layer includes the communications hardware and software drivers.

CCITT X.25 STANDARD

The CCITT X.25 standard defines a DTE-to-DCE interface and network. This standard closely follows the lower three levels of the OSI seven-layer model. "Closely follows" means that it follows the concepts of OSI rather than maps directly onto the model (see Figure 14.5). In fact, X.25 was conceived prior to the development of the OSI model and had been implemented by a number of organizations in Europe before OSI became a standard.

X.25 is made up of three layers. Layer three is referred to as the packet layer. This layer is responsible for transporting data across the network to its destinations. It sets up the paths between various communications nodes within the network and is also responsible for packet routing and for the control of internodal traffic. The Internet protocol (IP) and other protocols provide services at this layer.

Layer two is the data link control layer. The DLC layer establishes the communications link between devices over the physical channel. It is responsible for framing, error control, time-out levels and data formatting. It also maintains sequence control for frames on the communications link. X.25 uses the Link Access Protocol (LAP) and the Link Access Protocol-B (LAP-B), which are identical to the HDLC protocol for these services.

Layer one is the physical link layer that defines the electrical and mechanical aspects of the interface to a physical medium for the transmission of data, as well as the initial setup. This layer includes the hardware and the software driver for each communications device.

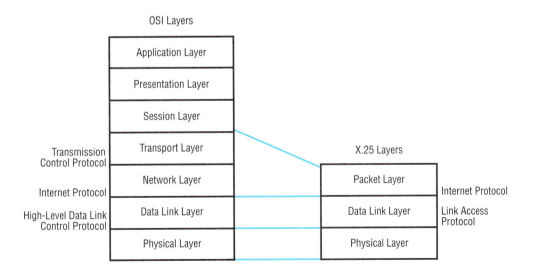

Figure 14.5   X.25 Layers as they Relate to OSI Layers

MANUFACTURING AUTOMATION PROTOCOL

The Manufacturing Automation Protocol (MAP) is a set of layered communications protocols (similar to those defined by the OSI model) that was developed by General Motors Corp. Its primary function is to manage factory automation activities. MAP uses elements of the IEEE 802.4 local area network standard and interfaces to wide area networks via the OSI upper-layer protocols. Many hardware and software manufacturers offer products that incorporate MAP, enabling computerized equipment from different vendors to communicate with each other in a factory environment. MAP uses either broadband or baseband transmission over coaxial cable and operates similar to a token-passing ring network.

CASE STUDY (CONTINUED)

The Bank of Scotts Valley will implement IBM's Systems Network Architecture because of the large number of SNA networks and the level of support available. The bank's data communications network planners have decided to break the SNA network into two domains. Domain A, located in Northern California, will support branches located in the northern part of the state. Domain B will be located in Los Angeles and will support the southern part of the state. Each branch contains a control unit communications node and its workstations are terminal nodes. The ATM networks will not be part of SNA, but instead will be connected to a Tandem computer that is channel-attached to the IBM processor.

The service center located in Los Angeles will be able to support connectivity outside of the SNA network. It will support the CCITT X.25 communications standard and have a dedicated link to an X.25 public data carrier. This will allow internetwork communications to other computers that do not support SNA but that have X.25 capabilities. It will also have OSI internetwork communications capabilities for communications with international networks. Figure 14.6 illustrates the Bank of Scotts Valley's SNA network.

Because each of the service centers maintains records for the accounts it supports, communications to the Northern California service center must be routed there from the Los Angeles service center. The computer in Los Angeles will take incoming requests from the OSI interface and convert them to an SNA format. At that point, the SNA-formatted request will be handled as if it were an interbranch activity. When either the Northern California or Los Angeles service center must communicate with OSI or X.25 networks, it will access an application program running in Los Angeles that is designed to reformat the communication into the correct format and transport it to the network interface.

REVIEW QUESTIONS

1. What does the ISO OSI model define?
2. What is SNA?
3. Are SNA and OSI compatible architectures?
4. SDLC is a protocol for what architecture?
5. What is layer two also known as?
6. True or false: The OSI model is designed to encompass both data processing and data communications.

7. What is X.25 used for?
8. What are the first three layers of the X.25?
9. What protocol is used with the X.25 architecture?
10. What does MAP stand for?

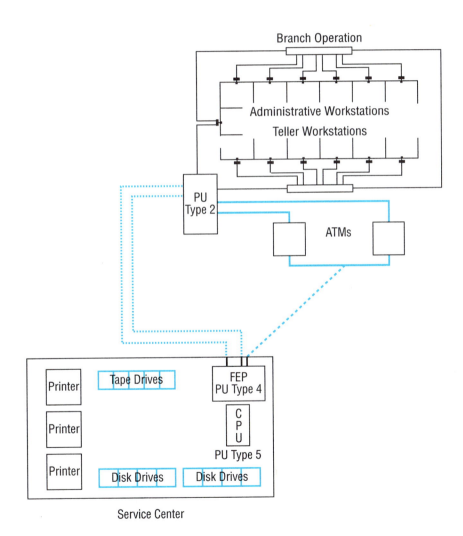

Figure 14.6 Bank of Scotts Valley SNA Network

CHAPTER
15

Protocols

INTRODUCTION

Two pieces of equipment that want to communicate with one another must use a protocol for controlling and exchanging information. A protocol formats data frames consisting of data and control information. The communications equipment at each end of a link uses the protocol's control information to determine the data's validity and its final destination within the network.

Another way of looking at a protocol is to compare it to the public mail system. The letter corresponds to the data and it must be directed to a specific person. An envelope contains the letter and bears the addresses of the sender and receiver. The destination address also may contain routing information for speedy delivery. This method of exchanging information is conceptually similar to a protocol packet or framed data communications.

The function of a protocol is to provide a handshaking technique between two pieces of equipment, multiple nodes, multiple networks or end-to-end sessions (user and application). Protocol functions are implemented as firmware or software processes and reside in the various communications devices attached to the network. Protocols assist in the transport of data between two distal points in the communications network using physical media. The physical media typically provide connections between terminal controllers and front-end communications processors or host computers, or from one computer or communications node to another.

Almost every manufacturer of data processing and data communications equipment supports some type of protocol. This includes both centralized terminal environments and networkwide communications activities.

Many companies originally provided only a protocol that was unique to their products.

At that time, there was no need to provide communications with other vendors' products. As multivendor networking became a reality, new protocols were developed that, in many cases, were different from those used for network or remote communications. This multiple-protocol environment often created incompatibilities between different manufacturers' networks, making it difficult for users to connect their networking hardware.

It is common today for one manufacturer to adopt and use the protocol of another manufacturer for internodal communications. One example is the adaptation of IBM's BSC protocol by many other vendors. Adapting other manufacturers' protocols is meant to serve as a compatibility feature, allowing direct connection of multivendor equipment. Since the introduction of international standards, many companies have implemented new protocols that will allow for internetwork communications.

DATA COMMUNICATIONS PROTOCOL CONCEPTS

Transportation of data across a communications network mandates that certain activities take place. Specific control activities occur at each end of the link to ensure that the data arrives in a sequential fashion, with notification to the sender if an acknowledgment is desired. Such notification communicates a successful reception.

Bit- Versus Byte-Oriented Protocols

Two general types of protocols exist, byte-oriented and bit-oriented. In byte-oriented protocols, character or byte strings are transferred in eight-bit (byte) formats. Control characters embedded within the header and trailer of the packet provide control indicators to the software. Byte-oriented protocols are generally found only at the second layer used with older protocols (see Figure 15.1).

In bit-oriented protocols such as SDLC and HDLC, bit streams are transported and only one bit pattern (01111110) is recognized (opening and closing flag). Bit-oriented protocols are generally considered more efficient because they require less overhead for transmission control than do byte-oriented protocols. (Figure 15.2 presents a bit-oriented protocol.) Bit-oriented protocols are usually synchronous and full-duplex in operation.

Protocol Functions

All protocols follow a set of established procedures for the movement of data. Protocol software frames the data bytes or bit stream with communications codes or special bit patterns

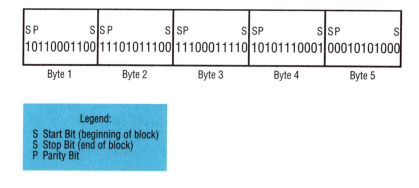

Figure 15.1   Byte-Oriented Protocol

that indicate specific control functions. These control functions are used to indicate transmission status and to identify the beginning and end of the byte or bit stream transferred.

The protocol software also establishes and maintains some type of sequencing control to ensure that packets and frames are not lost and are received in the order in which they were sent. This usually involves placing a sequence number in a field within the packet.

Protocol software also must maintain direction control to ensure that when one node is transmitting, all other nodes are receiving. This is especially important in a half-duplex environment.

The protocol software also manages start and stop control. Start and stop control provides an orderly transition through all phases of data communications. Start and stop control indicates the beginning and end of the packet byte or bit stream. It includes line turnaround in a half-duplex environment, indicators for the beginning and end of the packet flow, and proper linking and unlinking.

Protocol software must provide extensive error control to detect error conditions in the transmitted data. Upon discovery of an error in the received packet, the software requests retransmission of the data.

Protocol software must contain a function for time-out control, which is required to address deadlock situations that arise when a receiving node must wait to transmit because a response is expected from the sending node. Deadlock can occur when terminals and lines experience delay or are out of operation. If time-out control did not exist, a networkwide lockup could occur. Typically, time-out values are tunable in the software, based on the type of link used.

For certain protocols, transparency is needed to inform the protocol software that the data area begins starting at a certain byte within the packet. This control feature informs the protocol software to ignore any bit patterns that may indicate protocol functions. This is useful for transferring or downloading software across the link. Without transparency, the software that needs to be transferred could cause the protocol software to perform an unwanted function.

Depending on the protocol used, selected functions may not be required. Often, certain protocol functions may be implemented in such a fashion that they perform nothing more than basic activities.

Data Link Communications Codes

The standard code set used by the communications equipment often determines what control codes are available to the protocol software. The EBCDIC code set, for example, provides additional communications codes not available in ASCII. Specific data link control protocols selectively use the ASCII and EBCDIC standard communications codes differently. The protocol being used determines which codes are valid for that handshaking technique.

```
10001100111010111001110001111010101110001000101010 00
```

Figure 15.2 Bit-Oriented Protocol Frame

With bit-oriented protocols such as the SDLC protocol and the OSI HDLC protocol, ASCII and EBCDIC communications codes are not used because the code set employed is transparent to the protocols. Instead, HDLC and SDLC use bit groupings or binary counts to represent specific activities. Typical communications codes available in both ASCII and EBCDIC for byte-oriented DLC protocols include the following.

SOH: Start of Header. This is usually the first character after the synchronization characters and is used to indicate the start of the header information. The SOH is used to delineate the beginning of the frame, the control characters and the data.

STX: Start of Text. The STX character is used to indicate the beginning of the data field, which immediately follows the STX character.

ETX: End of Text. The ETX character indicates that there is no more data and immediately follows the last character of data. This may be placed where additional blocks of data will appear in the frame.

DLE: Data Line Escape. The DLE character works in conjunction with the STX and the ETX to provide transparency for the data being sent. Transparency allows communications control characters to be sent as data and prevents the transmission software from responding to their functions. This is used primarily when downloading software to remote communications nodes.

ETB: End of Transmission Block. The ETB character is used to indicate the end of a transmission block. The ETB is the same as the ETX except that when the ETX is used, more data blocks may follow.

ITB: Intermediate Text Block. The ITB character is used to indicate an intermediate end of transmission block. It is used to separate the message into sections for error detection without causing a reversal of the transmission direction.

EOT: End of Transmission. The EOT character indicates an end of the transmission block. It is also used to indicate "nothing to respond," and for line turnaround in half-duplex environments.

WACK: Wait Before Transmit. A WACK response indicates that the previous frame was received without error (positive acknowledgment), but the receiving station is not ready to accept another frame. The transmitting station will respond with an enquiry until a character other than WACK is received.

ACK: Positive Acknowledgment. The ACK is used to acknowledge receipt of the data. There are two forms of the ACK, the ACK0 and the ACK1. ACK0 indicates that the data was received without error and the receiver is ready to accept additional data. ACK0 is also used to acknowledge multipoint selection, point-to-point contention and even-numbered blocks of data. ACK1 is used to acknowledge odd-numbered blocks of data received.

NAK: Negative Acknowledgment. NAK is a negative acknowledgment informing the sender that the previous data block was received in error. Receipt of the NAK indicates that a retransmission of the block received in error is required.

ENQ: Enquiry. An ENQ character is used to bid for use of the link when in a point-to-point, contention-based mode. It indicates the end of a polling or selection request. It is also used to request retransmission of a NAK or ACK response if the original response was garbled or not received when expected.

RVI: Reverse Interrupt. The RVI is similar to the ACK and NAK. However, the RVI is a priority interrupt request to the station controlling the link to turn the line around for an important transmission.

TTD: Temporary Text Delay. The transmitter uses the TTD to retain the line even though it is not ready to use the link. The receiving station will respond with a NAK.

Error Detection

Several types of error detection techniques are available, depending on the protocols in use. Often, multiple error detection schemes are used at the same time. As mentioned in Chapter 10, some additional error detection may be available from modem manufacturers, either in the form of standalone error correction devices attached to the link or built into each modem.

Vertical Redundancy Checking (VRC). This form of error detection adds an additional bit to each byte, known as the parity bit. This additional bit will be turned on or off at the sending side, depending on the parity of the machine (odd, even or none) and the bit composition of the character sent. If the hardware operates in odd parity, then each byte that is composed of an even number of one bits will cause the hardware to set the parity bit to a one. This will make the number of one bits in the byte an odd amount. Also referred to as parity checking, VRC is not generally used because it adds overhead to the data streams being transmitted. Figure 15.3 illustrates an example of VRC or parity checking.

Longitudinal Redundancy Checking (LRC). This is used primarily with byte-oriented protocols. LRC creates parity bits that form a character for each bit row in a block. By placing a number of characters side by side in the buffer, each bit row generates its own parity bit. These parity bits create characters referred to as block check characters, which are transmitted to the receiving modem and terminal as part of the protocol frame. When the data is received, the data is reconstructed in the buffer and each bit row is validated (see Figure 15.4). A problem with this form of error detection is that if a block experiences a multibit error, it may escape detection on the receiving side.

Cyclical Redundancy Checking (CRC). CRC is the most extensive and complicated error detection and correction scheme available. It uses polynomial arithmetic to calculate 8-,

Bit Position	
1	0
2	1
3	0
4	0
5	0
6	0
7	1
Odd Parity	1

Figure 15.3 VRC Error Detection

16-, 32- or 64-bit cyclical redundancy check characters. CRC operates by calculating multiple binary-encoded characters that represent the sum of the data stream within the protocol frame. CRC is used extensively in HDLC and SDLC protocols. In SDLC, cyclic redundancy checking utilizes a generator polynomial. The CRC is usually the last field sent as part of the frame or packet.

Several other error detection methods are also available, including frame check sequence (FCS) characters (similar in function to CRC error detection) and forward error correction.

LAYER-TWO DLC PROTOCOLS

Asynchronous DLC Protocols

Many hardware and software manufacturers have developed asynchronous protocols for low-speed data communications. These protocols are used primarily within small computers and PCs. While these protocols are usually simple, several of them include extensive error-checking procedures. Blast is perhaps one of the best-known PC-oriented protocols; it provides for recovery if transmission is interrupted. XMODEM is a PC-oriented protocol that creates 128-byte packets and uses CRC error detection. Kermit, another PC-oriented protocol similar to Blast and XMODEM, also supports a 128-byte data packet.

Many other enhanced asynchronous protocols are available that include pseudo-blocking and extensive error correction techniques. Enhancements differ from manufacturer to manufacturer and are usually not compatible. In general, asynchronous protocols have the characteristics outlined in the following paragraphs.

Framing is at the character level and consists of a start bit before the data bits and a stop bit after the data bits. Because the asynchronous transmission method is used in telex transmission, an additional stop bit may be incorporated.

Although the data may be blocked in the application program, the data is sent one character at a time and not in blocks. Error correction is limited to character parity checking, except when error control has been implemented by the protocol developer under a particular manufacturer's specifications.

Asynchronous protocol speeds are usually limited to 9600 bps or less and are used

Bit Position	Information Characters					Block Parity Character
	1	2	3	4	5	
1	0	1	0	0	1	1
2	1	0	0	0	0	0
3	0	0	1	1	0	1
4	0	1	1	1	1	1
5	0	0	0	0	1	0
6	0	0	0	0	0	1
7	1	1	1	1	1	0
Odd Parity	1	0	0	0	1	1

Figure 15.4   Longitudinal Redundancy Checking

primarily with dial-up links. One reason these protocols are used in low-speed environments is the large overhead associated with asynchronous transmission (in some cases up to 37 percent). Some modems do provide asynchronous transmission at speeds up to 16,000 bps using special modulation techniques and add-on error correction devices.

Binary Synchronous Protocol (BSC)

Developed in 1966, BSC (also known as bisync) was created by IBM to support its computer communications activities. BSC is a character-oriented (byte-oriented) protocol that frames its data with communications control codes (described at the beginning of this chapter). BSC has been adopted as a *de facto* standard by many manufacturers because of the widespread use of IBM equipment supporting bisync since the 1960s. Early versions of BSC were provided to users in software form, but today it can be implemented in the hardware's firmware. Figure 15.5 shows a BSC protocol frame.

BSC is a half-duplex protocol that sends a single frame at a time and requires that a response be received prior to the next transmission. It operates in either multipoint or point-to-point configurations in either controlled or contention mode. In the controlled mode, the protocol functions in a polled mode using master and secondary stations over point-to-point or multipoint configurations. In the contention mode, BSC uses a primary station connected to a secondary station in a point-to-point configuration.

The BSC protocol detects errors using a combination of VRC and LRC techniques. Parity bits are generated by the transmitting station for strings of characters and are used to create a Block Check Character (BCC). Each BCC is appended to the protocol frame transmitted. At the receiving side, the protocol software regenerates the BCCs and compares them to those received in the protocol frame. If the comparison determines that an error has occurred, a NAK frame is returned to the sender (see Figure 15.6).

It is important to note that BSC is currently used in less than half of the IBM systems that perform data communications. Today it is mainly used with systems that do not have high data throughput requirements or do not support SNA. BSC is most commonly used on low-end systems. It also may be found on systems that have not been upgraded to IBM's newer protocol, SDLC.

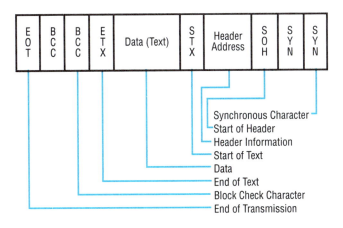

Figure 15.5   BSC Protocol Frame

Synchronous Data Link Control (SDLC)

SDLC is the layer-two DLC protocol currently considered to be the heart of SNA. (Figure 15.7 illustrates an SNA SDLC header.) It was developed in the mid-1970s and provides increased capability over the BSC protocol. IBM has stated that SDLC and the SNA architecture were developed as an overall strategy for its data processing and data communications environments. Figure 15.8 shows an SDLC frame.

HDLC, the layer-two protocol of the OSI model, is a superset of SDLC and ADCCP, which is a U.S. NBS protocol. HDLC is considered a superset because SDLC was developed by IBM prior to OSI development and was used as a model for HDLC. The SDLC protocol operates either in a full- or half-duplex environment in point-to-point or multipoint configurations. It may support peer-to-peer or primary-to-secondary nodes; however, it is designed primarily as a host control protocol. Multiple data blocks can be embedded in frames, and up to seven frames can be transmitted without acknowledgments between each transmitted frame.

SDLC is a bit-oriented protocol that uses bit strings to represent text. Bit patterns are transparent to SDLC, with the exception of a one-byte flag indicating the start or end of the frame. The flag consists of a 01111110 bit pattern. To prevent a data bit pattern from indicating a flag, a technique called zero bit stuffing is employed. After the opening flag is generated, if the sending side encounters a sequence of five one bits in a row, the protocol will insert a zero bit between the fifth bit and the bits that follow. The receiving side will detect the string of one bits and remove the inserted zero bit when it is encountered.

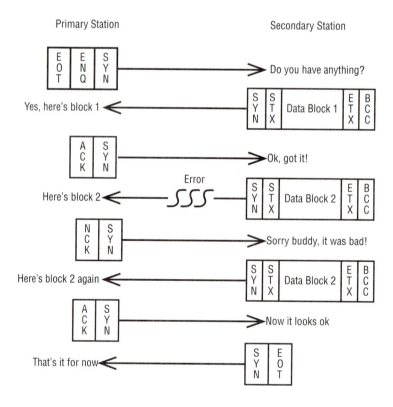

Figure 15.6 BSC Error Detection

Communications functions exist for many types of frame formats, including supervisory, unnumbered and informational frames. Unnumbered and informational frames transport data, and supervisory frames are used for control. The control field in each frame identifies the type of frame. Each frame also carries error-checking information in the form of a CRC field. One problem with SDLC is in its error correction. If an error is detected in the transmission, all contiguous frames after the error is encountered must be resent. This requires that a large buffer be established to hold all frames until the receiver acknowledges them as error free.

SDLC is designed for high transmission rates and supports satellite data links. Whereas BSC operates on a frame-at-a-time basis, SDLC can be configured to use extended formats. This extension supports transmission of up to 128 contiguous frames. Figure 15.9 illustrates the frame formats and control codes associated with the three types of SDLC frames.

High-Level Data Link Control (HDLC)

This protocol was developed by the ISO (ISO 4335) and is a superset of the SDLC protocol used in IBM's SNA. It is also used by many manufacturers as their synchronous protocol and is specified as the OSI layer-two protocol. A version of HDLC referred to as Link Access Procedure-Balanced (LAP-B) is in widespread use as the CCITT protocol that supports the X.25 standard. Many local area network systems also use HDLC for data link control. Figure 15.10 shows a basic HDLC frame format.

HDLC has many of the same characteristics of SDLC because it is a superset implementation. Normally, HDLC and SDLC are not compatible; however, depending on the implementation of the HDLC protocol, frame conversion from one format to another can be a simple process. Because HDLC is a standard definition, many computer manufacturers have adopted it. The HDLC standard defines types of stations, link configurations and data transfer modes.

SDLC	SNA	SNA	SNA	SNA
Link Header	Transmission Header	Request Response Header	Request Response Unit	Link Trailer
3 bytes	6 bytes	3 bytes	0 to *n* bytes	3 bytes

Figure 15.7 SNA SDLC Header Format

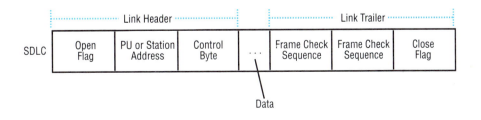

Figure 15.8 SDLC Frame

Types of Stations. Three types of stations can be identified:

- Primary stations that issue commands.
- Secondary stations that issue responses.
- Combined stations. Combined stations can operate as either a primary or secondary station, issuing both requests and responses.

Link Configurations. Two types of link configurations can be used with HDLC: unbalanced and balanced. In the unbalanced mode, one primary station and multiple secondary stations operate over point-to-point or multipoint links. Balanced mode uses a point-to-point configuration with the combined station concept in a peer-to-peer arrangement.

Data Transfer Modes. The data transfer modes indicate how a station will participate in a data transfer operation. The three data transfer modes are:

- Normal response mode (NRM)
- Asynchronous balanced mode (ABM)
- Asynchronous response mode (ARM)

NRM uses an unbalanced link configuration with a single primary and multiple secondary stations. The primary station controls data transfer to the secondary stations, but secondary stations can transfer data only when they are polled by the primary station. ABM uses a balanced link configuration with combined stations. Either station can initiate data transfer operations at any time. ARM uses an unbalanced configuration with a single primary and multiple secondary stations. Unlike NRM, ARM allows secondary stations to initiate data transfer without a poll from the primary station.

HDLC uses a frame format concept similar to SDLC that defines supervisory (S), information (I) and unnumbered (U) frames for control and data transfer. Figure 15.11 shows the basic format for the three types of HDLC frames.

Unnumbered Format

000	F	1111	DM	Disconnect Mode
010	P	0011	DIS	Disconnect
011	F	0011	UA	Unnumbered Acknowledgment
100	P	0011	SNR	Set Normal Response Mode
100	F	0111	FMR	Frame Reject
101	P/F	1111	XID	Exchange Station ID
101	P/F	0011	TST	Test

Supervisory Format

RRR	P/F	0001	RR	Receive Ready
RRR	P/F	0101	RNR	Receive Not Ready
RRR	P/F	1001	REJ	Reject

Information Format

RRR	P/F	INF	Information Frame

Legend:
- P   Poll Bit
- F   Final Bit
- RRR Next Received Count
- SSS Next Sent Count

Figure 15.9 SDLC Control Byte Information

The format of the frame fields includes the flag, address and control fields.

Flag Field. The flag field is used to indicate the beginning and end of a frame. Similar to SDLC, the flag consists of a 01111110 bit pattern. To prevent a data bit pattern from being mistaken for a flag, the same technique as used in SDLC, zero bit stuffing, is employed. After the opening flag is generated, if the sending side encounters a byte containing five one bits in a row, the protocol will insert a zero bit between the fifth bit and the bits that follow. The receiving side will detect the string of one bits and remove the inserted zero bit when it is encountered.

Address Field. The address field is normally an eight-bit field, but it can be longer if the number of devices in the network exceeds 127. The first seven bits of the address field are used for device addresses, and the eighth bit is used to indicate extended addressing, if implemented. The eighth bit indicates that an additional eight-bit address field is present. When an address field consists entirely of one bits, it is considered to be a broadcast address and all devices will receive the frames.

Control Field. The control field is an 8- or 16-bit field that consists of subfields for different protocol activities. The first subfield is a one- or two-bit field that identifies the type of frame (I, S or U) it resides in. Depending upon the type of frame, the next field may differ. For I types, the next subfield is a three-bit (seven-bit in extended format) sequence number used for the "next send" value. This field controls the number of frames that can be transferred contiguously without acknowledgments. This portion of the control field is also used for negative or positive acknowledgments to and from the receiver. If an out-of-sequence condition is detected in the sequence number, an error has been detected and frames represented by the overlapped numbers must be resent. For U and S packets, the second subfield is a one-bit field used to indicate the function.

The next subfield is a one-bit field indicating poll or final status. If a poll bit is indicated, the packet is a command type from the primary to the secondary station. The secondary station uses the final bit indicator to indicate that the last I type data frame is being transmitted. The last subfield in the unnumbered format is used for protocol functions and, for I and S frames, is the next received field.

The next field in the I frame and also in some unnumbered frames contains the data to be transported. This may be variable in length but is usually set to some fixed multiple of eight bytes. Following the data field is the frame check sequence (FCS) field, which

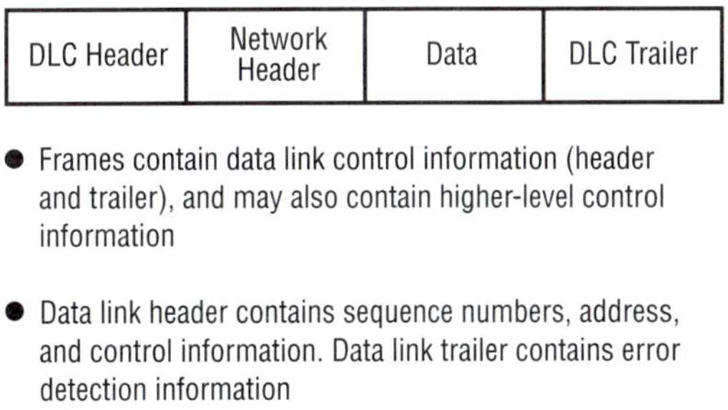

DLC Header	Network Header	Data	DLC Trailer

- Frames contain data link control information (header and trailer), and may also contain higher-level control information

- Data link header contains sequence numbers, address, and control information. Data link trailer contains error detection information

Figure 15.10 HDLC Frame Format

uses the standard CRC-16 or CRC-32 format. Table 15.1 lists the various command and response codes and frame formats that can be used with the HDLC protocol.

LINK ACCESS PROCEDURE-D (LAP-D)

The LAP-D protocol (ISDN Standard I.440/I.441) is designed to support ISDN basic and primary rate D channel activities. LAP-D is a variation of the LAP-B protocol used in X.25 networks. LAP-D's primary function is to communicate control information in a multiplexed environment between the user nodes and the central office. In an ISDN network, user nodes can be considered operationally equivalent to OSI layer two. Central offices are functionally equivalent to OSI layer three (network layer).

LAP-D provides two types of service: unacknowledged information transfer service and acknowledged information transfer service. In unacknowledged transfers, no acknowledgment is required from the receiver, and neither flow control nor error detection services are supported. This operates like X.25 datagram services and is used for rapid information exchange. With acknowledged transfers, a virtual connection is made and the protocol operates like HDLC with the same types of services, including error control, congestion control and acknowledged delivery. Both types of service can be supported concurrently

Frame Types:

- Information (I) frames always have information
- Supervisory (S) frames do not carry information
- Unnumbered (U) frames may carry some information

Basic Control Field Format

Frame Type	Bit Position						
	8	7	6	5	4	3	2	1
Information	N(R)			P/F	N(S)			0
Supervisory	N(R)			P/F	S		0	1
Unnumbered	M(2)			P/F	M(1)		1	1

Legend:
- N(S) Sequence Number of this I-frame
- N(R) Sequence Number of next expected I-frame
- P/F Poll/final bit
- S Supervisory frame type
- M(1)M(2) Unnumbered frame type

Figure 15.11   HDLC Frame Types and Control Byte Information

on the D channel. LAP-D frame structures are similar to HDLC frame structures and consist of the flag, address and control fields, described below.

Flag Field. The flag field indicates the start and end of a frame. Like the HDLC flag, the LAP-D flag consists of a 01111110 bit pattern. To prevent a data bit pattern from being mistaken for a flag, zero bit stuffing is used. After the opening flag, the sending side encounters a sequence of five one bits in a row. The LAP-D protocol will insert a zero bit between the fifth bit and the bits that follow. The receiving side will detect the string of one bits and remove the inserted zero bit when it is encountered.

Address Field. The address field in LAP-D (identical to HDLC) can be up to 16 bits in length. This is because the protocol must provide two levels of multiplexing to the devices it supports. At user sites, several pieces of equipment can share the ISDN interface and each device can support multiple types of traffic. A two-part addressing scheme is used to provide the multiplexing capability. It consists of a field identifier, command/response subfield, service access point identifier (SAPI) and a terminal end-point identifier

Information Frames
INF: Describes a Data Carrying Frame

Supervisory Frames
RR: Receive Ready Indicator
RNR: Receive Not Ready Indicator
REJ: Frame Reject Command
SREJ: Selective Reject

Unnumbered Frames
DM: Disconnect Mode Request
DISC: Disconnect
UA: Unnumbered Acknowledgment
SNRM: Set Normal Response Mode
SNRME: Set Normal Response Mode Extended
SABM: Set Asynchronous Balanced Mode
SABME: Set Asynchronous Balanced Mode Extended
SIM: Set Initialization Mode
RD: Request Disconnect
RIM: Request Initialization Mode
UI: Unnumbered Information Frame. Used to exchange control information
UP: Unnumbered Poll
RSET: Reset. Used to Reset NS - NR Control Field
FRMR: Frame Reject
XID: Exchange Station ID
TEST: Test

Legend:
NR Next Received
NS Next Sent

Table 15.1 HDLC Control Commands

(TEI) subfield. The SAPI field identifies the type of traffic and the TEI subfield identifies specific user devices.

Control Field. The control field defines three types of ISDN frames and, like HDLC, has supervisory, information and unnumbered formats. Additionally, subfields are used for sequence number control, command status and poll final activity just as in HDLC.

The I-type frames are the only ones allowed to carry data. However, again like HDLC, some unnumbered types of frames (response types) also can carry data. The control and data fields are limited to 260 bytes.

LAYER-THREE (NETWORK-LAYER) PROTOCOLS

There are several protocols for layer-three (network-layer) operations. Layer-three activities manage internetwork communications between similar or dissimilar networks. Layer-three protocol functions are considered to be the most complex because they must be designed to support many types of networks. In X.25 networks, layer-three protocols operate in what is referred to as the packet layer.

The network layer supports many types of functions, including data relay, addressing, congestion/flow control and error detection. Data relay activities support transport of the data packets from one network to another and are routed through to the receiving network. Address resolution for packets includes network-to-network addressing and dynamic addressing generation to assist in relay activities. Congestion and flow control are supported at layer three to avoid degrading the network's performance. Error control to manage traffic and resolve error conditions within layer three also may be provided, but error detection is not a specification of this layer. Layer-three protocols include IP and the Internet Control Message Protocol (ICMP).

Internet Protocol (IP)

IP was the result of a joint development effort by Xerox, DARPA and Stanford University. IP was designed to provide services between TCP and the Data Link Control protocol in the data link layer. Its function is to connect networks with minimal impact on each network. IP operates as a subnetwork-layer protocol and can connect networks with different internal protocols and performance. Figure 15.12 shows the IP PDU frame format. Figure 15.13 illustrates a U.S. Department of Defense (DoD) PDU frame format.

IP components within a given network define the format of internet packets they will be responsible for transporting. The protocol software in each node supporting IP must establish rules (via negotiations) for protocol and PDU management functions. These functions are based on control information passed between IP nodes contained within the IP header portion of the packet. The Internet protocol supports delivery of datagram packets from source location to destination; however, it does not provide acknowledgment, data error checking or retransmission. These functions are provided from the transport layer via TP or TCP. IP provides limited flow control to avoid congestion that slows network operation.

Values can be set via bit switches in the control portion of the IP header to provide information about the actions desired and agreed upon. IP supports two types of frames, data frames that consist of four parts and error-reporting PDU frames that contain three parts. The PDU consists of the fixed, address and option fields, described below.

Fixed Field. This contains the protocol identifier, which is not used if the sending and receiving nodes are in the same network. A length indicator defines the number of bytes in the IP header. A version number ensures compatibility with other IP implementations.

A PDU time-to-live (TTL) value can be used to ensure that the PDU will not continue to move through the network if it is not deliverable. The TTL is usually calculated in multiples of 500 milliseconds on entry into a network and is based on the number of nodes that the packet must traverse within the network. Each node decrements the value by one as it transports the packet. If the value becomes negative, the node discards the packet.

A segmentation flag is used to indicate that segmenting of a packet into smaller packets is allowed. Another flag, called the more flag, indicates that segmentation has or has not occurred. A third flag, the error flag, indicates that an error packet is needed. This occurs if the IP packet has to be discarded because an error is detected.

The last three subfields in the fixed part include the type of packet (data or error), segment length of the PDU (including the header information) and the checksum calculation.

Address Field. The address part of the PDU consists of subfields for the source and destination addresses. This is because they may be of different lengths depending on the source and destination of the packet. Addressing is handled across networks by establishing classes that define the type of address being used. This provides flexibility and allows a large number of small, intermediate and large networks to be interconnected. Three address classes have been established:

- Class A addressing uses a seven-bit network address and 24-bit host address.
- Class B uses a 14-bit network address and a 16-bit host address.
- Class C uses a 21-bit network address and an eight-bit host address.

Options Field. An options field may be included to communicate additional functions, such as:

- User-defined security
- Source routing that identifies the networks to be used

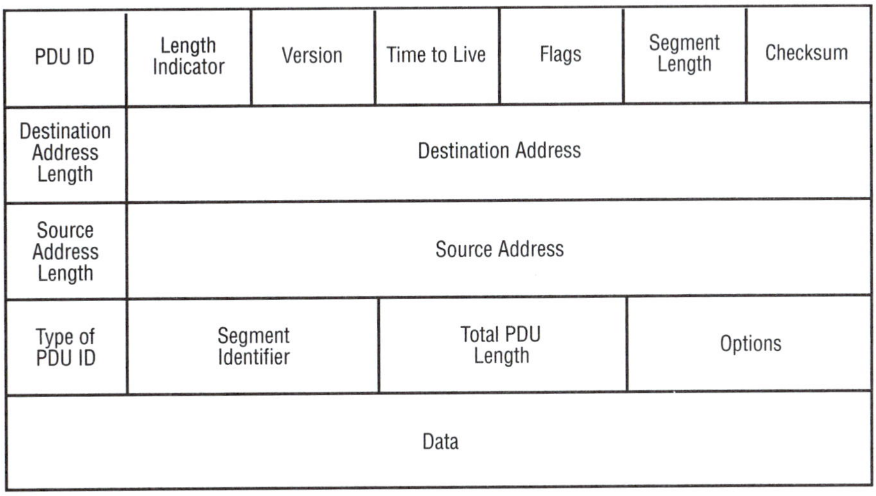

PDU ID	Length Indicator	Version	Time to Live	Flags	Segment Length	Checksum
Destination Address Length	Destination Address					
Source Address Length	Source Address					
Type of PDU ID	Segment Identifier		Total PDU Length		Options	
Data						

Figure 15.12 OSI Internetwork Header Format

- Route information that keeps track of the nodes visited
- Time stamping
- Priority for normal or expedited data transfers
- Quality of service, which specifies degrees of reliability and delay

The final part of the network PDU includes fields for the data and padding, if necessary, to provide a fixed-length packet.

Error PDU Format

An error PDU is created when a data packet cannot be delivered and must be discarded. This will occur only if the data packet contains an indicator requesting the creation of the error PDU. Formats of error PDUs are identical to that of the data PDU; however, they provide an additional two-byte field that contains a reason for discard rather than data. Twenty-two different discard classifications currently exist.

Internet Control Message Protocol (ICMP)

A companion to IP is ICMP. It is required in networks such as the U.S. DDN, and it must be implemented by every IP node. Figure 15.14 illustrates the ICMP header format.

ICMP is used by a gateway or destination host for error notification to a source host. ICMP uses the basic support of the IP packet or frame. This includes the IP headers as if the ICMP frame was data within the higher-level IP. ICMP is actually an integral part of the IP.

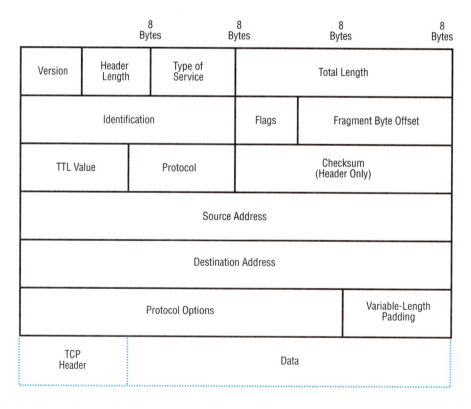

Figure 15.13 U.S. DoD Internetwork PDU Format

ICMP provides feedback to each of the gateways about network communications problems occurring within that specific network. Typically, message packets are created in a gateway node that detects the problem, then sent to other gateway nodes by the ICMP software. This occurs when a datagram cannot reach its destination or a problem exists with a gateway (e.g., no buffer space). It also can occur when a shorter route is available or when there are fragmentation problems.

ICMP message types include the following:

- Redirect — Used when a gateway has determined that greater efficiency can be achieved by redirecting the packet using a different link than the one specified

- Source quench — Indicates to a node or station that it needs to reduce its flow because of a congestion problem

- Time exceeded — Used when the time parameter of the datagram packet has been exceeded and the packet must be discarded

- Parameter problem — Indicates that a syntactical error has occurred and the parameter value in the IP header is unrecognizable

- Destination unreachable — Used when a network or node is unreachable for a variety of reasons

- Echo/echo Reply — Used for testing the links and connections between nodes

- Time stamp/time stamp reply — Used for monitoring the performance of the network

LAYER-FOUR (TRANSPORT-LAYER) PROTOCOLS

OSI layer-four protocols provide end-to-end integrity and guarantee delivery of packets across the network. One function of layer-four protocols is the segmentation of packets

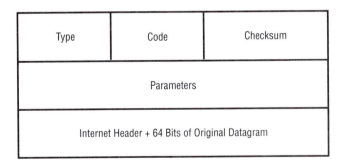

Return Codes:

0 Net unreachable
1 Host unreachable
2 Protocol unreachable
3 Port unreachable
4 Fragmentation required — Not specified
5 Source routing failure

Figure 15.14   ICMP Header Format

into smaller pieces. Segmentation applies to packets considered too large for transport across a particular network. Reassembly of those segmented packets into larger packets in the proper sequence, and sequenced delivery of the packet to its destination point, must also be guaranteed.

The two basic protocols at this level are the OSI Transport Protocol (TP), which is broken into five functional levels, depending on user requirements, and TCP, which offers the same capabilities as TP but is not an ISO-defined protocol.

Despite the fact that TCP is not an ISO protocol, it seems to be more popular than TP. TP, on the other hand, is used extensively in Europe and within the U.S. government.

Transmission Control Protocol (TCP)

TCP operates within the boundaries of the transport layer of the OSI model. It provides reliable interprocess communications between pairs of processes in distant hosts. TCP was designed for communications among dissimilar networks and was developed to support IP. As discussed, IP does not guarantee the delivery of packets or acknowledge a successful transfer. Figure 15.15 shows a typical TCP connection.

TCP interfaces with and manages the user's application data flowing from the upper-layer protocols such as the File Transfer Protocol (FTP) and TELNET Protocol. TCP interfaces with the lower-layer protocols and provides a translation service to convert application names to lower-level addresses for routing through the network. Figure 15.16

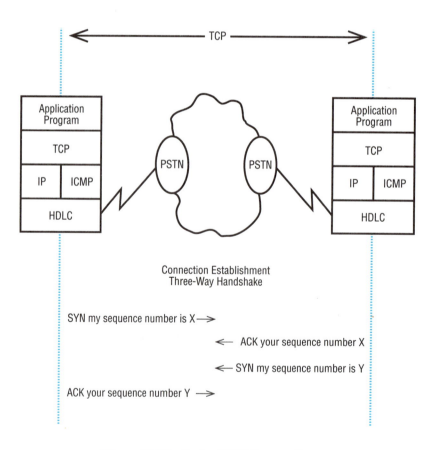

Figure 15.15   Typical TCP Connection

illustrates the header portion of the TCP data unit.

TCP is a virtual circuit protocol in that it establishes end-to-end connections using the concept of port and socket addressing. This establishes unique sets of addresses (ports) within the hosts for each pair of concurrent processes requiring communications.

Ports and sockets consist of unique network and node addresses and a generated circuit ID, which are used for packet routing and delivery. Like other protocols already discussed, TCP operates by taking protocol data units from upper layers of the network and establishing levels of service based on the negotiated end-to-end connection. TCP offers two basic data transfer services and provides several options that guarantee packet delivery and protection against duplicate packets.

Data to be transferred via TCP is broken into segments within the node's send buffer area (allocated in the memory of the node). These segments, known as transport protocol data units (TPDUs), are carried by the IP service for delivery to their destinations. The TPDU consists of TCP header information, control information and user data.

TCP provides many functions, including connection establishment, data transfer, segmentation and reassembly services, error control and flow control.

Connection Establishment. Before data can be transferred using TCP, the two end points must establish a connection and agree on the level of services required. Agreements must be reached on activities such as security, sequence numbering used for acknowledgment, window sizing and other options that will be required during connection establishment.

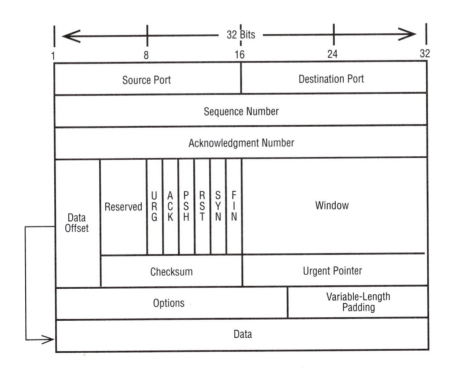

Figure 15.16 TCP Header

The activities involved in the transport of TPDUs are discussed below.

Data Transfer. Transfer of the TPDU across the network is accomplished via a mechanism that ensures the acknowledgment of each byte of the packet received. Embedded byte sequence numbers accomplish this activity by indicating starting and ending data byte offsets within the TCP frame.

Segmentation and Reassembly Services. Different networks often require packets to be a specific size, which can sometimes create a frame size incompatibility between networks and nodes. To address this issue, TCP performs packet segmentation and reassembly. A segment (frame) size is negotiated between the sender and the receiver during connection establishment. This may require that large packets be segmented (broken into smaller units) and then reassembled at the receiving node.

Error Control. A major activity of TCP is error control, which is required when packets either do not arrive or are damaged in transit. Acknowledgment packets containing sequence numbers of the last byte string received ensure that all packets are successfully transported. An incorrect sequence number returned to the sender by the receiver indicates that an error has occurred in transit and the packet needs to be resent. Timers are used by both the sender and the receiver. When the sender does not receive an acknowledgment in a specified period of time, it means that the packet was not received and should be resent.

Flow Control. Flow control logic is resident in each node of a TCP-oriented network and allows the receiver to regulate the arrival speed of the transported packets. Flow control between nodes is also managed using timer mechanisms that indicate congestion on the network. This is managed and controlled by using a negotiated window size between nodes. The result of this negotiation establishes the number of bytes that can be transported before an acknowledgment is needed.

Note that TCP is not recommended by the ISO. The ISO supports the Transport Protocol, Classes 0 through 4. TCP was developed primarily to support U.S. DoD networks. However, over the past few years, TCP has become available from a variety of vendors and is now widely used in the commercial sector.

TCP Formats. The transport packet consists of a 28-byte header and a variable-sized packet depending on the specific network. The header includes fields for addressing, sequencing, acknowledgment, service indicators and pointers, a flow control window for congestion management, checksum, options, padding and user data. The user data also may be part of an encapsulated upper-layer protocol frame that is treated as data by TCP.

Addressing. TCP addressing includes source port and destination port addressing. Each address is 16 bits long.

Sequence Number. Sequence numbers are contained within a 32-bit field and apply to the first byte of data within this segment. The sequence number corresponds to the byte offset of this packet as it relates to other segments for the packet. This can be illustrated by using an 800-byte packet and breaking it into 100-byte segments. In segment number 1, the sequence number begins at 0; in segment number 2, the sequence number starts at 100. This is piggybacked with the acknowledgment field and used for error and sequence control.

Acknowledgment Number. The receiver uses this field to tell the sending node the first byte of the next segment it expects. If an out-of-sequence number is received, the sender will be able to take corrective action and resend the missing or damaged segment.

Data Offset. This field is a four-bit pointer to the location within the segment of the first byte of data.

Pointers and Reserved Area. A reserved field follows the data offset and is not used at the present time. This field is followed by six one-bit flag fields indicating special activities, such as urgent data, acknowledgment, push data, connection on reset, synchronization of the sequence numbers and an end of data.

Window. This 16-bit field is used for flow and congestion control. It indicates how many bytes (segments) the receiver is willing to accept without requiring an acknowledgment.

Checksum Field. The checksum field is 16 bits long and is used for validating the entire segment (header and data).

The remainder of the segment includes a 16-bit urgent pointer for urgent data, any future options, padding and the user data.

OSI Transport Protocol (TP)

TP is really a suite of protocols supported by ISO standard 8073. TP can be viewed as supporting three types of network services with five classes of service. The three types of network services are:

- Type A networks — Provide services with an acceptable error rate and an acceptable rate of signal failures. Type A networks provide a reliable level of service to the user.

- Type B networks — Provide an acceptable error rate and an unacceptable rate for signal failures.

- Type C networks — Provide network connections with an error rate not acceptable to the transport service users.

TP Class 0: Simple Protocol (Type A Network). The CCITT developed Class 0 service to support the basic telex/teletype user. This is the simplest protocol class available and provides an end-to-end connection. TP Class 0 uses Type A network-level services for flow control management.

TP Class 1: Basic Error Recovery (Type B Network). Class 1 TP provides basic error recovery using sequence numbers contained within the protocol data unit. It was designed by CCITT to operate over X.25 Type B networks. TP Class 1 is used to synchronize the network in the event of a failure.

TP Class 2: Multiplexing (Type A Network). This class operates over a Type A network and provides multiplexing (multiple transport connections) across a single connection. It uses basic flow control with a credit allocation management technique.

TP Class 3: Error Recovery and Multiplexing (Type B Network). Class three combines the services of Classes 1 and 2. Additional capabilities are provided to manage networks with unacceptable levels of errors.

TP Class 4: Error Detection and Recovery (Type C Network). TP Class 4 is designed to operate across all types of networks and provides the greatest degree of control and recoverability. All services provided in Classes 0 through 3 are incorporated into TP Class 4 networks.

TP is designed to provide reliable internetwork communications between pairs of processes operating in physically distant nodes. TP operates by taking protocol data units from upper layers of the network, providing value-added services and transferring the PDU to the network layer for transport. Reliable network service, unreliable network service, data transfer, error control and flow control functions are incorporated into TP, as in TCP.

TP Formats. Ten types of TP formats exist, and each has three parts: a fixed part, a variable part and the data area. The fixed part contains parameters for header length, flow control, source and destination references, the protocol class, options, connect or disconnect reason, segmentation and sequencing. The variable part contains the called and calling transport IDs, PDU size, version number, security options and a checksum. It also includes additional options, fall-back protocol class, timers, requested packet transport rate and sequence numbers.

UPPER-LAYER PROTOCOLS

Many types of protocols fall within the definition of upper-layer protocols in the OSI model. But many of these protocols are in fact application services that provide end-user functions. They include TELNET, FTP, SNMP and other protocols for electronic mail and directory services.

TELNET Protocol

The TELNET protocol originally was designed for the Advanced Research Projects Authority Network (ARPANET). TELNET is an application protocol service that allows remote asynchronous terminals and terminal-oriented processes to communicate with each other across the network (see Figure 15.17). TELNET's design is based on network virtual terminal concepts that allow host access to be transparent to all end users. This allows the user to log on to a remote host using any defined terminal type and appear as a locally attached terminal. Like several other upper-layer protocols, TELNET uses negotiations for establishing levels of service between hosts and users.

TELNET permits the specification of pseudo-terminals, enabling the operating system on the host computer to treat the requesting remote terminal as a locally attached device. TELNET also permits the definition of I/O routines that enable an operating system to handle all I/O terminal activity in the same way, regardless of the type of device.

TELNET provides virtual terminal services that allow a common language to be used when performing connection activities. Virtual terminals are pseudo-device definitions that can be overlaid onto a real terminal, allowing the physical device to appear as another type.

TELNET uses a transfer protocol that defines the form of the data when transferred. In addition, it provides the control signals required for communications between the host and the physical terminal. It also describes the mode of data transfer (half or full duplex) and the data delivery method.

TELNET makes available a series of control functions for status and communications between the terminal and the host. Like other protocols already described, three major activities must occur within TELNET: initialization, data transfer and orderly termination. During the initialization phase (terminal setup), negotiations take place to agree on what format will be used in the communications activity. Data transfer is the actual communications activity and orderly termination deactivates the virtual terminal protocol activity in an orderly manner.

File Transfer Protocol (FTP)

FTP is another U.S. DoD protocol that falls within the definition for upper-layer activities (see Figure 15.18). FTP was developed because different computer manufacturers use different file formats for data storage.

FTP is a set of protocol services that allows file transfer between a host computer and the end user. FTP is similar in design to the TELNET protocol. One major difference is that FTP was designed specifically for file transfer rather than data access in a terminal environment. FTP specifies how files should be transferred from one computer to another over a data communications network. Like other DoD and OSI protocols, FTP is designed to support computers from different manufacturers. One additional point is that FTP is a set of services that uses TCP for data transfer.

Early in the evolution of data processing/data communications, a significant problem was how to transport files from one computer to another, regardless of computer type. Within the U.S. federal government, this problem was resolved with FTP, which was designed to shield users from file and storage variations between different types of hosts. FTP uses the concept of a source and destination file and provides for three types of data transfers: stream, block and compressed format.

File transfer using the stream mode is the simplest to use and is the default for all transfer activity. No options exist for special processing and no restrictions exist on different file types.

Block mode provides capabilities for restarting a failed transfer. This is accomplished by encapsulating the data records into FTP frames and using an error detection procedure embedded into each record to provide a file retransmission capability should a failure occur.

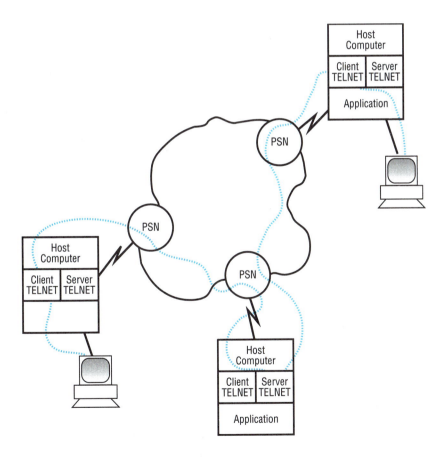

Figure 15.17 TELNET Connectivity

The compressed format mode can be used on top of the other formats to improve efficiency. The source host compresses the file data to be transported and the receiving host expands it on receipt.

Four different data types can be transferred using FTP: ASCII, EBCDIC, image and logical byte size. ASCII and EBCDIC use an eight-bit byte format and transfer each byte in an unmodified format. Image transfer provides no modification and delivers each byte in the exact form it was transmitted. Image file transfers are used primarily for object code (a program translated into a computer machine language) between similar machines. The final data type, logical byte, allows for the creation of a byte greater than eight bits in length. This may be used when sending program codes from one type of machine to another that use different byte sizes because of their architectures. For example, the 12-bit "slab" was at one time used in NCR computers, versus the eight-bit byte used by IBM.

Simple Network Management Protocol (SNMP)

While they can provide cost-controlled, efficient communications, multivendor networks also create an interesting challenge. With all of the different equipment, how do you

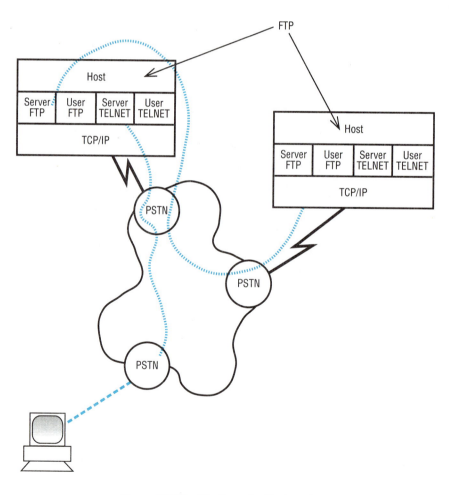

Figure 15.18   File Transfer Protocol

monitor and maintain the network? Several methods and products have been developed to address this problem. One such method is the Simple Network Management Protocol. SNMP is not an OSI protocol, and it uses the services of TCP/IP for its transport activities.

SNMP is referred to as a protocol but is really a protocol subsystem consisting of many components. SNMP was developed to provide network management capabilities across a wide range of interconnected products. Introduced in 1988, SNMP is supported by many communications hardware and software vendors, including IBM and Digital Equipment.

Three key elements make up the SNMP protocol environment: the structure of management information (SIM), the management information base (MIB) and the network management station (NMS). These components, working together, provide visibility into the operation and performance of a heterogeneous network.

Structure of Management Information. This component defines how each piece of equipment in the network is described in the management information base. The description includes information such as the device's line speed, bit rate, protocol and address.

Management Information Base. The MIB contains information about the overall structure of the network, including such items as test points and variable alarm information that the SNMP is expected to support.

Network Management Station. The NMS is usually a dedicated console that provides access to a database containing information on all network-defined devices.

While SNMP is defined as an application-layer process of the OSI model, it requires both TCP and IP. SNMP operates using datagram packets to carry status information between SNMP software resident in each network node. SNMP also provides interface capabilities to support network elements not designed to SNMP specifications.

Two problems that exist with the protocol are the large number of packets needed to support the network and its connectionless orientation. A large number of packets are required to support the network because SNMP must send a packet out in order to receive one. Connectionless service could cause a problem in that packets carrying important information might not be delivered. Consequently, this type of service does not guarantee delivery.

CASE STUDY (CONTINUED)

Communications between each of the workstations at the branch level, as well as from the branch to the service center, will use SNA SDLC in a full-duplex environment. To guarantee security, the bank has decided that data will be encrypted to scramble the EBCDIC code set whenever it is transmitted. One of the major features of SDLC that is important to the bank is the protocol's ability to provide a high level of error detection. SNA will be the transport mechanism between the branch and the service center. Within the branch, a token-ring local area network will carry the SDLC frames between the server and the workstations.

The Los Angeles service center will be responsible for converting data intended for international communications. The computer at that center will convert the SDLC frames to either an X.25 LAP-B datagram-type packet or an OSI HDLC virtual circuit-type packet. The computer also will be programmed to recognize and decode TCP/IP-type packets and convert them into SDLC frames. Figure 15.19 illustrates the Bank of Scotts Valley's protocol links.

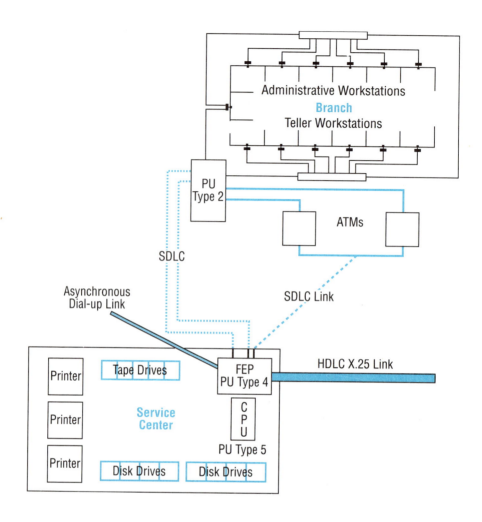

Figure 15.19 Bank of Scotts Valley Protocol Links

REVIEW QUESTIONS

1. Define the term "protocol."
2. What functions does data link control accomplish?
3. In what layer of the OSI or SNA protocol stack is the DLC protocol?
4. What older transmission method sends one byte at a time?
5. What function in bit-oriented protocols do control bits perform?
6. What control codes in byte-oriented protocols accomplish line turnaround?
7. What does a NAK do?
8. Name the three types of error detection in use.
9. What is the major difference between asynchronous and synchronous protocols?
10. What are IBM's current synchronous protocols?
11. What BSC response does a secondary station send when it is not ready to receive the next frame or packet?
12. For which architecture are TP and IP defined?
13. What is SNMP?

PART VI

LANs, Troubleshooting, Network Management and Future Trends

CHAPTER
16

Local Area Networks

INTRODUCTION

A LAN consists of hardware and software that provides an interface for directly attached computers distributed over a limited area. With this arrangement, users can access and manipulate data in a simple, efficient and inexpensive manner on a local level rather than via the host computer.

Local area networks represent the culmination of 25 years of technology development. LAN technology was first used by the cable television industry for the transport of multiple television channels over coaxial cable to locations that could not receive broadcast signals. Because of CATV industry requirements for very wide bandwidth, a system of transmission was developed using transmitters, receivers (transceivers), coaxial cable and connectors. This transmission system can carry dozens of television signals (multiple channels) over a single transmission medium. A major goal was the elimination of cross-channel interference between the various television signals. Xerox first employed CATV technology for local area networking in its Ethernet system. (Ethernet will be discussed later in this chapter.)

Local area networks today provide connectivity between all types of intelligent devices over short distances. LANs usually are restricted to 10 kilometers or less, and most commercial systems are limited to a few thousand meters at most. Connections are accomplished using a variety of transmission methods and communications links. The cable and wire available includes coaxial cable, twisted pairs and fiber-optic cable. Throughput rates (bits per second or packets per second) and user services vary depending on the LAN technology and transmission technology used.

IEEE PROJECT 802

Local area networking got its official start when the IEEE established Project 802 in February 1980 at the request of several of the organization's members who wanted to develop a standard to specify how computers and intelligent devices could communicate over a limited distance. Project 802 continued for more than two years, resolving a number of technical issues and defining and documenting a set of technical specifications to be submitted to the main body of the organization. The results of these activities led to the development of the IEEE 802 and ISO 8802 international standards.

At the formation of Project 802, a large segment of the group wanted the IEEE membership to accept Xerox's Ethernet LAN as a standard. Designed and implemented at the Xerox Research Center in the early 1970s, Ethernet was developed to provide communications between Xerox's Palo Alto Research Center (PARC) and other Xerox facilities. The original Ethernet operated at a speed of 2.96 Mbps. By the end of 1980, Xerox had installed more than 30 Ethernet systems supporting more than 1,000 attached devices. It was in the best interests of Xerox and its installed customer base to try to have the Ethernet specifications adopted as standard.

The IEEE 802 group agreed to look at several different implementations because other manufacturers were also developing LAN technologies. Project 802 established a number of working groups to evaluate the different technical specifications. This evaluation led to recommendations for the creation of the IEEE LAN standards.

Project 802 Activity Log

February 1980. The IEEE 802 Committee was formed to pursue the specifications for local area networks and produce a working draft (Draft A).

December 1980. The committees decided to pursue multiple access methods based on submission of a joint publication on Ethernet from Digital Equipment, Xerox and Intel.

November 1981. Draft B was circulated for voting and suggested revisions among IEEE membership.

May 1982. Draft C was circulated for voting and suggested revisions among IEEE membership.

December 1982. The 802 final draft was accepted by the IEEE. Immediately after acceptance by its membership, the IEEE, U.S. National Bureau of Standards and ECMA endorsed three LAN standards, which became the ISO and IEEE LAN standards. IEEE 802 and ISO 8802 LAN standards are listed in Appendix A. Figure 16.1 lists the major IEEE 802 standards.

LAN DESIGN

The objectives for developing LAN technology were determined by user requirements for locally shared access to common resources. Over the years, these objectives have become the overall guidelines for LAN design and are discussed below.

Media Connectivity

Media connectivity addresses the ability to link together the different devices that make up the network. Network users need to access and connect many types of devices regardless of their communications protocols and operating speeds. A flexible connectivity capability permits each workstation to access many network resources. The connection method must be cost-effective and provide the ability to extend and enlarge the network quickly when required. An important point to remember is that a cost-effective network should take advantage of any on-site wiring systems. The existing wiring must be able to support a bandwidth wide enough for all planned devices over the life of the system.

Internetwork Connectivity

Internetwork connectivity is required so that LANs can access wide area networks, if necessary. Users often need connectivity to IBM SNA networks, public switched networks or X.25 packet networks. The connection may be either direct or via gateways and bridges.

Network Management

Network control and management are also design considerations. Regardless of the size of the LAN, network control and management may be required to maintain acceptable uptime and performance. When networks go down or grow rapidly and change configuration, the need for network control and management becomes evident.

Cost Control

Cost control may require that end users share the expense for incorporating and maintaining a local area network. Frequently, users manage and track costs associated with the implementation and maintenance of networks. It is common for management to require expense breakdowns not only for the network components, but for usage as well. This information is required to justify the acquisition of new software or hardware when the network needs to be expanded. If needed, the capabilities for managing this function should be provided by the LAN product vendors.

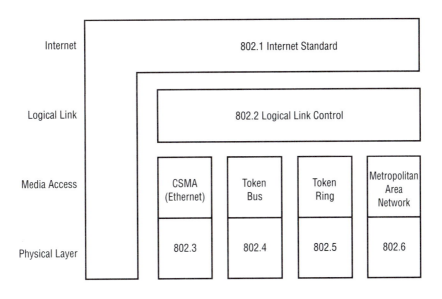

Figure 16.1   IEEE Local Area Network Standards

Security

In light of computer hackers' facility with obtaining network access, security should be integral to the LAN. Security ensures that network and data integrity are maintained. Security activities include log-on and password access control, workstation access control and public and private file access control using passwords, data compression and encryption.

Integration

Local area networks should incorporate the technology necessary for easy integration of other networking services. The integration of data, imaging and process control systems into a single data communications network may be needed in the future. The LAN should provide capabilities for future integration of company operations without impacting the user base.

BASEBAND AND BROADBAND LANS

A LAN can be described as baseband or broadband, depending on whether it was designed to use digital or analog signaling techniques. Many vendors offer LANs that support both types of transmission, such as Ungermann-Bass Inc., which offers the NET/1 network.

Baseband Transmission

The term "baseband" defines a single-channel transmission methodology that is mainly used for digital communications. The workstation uses digital signals to produce electrical signals (voltage) corresponding to the data it wishes to transmit. These electrical signals are placed directly onto the baseband cable. Baseband transmission allows the transmission of only one device's signal on the wire or cable because the device requires the entire bandwidth for digital transmission. Time-division multiplexing can be used if multiple devices must transmit simultaneously. However, multiplexing is not common in baseband LANs.

Baseband is a popular transmission method because of the higher costs associated with the equipment needed for broadband analog conversion. In addition, baseband systems are usually less complex than broadband systems. Many vendors' LAN configurations use baseband transmission, but they are usually more limited in available bandwidth (data rates) and throughput than broadband systems. These vendors include IBM, Datapoint Corp., 3Com Corp. and Ungermann-Bass. Figure 16.2 depicts a baseband LAN.

Broadband Transmission

Although broadband LANs have more capabilities than baseband LANs, they are more difficult to design, implement and maintain. They are also more expensive, primarily due to the analog components required for modulation. Differences between baseband and broadband systems depend upon the characteristics of the transmission medium (normally coaxial cable for broadband), its length and the associated components being used.

Broadband transmission provides multiple channel capabilities dispersed across the entire bandwidth of the medium. In addition, the various channel carrier waves are modulated to represent the information they carry.

An advantage of broadband transmission is its ability to accommodate several independent transmission sources simultaneously, unlike baseband systems, which can handle only a single transmission path. Through the division and allocation of its available bandwidth, a broadband system can service data, text, voice and video applications at the same time by allocating channels to each function. Figure 16.3 illustrates a broadband LAN.

Channel Bandwidth Allocation

Because baseband uses the entire bandwidth for transmission, a single channel is defined for the entire link. Digital signals placed on the medium radiate in both directions using all of the available bandwidth. Baseband transmission is used primarily by Carrier Sense Multiple Access (CSMA) networks, which are described later in this chapter. For broadband transmission, the signals are transmitted in a single direction. This method may be used for either token-based or CSMA networks.

Two-way broadband transmission can be achieved by employing one of two basic techniques. The first technique uses a single coaxial cable with its total frequency spectrum split for the allocation of transmit and receive channels. The second method uses dual cables, each carrying channelized signals in the opposite direction. Both techniques require that a head-end remodulator be installed at one end of the cable to translate the forward channel frequency into the return one. Single-cable systems offer two ways for the available frequency spectrum to be divided for two-way communications: midsplit and subsplit.

Midsplit. Midsplit technology provides a more equitable frequency allocation between the inbound and outbound channels than subsplit technology, which has a much smaller inbound bandwidth (see Figure 16.4). Midsplit frequency allocations from 5 to 108 MHz are reserved for the inbound signals, and the outbound signals use 162 to 400 MHz. The frequencies from 108 to 162 MHz serve as a guard band to prevent interference between the inbound and outbound frequency bands.

Subsplit. Subsplit systems provide frequency allocations for the inbound direction from approximately 5 to 30 MHz and in the outbound direction from 54 to 400 MHz (see Figure 16.5).

In either technique, frequency allocation varies according to the specific vendor's product. Most broadband systems that support highly interactive applications, such as those

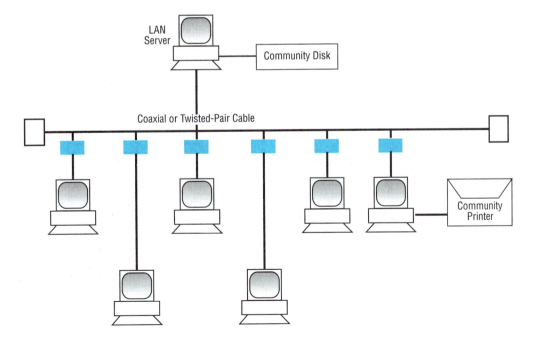

Figure 16.2   IEEE 802.3 Baseband Bus Network

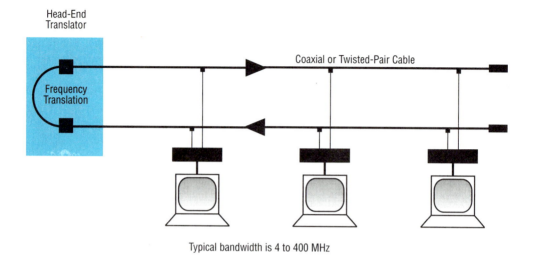

Figure 16.3 Dual-Cable Broadband Bus Network Using a Separate Cable in Each Direction

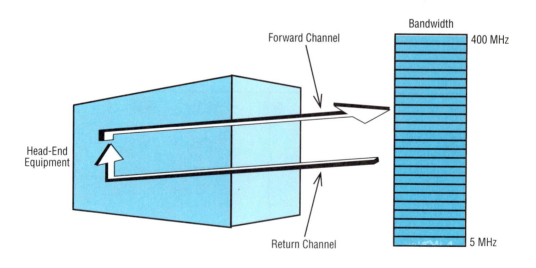

Figure 16.4 Broadband Midsplit Technology Using a Single Cable with Separate Inbound and Outbound Flows

found with data processing and process control systems, are usually midsplit because an equal amount of traffic flows in each direction. Broadband networks that typically handle large amounts of video processing are usually subsplit because they have more outbound than inbound traffic. Many single-cable broadband LAN vendors offer both midsplit and subsplit systems.

LAN CONTROL

In order to transmit messages across a network, a communications path must be established using circuit switching or packet switching. Data is placed onto the media by the LAN node and is then transmitted to its destination using either centralized or decentralized control.

With centralized control, a central node receives all inbound data and processes it for routing to its destination. Centralized control costs are initially high, but the incremental costs are lower. Centrally controlled environments require redundancy to ensure reliability, because a controller failure will disrupt the local area network operation. Traffic is easy to control from a central node, but routing software for handling and switching traffic can be quite complex.

In a decentralized environment, the medium is shared by a large number of users. In some LAN configurations, data can be multiplexed onto the medium, which requires that each node has its own hardware to perform multiplexing and demultiplexing. As packets travel through the network, each node receives all packets but selects only those messages intended for itself, ignoring or passing all other packets to the next node. Each node incorporates software and hardware to perform this packet selection process, as well as the routing functions necessary to forward other packets to their proper destinations.

Decentralized control is more reliable than centralized control, because a node failure does not necessarily halt network operation; rather, the failed node is simply bypassed. Software updates are more difficult in a decentralized environment, however, because each node requires the new software and a method must be developed for its distribution.

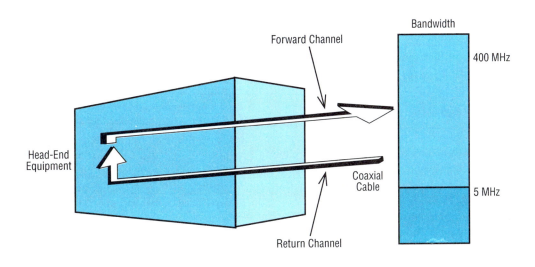

Figure 16.5 Broadband Subsplit Technology

MEDIA ACCESS CONTROL

Media access control (MAC) is the technology used to access the media. It is responsible for the access methods required for managing and controlling network traffic in a local area network. If media access control is centralized, a central controller determines when access and transmission by each station can occur. It accomplishes this by using polling techniques similar to those used with wide area networks. Stations transmit when requested to do so, or when a service request is honored by the central controller. Overhead associated with polling does, however, decrease the throughput of the network because it requires additional packet traffic for control.

Failure of the central controller disrupts the entire network. However, network node failures have minimal impact on overall operations. In this type of access, the failed node is taken off-line. Fault diagnosis and hardware/software updates are relatively easy in a centralized environment. Most centrally controlled LANs use deterministic access control to avoid contention and collision.

Decentralized media access control permits each node to be responsible for its own access to the network facilities and for resolving contention and collision. Most decentralized environments use nondeterministic access.

Deterministic Access

When deterministic techniques are used, one method for controlling access is by token passing. A token is a specific bit pattern that indicates whether the media is available for use. It is passed from node to node on the network. The node in current possession of the token acts as the master for all other nodes on the network, and it may require them to respond to its request for data. After transmitting, the node passes the token and associated control to its successor in a predefined order and within a prescribed amount of time. Token control and recovery procedures are complex, but this type of access control is reliable and efficient.

Nondeterministic Access

In a nondeterministic environment, network nodes must contend for access and control of the media. If two or more terminals contend for the media simultaneously, collisions will cause the transmitted data to be invalid and require data retransmission. Collision detection and retransmission control are straightforward and are based primarily on timing algorithms. This type of access control is efficient in low-traffic conditions but is not as efficient as deterministic access for high-traffic conditions.

Access Methods

LAN media access methods are either contention based or noncontention based. The most common standard methods are token passing (noncontention) and CSMA (contention). Many differences exist between the two access methods and their specific implementations. The IEEE provides a standard for both token passing and CSMA. Each method has its strengths and weaknesses, and the selection of a particular method should be based on the requirements of the applications.

NONCONTENTION-BASED ACCESS

Token-Passing Ring

Token-passing LANs most often are associated with ring topologies but may also use the bus topology. Token-passing rings use special bit patterns referred to as tokens, which are passed around the ring from node to node. In this type of LAN, no central authority controls the token (see Figure 16.6).

The token normally consists of eight bits (see Figure 16.7). Token availability is represented by either a binary 1 or 0 in one of the bit positions. A zero bit indicates that the token is available and a node wishing to transmit may take control of the token as it passes by. A binary 1 is used to indicate a busy token (information has been appended to the token). The remaining seven bits represent different activities such as monitoring, reservation schemes and prioritizing. The functions of these bits vary according to specific products. The monitor bit, which provides control capabilities, is used for the welfare of the ring operation.

As an illustration, if two tokens happen to be generated onto the ring at the same time, one of the workstation control interfaces would have to correct this condition. The interface, using a timing mechanism and the monitor bit, can remove damaged tokens from the ring and create a good token to restore operation. Lost or duplicate tokens can be caused by a damaged interface or a hit on the line.

A node gains use of the ring when in possession of an empty token. The workstation marks the token as active and appends the data behind it. Because only one device at a time may transmit in a token-ring LAN, packet data byte sizes are determined by the length and number of nodes on the ring. If a station has more information to transmit than a data packet can handle, segmentation and reassembly will take place in the node's network interface. The sending device's interface stores the data in a buffer and transmits it in separate packets using a sequence number. Figure 16.8 illustrates the frame structure of an IBM Token-Ring network.

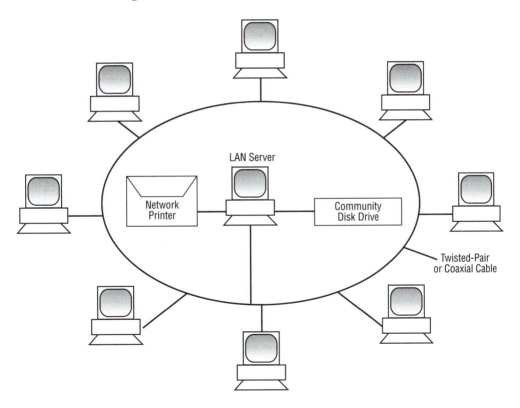

Figure 16.6 IEEE 802.5 Centralized Token-Passing Ring Network

Token-Passing Bus

A token-passing bus establishes a logical ring structure (see Figure 16.9). Because each interface unit is directly attached to the bus, the logical ring token is passed from device to device using an addressing scheme established during network implementation. The device in possession of the token has the right to transmit. If it has nothing to communicate, it passes the token on to the next device in the logical ring. Each node maintains the address of the next node to which the token must be passed.

A node possessing the token may use the bus for a specified maximum hold time. When this time expires and the transmission is completed, or the device has no data to send, the token is passed to the next device. A specific set of algorithms governs interface operation. All activities on the bus are synchronized to a slot time equal to twice the maximum propagation delay plus the interface's internal response time.

Error conditions are handled by controlled contention mechanisms. As an example, device A passes the token to device B, but B fails to respond. Device A, via a time-out mechanism, recognizes this failure. Device A is responsible for reestablishing linkage for the logical ring. Device A must reissue the token, which must then be followed by carrier-free frames or quiet windows, to be broadcast over the channel.

Devices with data to send could, at this point, respond to these windows by demanding membership to the ring via a set-next-interface frame. This demand would indicate the new member's address. Device A then would respond by issuing a token link-up to the new member's address, restoring operation to the ring.

With token passing, either bus or ring, the size (number of bytes of data) and number of devices have a great affect on the throughput. Of the token-based topologies, token-passing rings are the most common. Token-passing buses are the second most frequently used.

Token-Passing Fiber Ring

Token-passing fiber ring networks operate identically to token-ring networks that use coaxial cable or twisted-pair wire. The two major advantages of fiber are its speed and its ability to filter out electromagnetic interference. At the present time, throughput rates are

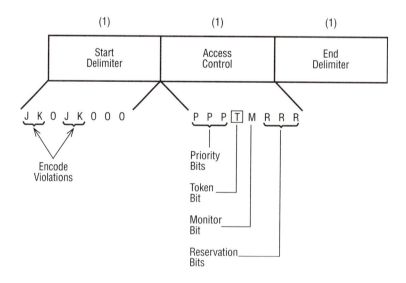

Figure 16.7 IEEE 802.5 Token

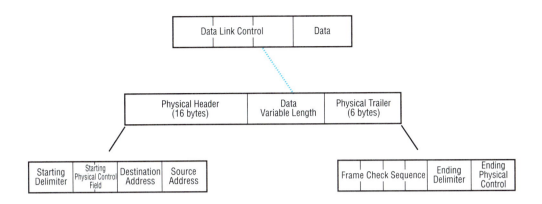

Figure 16.8   IBM Token-Ring Frame Structure

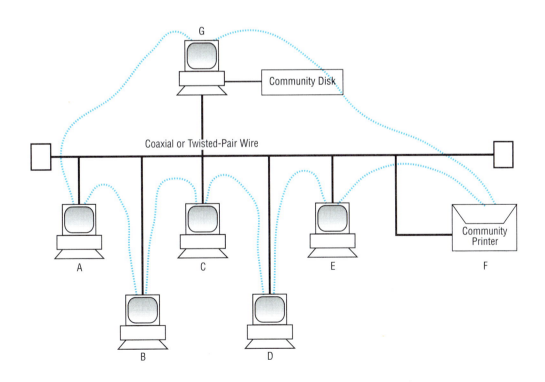

Figure 16.9   IEEE 802.4 Token-Passing Bus Logical Ring Structure

in the 100-Mbps range.

Several methods have been developed to interface LAN drivers to the fiber-optic (FO) media. LED or laser emitters are the most common devices used. Interfaces include EIA-232-to-FO interface drivers, RS-422-to-FO drivers and baseband FO drivers.

CONTENTION-BASED ACCESS

Contention access methods most often used with LANs are based on a modification of the ALOHANet network approach, named for the University of Hawaii's system. The ALOHANet provides a large number of terminal users with inexpensive and easy access to central computing facilities using radio links. The ALOHA system is a broadcast radio system covering the Hawaiian Islands; the central processor is located in Honolulu.

Several hundred terminals have access to the ALOHANet using a time-sharing system. In the original ALOHA system, stations transmitted without attempting to determine if the channel was available. This allowed data packets from different sources to be transmitted at the same time, creating the possibility of a collision as they arrived at the central processing unit. A collision caused the destruction of the entire data packet. Extensive efforts have been made to develop variants of the ALOHA method that can be used in local area networks. Variations of the ALOHA version include the CSMA techniques described in the following sections.

CSMA

CSMA is a contention-based access method used in many bus-oriented LANs as well as in Ethernet. With CSMA, devices must listen to the channel before sending in order to determine if the carrier has data traffic. If the bus is busy, all other stations are able to sense the traffic and hold transmission until the bus is free. Figure 16.10 depicts a CSMA frame structure.

With CSMA, a node must listen to the medium to determine if another node is transmitting. This access method is often referred to as Listen Before Talking (LBT). If the bus is free, a station may proceed. If two or more devices attempt to use the medium at the same time, a collision will occur and the data from both devices will be destroyed. CSMA resolves this problem by specifying what a station should do if the channel is busy. Three methods of resolving contention are in use: Nonpersistent, 1-Persistent and P-Persistent CSMA.

Nonpersistent CSMA. Nonpersistent CSMA requires that a station wishing to send data listen to the medium, and if the medium is idle, it may transmit. If the medium is busy, it waits a specified amount of time calculated from a probability algorithm. This is accomplished using logic built into the interface that provides a random access to the medium. When an interface encounters a busy condition while attempting to access the channel, a random wait time is invoked. If, on the next attempt, the same condition is met, the cycle is repeated until access is accomplished. The use of random timing reduces the possibility of a collision. If several stations have data to send, there may be wasted idle time following a transmission. To avoid channel idle time, the 1-Persistent access method can be used.

1-Persistent CSMA. This CSMA technique enables a station that needs to transmit to listen to the medium and determine if it is idle. If it is idle, the station may transmit. If it is busy, the device will continue to listen until the channel is idle, then it will transmit immediately. If a collision is sensed, due to lack of acknowledgment, the cycle is repeated. Although this method reduces idle time, a collision is more likely with 1-Persistent because transmission is immediate rather than random, as with Nonpersistent CSMA. A compromise that attempts to reduce collisions and idle time is referred to as P-Persistent CSMA.

P-Persistent CSMA. Using the P-Persistent technique, a device first determines if the bus is free, then it transmits with the probability of a variable (P) plus one time unit equal to the propagation delay time. If the bus is busy, the device will continue to listen until the channel is idle, then it will repeat the first step. To make this access method feasible, different P values are established for each device to retry. These retry intervals involve spacing retransmission attempts further and further apart to maximize channel use at the cost of message delay.

A major problem with CSMA is that when two frames do collide, the medium is unstable for the duration of the transmission. For long data strings, the amount of time wasted can be considerable. This problem can be reduced if a station continues to listen to the channel after transmission has begun, thereby enabling the device to detect the collision. This access method is referred to as CSMA with Collision Detection (CD).

CSMA/CD

A CSMA/CD-based network station continuously monitors the channel after it initiates transmission. Because local area networks operate in a limited geographic area, feedback is not a problem. If a collision is detected during transmission, the device immediately ceases transmitting the data and sends a brief jamming signal to ensure that all stations are informed that a collision has occurred. After transmitting the jamming signal, the station waits a random amount of time, then attempts to transmit again using CSMA.

Collision detection saves transmission time. However, a comparison of delay between token passing and CSMA/CD indicates that the delay factor is less of a problem with token passing, because token-based system nodes do not have to contend for the link. A number of factors do affect the performance of both token passing and CSMA/CD. Currently, the most common contention-based access method is CSMA/CD, but another contention-based access method is available, CSMA with Collision Avoidance (CA).

CSMA/CA

CSMA/CA employs some type of priority scheme to safeguard the data communications of high-priority devices. The needs of these devices are catered to before the needs of the low-priority devices.

Preamble	Destination	Source	Type	Data	CRC

Preamble	64 bits
Destination Address	48 bits
Source Address	48 bits
Type	16 bits
Data	368 bits minimum; 12,000 bits maximum
Frame Check (CRC)	32 bits

Figure 16.10   CSMA Frame Structure

CSMA/CA is implemented by using a delay after each data transmission that is proportional to the priority of the node. In other words, high-priority devices experience short delays while low-priority devices experience long delays. Using a priority technique of this type, packet collisions are usually avoided but may still occur on occasion. A solution is still required for handling collisions; this may be either collision detection or retransmission based on a negative acknowledgment.

LAN PERFORMANCE

LAN performance is affected by system parameters such as transmission rate, cable length, data packet size and software overhead. These factors determine the filtering rate or the packet per second (pps) rate of the LAN. Generally speaking, the bit rate specification of a particular LAN technology does not imply that the LAN can actually move data at that rate. The LAN's effective throughput rate is the only true indication of its actual performance. The effective throughput rate is a measurement of how many bytes of data can be transported to their destinations over a specific time interval. This is often a difficult figure to obtain due to the amount of overhead associated with a particular LAN product.

A LAN's throughput delay is important if optimal results are to be achieved. Throughput is of particular importance when LANs are interconnected using a gateway or bridge, because of the added overhead. Delay is a measure of the total transfer time of the data, defined as the time interval from the creation of the data at the origin to its reception at the destination node. This transfer time includes queuing and access delay at the sending node, the transmission time of the data and the propagation delay created by the media length.

The importance of proper design and planning of a LAN cannot be understated. Topology, access methods, media, growth, changes to the system and costs are all important factors.

Table 16.1 lists some of the differences between token-based systems and CSMA systems. The table does not imply an endorsement of one type over the other, but it does illustrate potential areas of concern.

CASE STUDY (CONTINUED)

A major part of the Bank of Scotts Valley's branch data communications is planned around local area networking capabilities. Use of a LAN provides major benefits, including a reduction in the number of point-to-point links needed in each branch over what is required in a wide area network terminal environment. Another benefit is the reduction of costs associated with branch support. The incorporation of medialess workstations can reduce hardware expenses and still maintain improved response time because the workstations operate in a local environment.

A 16-Mbps token-ring LAN is selected for branch operations. Each teller window will have a medialess workstation connected to the ring. This workstation will be an Intel 80286-based PC with 640 KB of memory. In addition to administrative workstations, which are fully configured PCs, each ring will have a LAN server that supports a laser printer and large disk storage. An additional administrative workstation will serve as a gateway for traffic between the service center and the branch and will be used for routing activities. Operational software in support of the tellers will reside on the LAN server and provide inquiry, deposit and withdrawal capabilities. The gateway node will function under control of the server. The server takes teller workstation requests and reformats them for transport by the gateway to the host computer.

Dual rings will be installed at each of the branches using unshielded twisted-pair wiring to take advantage of media already installed at each branch location. A dual-ring configuration was selected because it will provide a back-up capability if the primary ring fails. One administrative workstation within each branch will be set up to monitor and control the LAN. It will monitor the branch network, contain diagnostics and maintain performance statistics that can be accessed by the service center if required.

The bank's information services department intends to continue to expand the use of local area networks and, at some point in the future, to have all users interconnected via token-ring LANs and communications processors located throughout the bank. Figure 16.11 illustrates a typical local area network installed at a branch location.

Concern	Token-Based Networks	CSMA Networks
Delay	Measured	Degrades when Load Increases
Prioritized Packets	Supported	Not Supported
Throughput under High Load	Improves with Load	Degrades with Load
Product Availability	Widely Available	Widely Available
Availability of Off-the-Shelf Components	Wide Variety of Products Available	Wide Variety of Products Available
Cost	Reasonable Costs Implementation on Chip Sets	Reasonable Costs Implementation on Chip Sets
Medium of Choice	Any Medium	Any Medium
Availability of Test Equipment	Wide Variety	Wide Variety

Table 16.1 Comparison of Token-Based and CSMA LAN Technologies

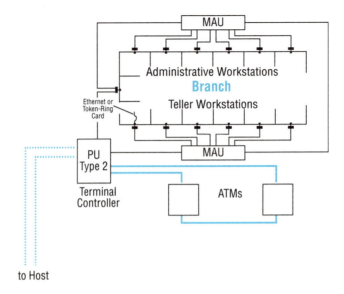

Figure 16.11 Bank of Scotts Valley Branch Token-Ring Network

REVIEW QUESTIONS

1. What do the IEEE 802 standards cover?
2. What does CSMA stand for?
3. What standard is Ethernet an implementation of?
4. What is the principal transmission technique used by CSMA?
5. What does a token-ring network do?
6. What is the most popular transmission medium for LAN implementations?
7. What type of implementation does CATV use?
8. Describe broadband.
9. In what way does baseband differ from broadband?
10. Why is LAN technology considered a state-of-the-art network approach?

CHAPTER 17

Network Troubleshooting

INTRODUCTION

Network failures happen! When a network goes down, the results can be serious. Today, companies are so highly automated that when communications or network failures occur, a potential loss of millions of dollars is not unrealistic.

Problems occurring within a data communications network are usually difficult to identify, isolate and correct in a timely manner. In addition, problems often exist that no one is aware of. Once a problem is detected, network components must be examined to determine exactly where the problem lies. A systematic approach to testing each component is needed to determine if the line or device is functioning correctly.

During the analysis of network components, the following items should be tested:

- Communications software parameters and activities
- Communications support hardware, such as multiplexers and modems
- Front-end processors and terminals
- Lines (both dedicated and switched)

After the problem component is identified, correcting the problem on the line or in the device may be a major task, because a wide variety of equipment and methods exist for problem identification and correction. Every organization should have a disaster-recovery plan in place to address problems, regardless of the degree of failure encountered.

This chapter provides a template for error analysis and a corrective action program for identifying and resolving problems.

TYPES OF ERRORS

Specific categories that must be included in a problem-analysis methodology include the following:

- Software errors
- Computer and communications hardware errors
- Network link errors

Software Errors

Software problems can occur in any of the program components that make up the network environment. Application processes that are not properly tested prior to installation in the production environment can terminate abnormally when conditions occur that the program cannot handle. Often, these software errors are insidious in that a program may operate for an extended period of time without experiencing a failure. For example, consider a program that computes numerical values. It operates for an extended period of time without failure but one day encounters a number larger than it can handle. When it tries to perform this arithmetic function, it may cause an arithmetic overflow error that abnormally terminates (crashes) the application process.

Communications system software is also subject to errors. Terminals or lines whose characteristics were incorrectly specified to the software certainly can create problems, including bit rates or operational values such as fall-back rates that are mismatched between devices. This type of error can take the device or line down. For example, a line time-out parameter value might be set lower than what is acceptable for occasional delays caused by congestion. When congestion on a link is encountered, a device attached to that line, when attempting to respond, will not be able to do so. This causes a time-out condition to occur in the control software. If the number of time-outs that take place is greater than what is specified, the link will be taken off-line. Another example is an error threshold retry value not set high enough for a line that experiences frequent bit errors. If this limit is set lower than what is acceptable, the software will continually take the line down due to the excessive number of errors.

Hardware Errors

Communications hardware errors are often difficult to detect; hardware analyzers as well as software diagnostic programs are usually required to locate and correct them. One reason for this difficulty is the sheer number of hardware components that make up a typical network. Hardware is also difficult to diagnose because errors are often sporadic and the network requires extensive monitoring to locate and identify them. In many cases, hardware diagnosis requires that the network be taken down, which can compound the problem as well as upset users.

Network Link Errors

As with the other types of network errors, both software and hardware diagnostics are required to identify, locate and correct line problems. Many times, link errors occur only once, making this a difficult area to correct. An error may occur within the telephone company's network, requiring the telephone company to perform the diagnostics. However, the user must first discover the problem and determine that it does not lie in the organization's own software or hardware.

PROBLEM ANALYSIS PROCEDURES

To respond to problems on a network, you need a step-by-step procedure for error identification, resolution, documentation and notification; in other words, it is important to have a systematic approach to identifying and resolving network errors. Every organization should have a disaster recovery plan in place to address problems, regardless of the degree of failure encountered.

Documentation. The first component of a problem determination system is good documentation; the communications network must be mapped out in detail and kept up to date. The map must include transmission paths, routing, hardware identification and software characteristics.

Transmission Paths. Each and every transmission path (both hard-wired and leased-line) must be documented. This includes the rated bit speed, the organization or vendor responsible for its maintenance and a contact if a problem occurs. If it is an internal link, notes on accessibility must be included that describe access details.

Routing. A routing map should show where the lines run and how to access them for repair. If a line traverses restricted areas, details on how to access it, including any legal restrictions, are necessary.

Hardware Identification. All network hardware must be identified as to the type, operational characteristics and line addresses used. Ownership and maintenance responsibilities also must be identified, as must contacts authorized to repair the components.

Hardware Monitoring Components. It is important to place network-monitoring functions where they will provide complete visibility into the operation of the entire network. At minimum, major lines and hardware and software components must be monitored. In many cases, end points such as modems and terminals can be bypassed if cost is a concern. These points normally have self-contained diagnostics that can be run locally.

Software and Performance Characteristics. All software must be identified, and important configuration information must be accessible in order to determine operational parameters and performance characteristics. All staff members responsible for the care and maintenance of the software should be identified, along with information on how to contact them.

Problem Resolution Plan. A written plan that addresses problem resolution should be developed and kept updated. Step-by-step procedures must be defined for troubleshooting and resolution. Network schematics as well as related hardware and software data also must be part of the documentation.

Tools. You should have software in place for real-time performance monitoring of the overall software environment and the hardware components. Performance must be monitored because it is often difficult to detect errors when the network is experiencing problems but has not yet failed. Performance can be monitored with software monitors and hardware monitors attached to the network.

Network Performance Parameters. To determine whether the network is experiencing a problem, operational values need to be developed for both normal and peak operational periods. Extensive testing and statistical analysis will be needed to establish benchmark figures for comparisons. This information should include activities such as average response time, I/O queue wait times and channel/line busy activity. Transaction rates, numbers for errors encountered and the number of retry on errors performed also should be tested.

Problem Determination

Once a problem has been detected, follow these steps:

1. Identify the problem area. Using the tools and procedures described earlier in this chapter, determine exactly where the problem resides.

2. Determine whether the problem is catastrophic or noncatastrophic. The nature of the problem normally determines how it is to be resolved. There should be procedures in place for catastrophic and noncatastrophic failures. Catastrophic failures require immediate attention to bring the network back online again. Noncatastrophic failures often can be bypassed and resolved during normal maintenance.

3. Determine whether an alternate path can be taken to bypass the error. In some cases, standby equipment is available and can be brought quickly into service. The availability of back-up links should be documented.

4. Determine whether the problem can be resolved without taking the network down. Regardless of the size of the network, bringing the network down should be the last resort unless it is planned well in advance and users have had ample notification. Downtime can be costly for a company.

5. Determine the mean time to repair. It is important to keep users informed of the status of the network. You should determine the mean time to repair the problem and notify users.

Problem Resolution

The following items are important for resolving network problems.

Trouble Tickets. When a problem is encountered, create (open) a trouble ticket to document the problem area and track the problem. The trouble ticket should specify the time the problem was first encountered, its location and successful corrective actions taken.

Automatic Tracking System. An automatic tracking system is often developed to record the status of the troubleshooting activity. Categories of problems should be defined that govern the types of actions that must be taken (e.g., critical versus noncritical). After the problem is resolved, the trouble ticket must be closed and its statistics should be included in a historical database for future reference.

Vendor Notification. If the problem occurs with leased or vendor-provided equipment, notify the vendor as soon as possible so that the vendor or equipment provider will participate in problem resolution activities and can take steps to prevent the problem from recurring.

Repair Scheduling. Often a network can be operationally maintained by bypassing the problem area. You should make sure that the component in question is scheduled for repair. This is an area that is easily overlooked if standby equipment is placed into service and the failed device is taken off the network.

User Notification. Keep users informed; an educated user understands that network failures are to be expected and will be assured that problems are being attended to if you provide status information. Such ongoing communication encourages user confidence.

SOFTWARE DIAGNOSTIC TOOLS

Software diagnostics are valuable for determining hardware, software and network errors. They allow network providers to monitor and maintain an acceptable level of performance within the CPU and in the communications components of the network.

Software performance monitors such as The System Center's NetMaster and IBM's NetView can take snapshots (view the operational status) at selected time intervals (usually one-second views) of all active network components and programs. The information gathered can be displayed in a real-time environment (monitored online) or can be collected and summarized for batch print-outs. These are useful tools in determining real-time performance and for long-range planning purposes.

HARDWARE DIAGNOSTIC TOOLS

Hardware Monitors

To ensure that the communications network is performing at its best, it is important to be able to view hardware performance. Access to real-time hardware performance information gives you the ability to determine if the total environment is functioning properly. Hardware monitors provide a picture of the internal processing activity of the computer and communications network. For more detailed information on these devices, see Chapter 18.

Modem Diagnostics

Modem diagnostics are generally included as part of the modem's circuitry. The diagnostics ensure the integrity of the modem and the attached lines. Diagnostic features are usually found in high-end modems and depend on the intelligence and type of modem. Diagnostics that are usually internal to high-end modems include loopback testing, frequency bandwidth diagnostics, signal levels tests and system status indicators.

Loopback Testing. Loopback testing includes local and remote capabilities for both analog and digital transmission. It ensures that a signal can be propagated across the entire link. Loopback tests are usually provided in the form of a random bit generator within the modem that produces a special bit pattern that can be verified at both ends of the link.

Frequency Bandwidth Diagnostics. This type of testing is used to monitor and detect out-of-frequency conditions, since modems operating at specific frequencies may drift from their assigned frequency over time. Frequency bandwidth diagnostics make sure that frequency drift can be detected so that the operational spectrum is accurate.

Signal Level Tests. Modems must operate within a specific signal strength range as dictated by specifications set by international standards groups as well as federal regulatory agencies. An important test is the line signal level (DBM level) test, which checks the output signal strength of the modem. This provides information on whether the modem is operating within an acceptable signal strength range.

Signal Status Indicators. Many modems provide signal status indicators (front-panel LEDs) that validate the correct operation of the modem when it is active. Specific indicators are usually provided for major functions such as carrier detect, dataset ready, clear to send, request to send and transmit/receive activities. These LEDs enable you to determine which of the modem's circuits are performing properly.

NETWORK HARDWARE DIAGNOSTICS

Hardware monitoring is desirable and may be required for many types of networks. This activity detects and allows correction of communications problems before they have the chance to substantially affect the network's performance. Network diagnostics cover a wide variety of activities; the major types of diagnostics include EIA-232/EIA-449 operation and interface performance, line monitoring for signal quality and noise, terminal monitoring using self-checking routines provided by the manufacturer and, on the network itself, the use of network controllers and monitors. Following are some of the hardware tools available to perform these functions.

Protocol Analyzers

Protocol analyzers are also referred to as line analyzers, data analyzers and datascopes. These devices are used to monitor and evaluate both line activities and data frame/packet formats. They can be used to determine the operational status of a line, device or communications software process.

Generally speaking, a protocol analyzer is an intelligent device such as a personal computer with a CRT and keyboard. It usually provides a full-screen display and is both programmable and menu driven. The manufacturer usually provides a simple programming language to set the analyzer to an operational status and set alarms and triggers. Many analyzers include a diskette or disk drive for off-line storage, as well as a cartridge tape for backup. Most protocol analyzers are also able to support multiple host software protocols.

An analyzer can be set to capture and store information based on triggers programmed into it. A trigger is a predefined value such as a number that, when exceeded, indicates an unacceptable error level. The events that will be used to trigger the program can include specific line items or transaction types, specific packets or frames and certain types of error conditions. The frames that meet the set conditions either will be captured or counted for real-time or batch analysis. Batch capture and analysis let you leave the analyzer unattended and still capture events and desirable information.

Many protocol analyzers include integrated timers that can be used to capture information such as line turnaround time, which is the number of milliseconds needed to reverse the direction of the line in half-duplex operations. Other information that can be captured includes:

- Response time — The amount of time it takes for a terminal to respond to a polling request

- Host response — The amount of time it takes the host to reply to a terminal activity

- Retransmit requests — The number of times a retransmit request is generated because of an error

The protocol analyzer setup is usually straightforward and must follow the manufacturer's format. Most manufacturers provide a simple, menu-driven set-up program that usually includes capabilities such as selection of a specific protocol, selection of the bit rate of the line to be analyzed and selection of the events that need to be monitored, such as the number of retries on each transmission error.

Many companies produce protocol and data analyzers. When selecting analyzers, it is important to ensure that they are compatible with one another, because you might have to capture and integrate data for review from several remote analyzers. Companies providing this type of equipment are Digitech Industries, Atlantic Research, Hewlett-Packard and Digilog.

Breakout Boxes

Breakout boxes allow you to view signals being transferred across the link between the terminal (DTE) and the modem (DCE). A breakout box typically has two rows of LEDs to monitor the electrical signals flowing between the two devices (DTE and DCE). These LEDs are sensitive only to electrical pulses present on the line and indicate signal activity.

The breakout box is powered by either a DC external power source or an internal battery. It usually includes two pairs of ribbon cables for attachment to the DTE and DCE. Some breakout boxes also have an audio monitor.

Many breakout boxes are supplied with bit error rate testers (BERTs), which can generate pseudo-random bit patterns that can be transferred across the link. Additional features include a three- or four-digit display for errors, error injection for proof of operation and support for synchronous or asynchronous transmission.

Status Activity Monitors

Analog diagnostic status activity monitoring tools enable you to test and monitor the analog communications circuits for a variety of conditions. One of these conditions, signal loss, is the difference in the signal amplitude (power level) between the transmit and receive ends of the link. Loss is evaluated by measuring the amplitude at a reference frequency. Normal leased-line levels are -10 dBm at the transmit end and -26 dBm at the receiving end for an approximate 16 dBm loss.

Noise is another condition that needs to be analyzed. When line noise levels exceed the established signal-to-noise ratios, the devices at each end of the link cannot distinguish between the data signal and the noise present on the line.

Another type of problem is attenuated distortion, which causes different frequencies within an allocated bandwidth (channel) to shift their timing (speed up or slow down). This causes the information being carried to change its value.

Status activity monitors also can detect other analog problems such as delay distortion, phase jitter, nonlinearity and transients (such as gain/phase hits and dropouts).

Testing analog circuits typically consists of level tests to ensure that all lines and components are functioning at the proper transmit and receive levels. Frequency response tests are implemented to ensure that all lines are functioning within the correct frequency bandwidth. Noise level tests determine whether the proper signal-to-noise levels are being maintained. Peak-to-average ratio tests are used to determine delay distortion, amplitude distortion and noise.

Depending on the manufacturer, these devices are usually equipped with features such as an oscilloscope/CRT, automatic frequency sweep capabilities, a very wideband frequency range and intelligence to capture and summarize statistics. Many companies manufacture this equipment, including Hewlett-Packard and Halcyon.

Cable and Fiber Analyzers

Cable installation errors and manufacturing flaws can create continuity and bit rate problems if they remain undetected. Cable analyzers are designed to evaluate cable conditions to ensure that they comply with the manufacturer's operational specifications. Many types of analyzers are available for all types of media. They include simple devices such as those that evaluate interface cables as well as much more complex devices, such as time-domain fiber reflectometers, which analyze high-speed fiber-optic cable.

Network Control Monitors

Network control monitors, which can be either a part of a network control center operation or integrated into the front-end processor or CPU, provide visibility into the entire network for monitoring performance and detecting error conditions. For monitoring to be effective, it must be nonintrusive (i.e., it should not burden the system or affect performance of the network).

The network control monitor should provide a means for the rapid diagnosis and identification of the problem. It must enable operators to invoke tests that may or may not intrude on the network's operation. The network control monitor must be programmable to establish operational levels. When these levels are exceeded, the monitor will notify the operator. It also should provide information about error rates, network response times and the status of all communications equipment on the network.

After the problem has been identified, the network control monitor must be permitted to isolate and take off line the portion of the network having problems. This means having the ability to shut down lines, modems, multiplexers and even nodes. The network control monitor should enable the operator to reconfigure the network so that operations can resume.

Administrative responsibilities of the network control monitor include maintenance of a database for network configurations as well as the provision of online statistics. Port use, equipment reliability and error rates are also important.

A second system or a shared back-up facility that can be brought online via switches should be available if an emergency occurs. These systems are called hot standbys.

LEVELS OF MONITORING AND CONTROL

Several levels of monitoring and control can be implemented to achieve network visibility. One level is manual patching, which requires that modems and ports be wired through patch panels and manually switched in the event of a failure. Another level is electromechanical patching, which uses automated patch panels controlled by a local or remote terminal or computer. The use of a matrix switch is an alternate method that permits access to the communications lines. Matrix switches provide an electronic method for line control and can be managed by a network monitor or network control center equipment.

For a higher level of network control, a network control center is required to integrate all monitoring and control functions. All points in the network are wired so they can be reached with network monitoring. Error conditions can be detected and corrected rapidly and the network can be reconfigured from a central point.

CASE STUDY (CONTINUED)

At the outset of its data processing and data communications planning sessions, the bank recognized that its number one priority is to keep the network up and running as much as possible. The planners realized that bank operations would come to a standstill if the network or service center came down. They also recognized that components do in fact fail, so they devised a plan to ensure that downtime would be kept to a minimum. The bank's approach to maintaining healthy network operation involves the following activities:

- The establishment of a help desk staffed by data communications network support personnel who can provide telephone assistance to any user who might need it. This might range from application support to troubleshooting activities that terminal and PC users can perform.

- The establishment of a troubleshooting system with several levels of response. The system defines actions that users and support technicians should follow if a problem occurs.

- The acquisition of local and remote software diagnostics to assist in problem determination. At each branch, an employee will be trained to run the diagnostics and interpret the results.
- The establishment of a regular schedule of preventive maintenance for branch and service center hardware.
- The complete testing of all software changes in parallel for an extended period of time before placing them into the production environment. This prevents changes from causing the network to crash due to unforeseen problems.
- The establishment of hardware reserves to ensure that critical components can be placed into immediate service if an operational unit fails. This necessitates additional funding; however, the bank believes that having standby components ready provides an additional level of safety.

REVIEW QUESTIONS

1. What are the three major types of errors encountered within a data communications network?
2. Name the basic procedures used to identify and resolve errors.
3. What devices perform analog and digital loopback testing?
4. What functions do protocol and data analyzers perform?
5. What function does a timer perform when used in a protocol analyzer?
6. What function does a breakout box perform on the network?
7. What is BERT an acronym for?
8. What functions do SAMs perform?
9. What product is used for monitoring the entire communications network?
10. Why should network control centers be required within medium to large communications networks?

CHAPTER
18

Network Management and Control

INTRODUCTION

Network management has become a critical issue in the 1990s. Global networks that use multivendor equipment, often in a complicated bridged environment, are rapidly increasing in numbers. Controlling the resources of these networks is a vital aspect of data communications.

Managers responsible for network communications require network visibility and control to provide end users with an acceptable quality of service. As discussed in Chapter 17, keeping the network up and providing acceptable levels of service are paramount to a successful communications environment.

Network management often is overlooked during the planning and implementation stages for one of the following reasons:

- The planned network is too small to need network management.

- The vendor will provide the necessary network management, along with the hardware and software.

- It is regarded as an unnecessary function.

But it is important to include provisions for network monitoring and management in any network plan, because the network will probably expand at some point and may require monitoring and control to maintain acceptable performance.

Proper planning is a major factor in successful network operation. Before a network is installed, consider how the network is to be maintained to achieve optimum performance. A network control center may be needed, depending on the size of the organization, the number of devices needing support and whether internetwork communications are required.

When deciding whether to implement a network control center, consider these questions:

- Can the size of the network justify the cost of implementing the center?
- Network control centers are expensive to maintain and staff. Will these costs be justified?
- What is the liability if the network goes down for a prolonged period of time?
- What will the costs be in terms of lost revenue if the network goes down and service cannot be restored quickly?
- If the network goes down, are alternate methods available for backup?
- Is network performance a key issue?

Networks with light traffic loads may not require network monitoring. In this case, preventative maintenance and testing may suffice. Often, network control centers are not economical; in these cases, the back-up problem can be solved if an alternate data center with communications is in place.

NETWORK CONTROL CENTERS

Measurement and monitoring of networks that connect large quantities of dissimilar equipment are essential in controlling performance. Specialized equipment and techniques are usually needed to gather and analyze performance data on fully distributed networks where there is no central control facility. The network control center should perform the following functions:

- Performance monitoring
- Configuration control
- Fault isolation
- Access security

Performance Monitoring

Most performance monitors provide programming capability to set parameters for monitoring a variety of conditions over specified periods of time. Factors that should be monitored to maintain peak performance of the network include message delay, channel throughput, message overhead, network stability and traffic control.

Message Delay. The amount of packet delay (normal packet load versus abnormal packet load) that can occur during peak periods is a key factor in determining acceptable network performance. Delay is the result of congestion on the links caused by resource contention or equipment malfunction.

Channel Throughput. The total number of packets flowing over a specific period of time should be monitored and charted. This can be used to indicate performance degradation.

Message Overhead. The number of packet retransmissions required due to error conditions must be monitored continuously. This count is a major indicator that provides key information about any problems that might exist.

Network Stability. Statistics that relate to the number of network failures and restarts experienced over a specific period of time should be developed.

Network Response Degradation. Various traffic conditions must be identified and traffic activity monitored to indicate network or application degradation.

Configuration Control

Configuration control tools (hardware and software) aid in supporting and tracking user devices. The variety of equipment (e.g., modems, computers, terminals, storage devices and printers) that can be connected to the communications network require a variety of interfaces.

Configuration software used with network management control tools defines and records values for node or device connections along with specific target information to be captured. This information is useful for discovering any changes to the network configuration by other than authorized personnel.

As an example, a user could change the bit rate (depending on the application) from 1200 bps to dial out or 9600 bps to access the host. The configuration software should be able to define parameters to allow or disallow this mode of operation, providing a level of control. At minimum, it should indicate the condition to the network manager.

Configuration tools can be used in two different ways: initializing the connection installation and using the update mode for day-to-day maintenance.

Fault Isolation

In addition to monitoring the network's configuration, network managers must be able to monitor the device connections to the cable and detect any device malfunction. Cable connectivity can be determined by simply polling the devices on the network. The network control center should be set up to initiate self-tests and to issue data loopback commands to devices on the network.

Automatic failure detection can be provided if the correct hardware and software is present. Automatic failure detection involves reporting a failure in the network to the network control center, which then executes testing functions to isolate and correct the problem. An inherent problem with any network is the failure of one or more components. However, with the proper test procedures, a fault can be isolated and corrected, ensuring the availability of the network.

Access Security

Data transmitted between computer resources may be sensitive or confidential. To ensure the protection of private information, access to devices on the network can be controlled through the software and the network control center.

Via program control in the network control center, a database can be set up to identify authorized users. This database file identifies access groups (who may talk to whom). All transmissions are routed to the network control center, which authorizes who is able to communicate on the system. A call scenario then might be as follows.

A specific user initiates the transmission. The network control center first verifies the validity of the calling node as a user of the system by examining an internal device address and a user password (ID). This provides a restriction that eliminates intruders from logging on to the system. If the sending device is invalid, the session is terminated immediately. If the check is valid, the sending device is acknowledged and queried for the destination address.

The destination address is then checked against the receiving device's user group. If common group membership is determined, a session is established. Protection of session data is ensured with encrypted data sessions; the node is equipped with an encryption chip and enhanced communications protocols.

NETWORK CONTROL CENTER ADVANTAGES

The network control center permits real-time analysis of network performance, allowing dynamic reconfiguration and modification of the network. It also allows quick response to problems, thereby minimizing downtime. Implementation of a network control center provides centralized control over maintenance decisions and assists in establishing performance criteria. Another advantage of the network control center is that it assists in reducing response time for repairs and helps to reduce maintenance expenditures. A network control center also maximizes network use before network growth creates costly modifications.

NETWORK CONTROL CENTER EQUIPMENT

Network Control Center Console Monitor

The network control equipment should be passive; it should not interfere with the operation of the network. Therefore, the manner in which the center is attached is important. The network control center normally uses a network monitor to gather statistical information. The monitor provides information to an intelligent device (usually a microcomputer) for data analysis. A storage device (hard disk) is needed during high network traffic conditions to store data for later report generation.

Artificial Traffic Generator

Artificial traffic generators consist of software or hardware designed to enable users to stress test the network to determine weak points. They can be used to present a known random distribution of traffic load to the network while data analysis software captures the information. The data gathered by the software generally includes:

- Time tagged frames — Test frames containing time and date stamps that can be used for performance tracking.

- Source and destination address — Both the sending and receiving node addresses should be included for tracking and routing activities.

- Retries — The number of retries required to move the packet from its source to its destination.

- Total transmission attempts with a valid CRC check — The total number of transmission attempts in which the packet is received correctly. The valid CRC check helps to track nondata packet errors that may result from time-outs, equipment problems or congestion.

This data can provide valuable information for determining the quality of network performance. It also aids in long-term tracking to predict and plan for expansion. This stored statistical information serves two basic purposes: It provides information to the network manager on current and predicated network performance, and it is used to develop reports that provide information such as packet type, data size, interarrival time, channel delay, communications delay, collision count and throughput.

The traffic generator (which is a processor in itself) is connected to communications nodes by links that generate experimental conditions. A console CRT and printer are used for network control center monitoring of real-time information and to produce hard-copy reports.

A variety of vendors provide network control center equipment. Software is offered by Proteon Inc. and IBM, among others. Hardware vendors include IBM, Codex, AT&T and Network Equipment Technologies (NET). A variety of functions are provided by the equipment, including electronic software metering, audit trail and report generation, menu managers and editors. Additional network control hardware functions include resource assignment matrix monitoring, universal network users, workstation inventories, resource databases, alarmed packet counts and reporting and automatic line test and fault isolation.

CASE STUDY (CONTINUED)

The Bank of Scotts Valley cannot yet afford to establish a network control center for monitoring its communications network. This does not mean that the bank's managers think a monitoring function is unnecessary. Data communications operations and technical support personnel have implemented IBM's NetView software on the mainframe and the distributed network, enabling them to use the existing hardware for monitoring and control.

The bank's planners also have provided plans for a separate network control center to be located at a third site when it can be cost-justified. The remote network control center will provide network monitoring and dynamic network reconfiguration, and it will serve as a disaster recovery center should one of the service centers experience a failure.

Equipment to be installed will include a back-up IBM 4341 mainframe that will operate as a hot standby, an IBM 3745 communications processor and redundant communications links to each of the service centers. A network controller will tie the entire network together, and all network links will pass through the network controller. Figure 18.1 illustrates the bank's proposed network, which includes the remote network control center.

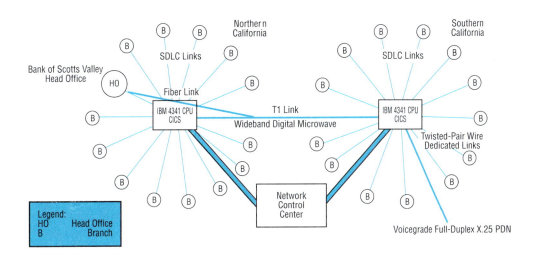

Figure 18.1 Bank of Scotts Valley Service Centers and Network Control Center

REVIEW QUESTIONS

1. Is the network control monitor a required component in a communications network?
2. Are frame error counts important to performance?
3. Can dynamic configuration be accomplished using a network control monitor?
4. What are the functions of a network control center?
5. Are network control centers a required component for all communications networks?
6. Is a hot standby a required component in network management?

CHAPTER

19

Future Trends

THE NEXT GENERATION

Data communications continues to evolve at a rapid pace. Global heterogeneous networks are becoming the norm for many international organizations, and multiple networks that support different types of hardware and software are common today in large corporations. These companies are the driving force behind the development of new hardware, software and standard link technologies. Users need new software and hardware to meet increasing demands for worldwide high-speed data communications.

New technical capabilities will be required to meet the ever-increasing demand for data. As the world becomes more digitized, bit rate requirements will grow exponentially, due in part to the demand for digital imaging and full motion digital video. Digital video and imaging require a large number of bits to represent each graphics frame; it is not uncommon to see a single video frame requiring millions of bits. Data processing and computer-developed information also will continue to grow and require communications as companies shift to remote distributed processing.

This chapter describes the hardware, software and services we can expect in the future, based on current directions and demand. Some of these capabilities are just over the horizon, such as the SONET communications network. Others will not be operable for many years.

The next generation of communications hardware and software will be based on new high-speed link capabilities made available by public and private telephone service providers. Communications processors, multiplexers and modems will be designed around the link service capabilities made available. High-speed fiber technology supporting speeds well into the gigabit-per-second rate is under development, and new hardware and software will be developed to use this high-speed capability.

Three of the basic limitations we have had to live with for some time are rapidly diminishing as hardware and software improve. One such limitation is link capacity and the ability of equipment to manage communications activities at very high bit rates. Specifically, hardware cannot be built until manufacturers know what type of link and bit speeds will be available in the future. Software manufacturers also must develop new protocol and management software that can support the high bit rates provided by the new hardware. Finally, costs must continue to decline as technologies improve in order for companies to shift to them.

The next generation of data communications equipment probably will use high-speed, single-mode multifrequency fiber optics operating at very high bit rates. The fiber will be directly coupled to computers capable of handling gigabit-rated links and having processing rates well into the billions of instructions per second. Future hardware will mandate new microprocessors and greatly increased memory capacities to handle the high-speed data communications rates.

Computers

Performance limitations relating to memory capacity and processor speed are based on the physical properties of the materials and the etching technology used. Only so many circuits can be etched onto a specific size of silicon wafer (semiconductor chip). The smaller the etched circuit, the more heat generated by friction of the electron movement. When the heat reaches a certain temperature, the chip fails.

Another limitation to the development of higher performance computers and processors is the circuit speed of the chip. Depending on the circuit material used by the semiconductor manufacturer (e.g., gold, silver, etc.), the circuit speed of the chip can vary greatly between different chips on the printed circuit or etched circuit board. Also, manufacturing costs of specific circuits vary, depending on the material used in chip construction.

A new generation of computer is emerging with major improvements in capacity and performance. New architectures, new materials and improved semiconductor/printed circuit board etching technology is enabling semiconductor manufacturers to reduce size substantially and increase the durability of processor and memory chips. A benefit of that reduction is a gain in circuit performance and ultimately a faster computer. Improvement in memory capacity (more memory in the same physical space) will allow much faster memory access speeds, contributing to the computer's performance.

Originally, memory and processor chips had only four-bit wide paths that were used for data movement within the CPU. Now it is standard to find computers supporting 32, 64, or higher bit paths for connecting the computer's internal components (memory, logic, I/O control). In the near future, we will probably see microprocessors and computers capable of supporting 128-, 256- and 512-bit bus interfaces. This, however, will require new architectures and bus technologies to be designed to support the new bus structures. Larger bus pathways and new computer architectures will provide a capability for much faster data movement within the computer or processor.

Another rapidly developing area is parallel processor architecture. This type of processor architecture will support hundreds or thousands of interconnected microprocessors and will provide parallel processing capabilities for concurrent applications. Parallel processing involves the use of dedicated microprocessors for each active application or process within an application. Each task or activity is assigned to a specific processor for the duration of its execution.

Another way parallel processing can be used has to do with the overall management of the computer. Dedicated processors can manage activities such as I/O control between independent storage devices and data movement within the CPU. One processor can hand off a request for services to another processor (e.g., an I/O processor) and then return to what it was doing before the request. It then periodically checks the I/O processor for the information it had requested.

New and faster semiconductor-based components will be developed from superconducting materials (after the technology is perfected and products can be economically manufactured). Superconducting involves the ability to move electricity or signals across a wired medium without a current loss caused by resistance of the wiring material. Superconductors have incredible potential; when ambient-temperature superconducting is perfected, it will allow the construction of highly efficient motors and generators. It also will provide the ability to transport electrical signals (e.g., electricity, semiconductor signals, etc.) without a reduction in the strength of the electricity or signal. Superconductor development is ongoing and, once perfected, will provide a tremendous speed and reliability improvement to computing and communications.

Local Area Networks

Local area networks represent the fastest growing area of data communications, and it is reasonable to assume they will continue to grow at an accelerated rate for quite some time. Future growth will be fueled in part by the practical use of FDDI, which provides 100-Mbps fiber capability, and the availability of more efficient gateways and bridges.

FDDI is in the process of being accepted as a standard. It is currently offered by many vendors and is very likely to be finalized as a standard for LAN connectivity in the near future. FDDI will provide high-speed transparent backbone connections between LAN nodes. While this will have little effect on overall performance for self-contained LANs, it will provide interconnect capabilities between different types of LAN technologies, such as Ethernet and token-ring networks.

The introduction of intelligent gateways and bridges providing transparent routing and relaying will allow workstations and servers to maximize resources. The relaying bridge or gateway will use a logical or generic node address provided at the workstation by the user or the software to generate a physical address for the node receiving the data or packet.

Greater speed and processing capabilities also will be available in the future. New LAN workstation interface hardware that supports much higher speeds will be available with new processors capable of maintaining higher I/O bit rates. It is expected that many computer manufacturers will incorporate LAN functions into the computer's motherboard, probably in the form of semiconductor logic installed like the optional math co-processor chips used today.

Some vendors are incorporating LAN software into their operating system software, such as IBM with its Operating System (OS/2) and Microsoft with its Microsoft Windows environment. Other vendors of network operating systems, such as Novell, are likely to provide program interfaces that will allow their software to function as an extension of the operating system. Users will then be able to invoke LAN functions via the graphical user interface similar to other application processes.

Hardware and software capabilities built into future equipment will provide greatly improved throughput efficiency. They will also allow a much larger number of nodes to be attached to a single network.

Communications Processors

Improvement in communications processors and substantial reductions in manufacturing costs will provide users with economical, high-speed capabilities that are now too expensive for many organizations. Communications processor capabilities will include the ability to directly connect high-speed fiber-optic links into optical multiplexers contained within the communications processor. These links, in turn, will connect directly to fiber-optic buses.

Communications processors, like computers, will be assembled using advanced semiconductor memory and microprocessors operating in parallel. The processors will be able to handle extremely high-speed communications links to support multiplexed data and full-motion digital video capabilities. As new hardware allows faster I/O activity, the restrictions on the total number of bits per second that the processor can handle will disappear.

Communications processor software probably will be given more responsibility for monitoring and managing the network. Many communications functions resident in the host computer may be incorporated into the communications processor's software.

Multiplexers

Multiplexers will continue to evolve and provide an extensive array of services for small organizations that cannot justify a full-blown communications processor. Like communications processors, multiplexers might have direct channel interfaces for fiber optics, provide extensive drop and insert capabilities for low-speed links and have logic to support fractional DS-1 and DS-3 links. Some multiplexers may provide bridging and gateway capabilities and support network management and high-speed protocols.

Modems, CSUs and DSUs

Modem, CSU and DSU manufacturers will continue to enhance their products to use developing channel and bandwidth capabilities. As higher speeds supported by the SONET network and High-Performance Parallel Interface (HPPI), which is designed to support rates of 800 Mbps and higher, are implemented by the various carriers, we can expect manufacturers of traditional modems, DSUs and CSUs to offer optical modems supporting these new standards.

Media and Cabling Systems

Media and cabling systems will continue to evolve as new protocols and transmission components are developed. Several companies are experimenting with 100-Mbps transmission using unshielded twisted-pair wiring over limited distances. Fiber-optic cable bit speeds and distances will continue to increase at a rapid pace with the development of supporting component technology. High gigabit-per-second rates over thousands of miles of cable without repeaters will soon become a reality. The use of infrared and other waveband wireless radio frequency transmissions will become more popular for limited-distance applications as error detection and correction become more mature. FDDI will become a standard for both wide area and local area networks in the near future.

Application Development Software

Program creation (writing program code) has always been somewhat of a problem for application programs developed for use in data communications networks. Programmers have had to be careful when developing code because of the critical placement of screen items such as the cursor and protected fields. Often, separate programs are used to develop screen formats, provide error detection and access databases, which can create alignment problems.

New application development tools for creating application programs or screen formats will allow programmers to correct field misalignment problems and other specification problems automatically. Additional application development tools will provide simple procedures for creating, maintaining and modifying online application programs. They most likely will be driven by English-like statements used to develop the logic and by mouse/trackball placement of positioning elements for screen formats.

Communications Control Software

Communications control software will become more intelligent with the addition of artificial intelligence (AI) or fuzzy logic routines resident in the program code. This will allow the software to manage much of the routine maintenance normally handled by a systems programmer or operator. Today, when terminal environments change, many software programs need to be modified in order to function in the new environment. It is not difficult to make an incorrect change or to forget a change altogether. When AI technology is incorporated, maintenance software automatically will update all relevant software to ensure that a system's integrity is maintained.

The communications control software of tomorrow also will integrate extensive monitoring, management and dynamic change capabilities. Much of the control software will be incorporated into the hardware in the form of ROM semiconductors and will be developed using worldwide standards, which will allow use on many different vendors' systems. Other activities, such as backup and recovery, will evolve and provide a secure point-of-failure restart capability. Security will be supported extensively from within the communications control software to control unauthorized access to the network.

STANDARDS

Standards that apply to both software and hardware will continue to be developed by the national and international standards' organizations and will be implemented by a larger number of vendors worldwide. This implementation is being driven primarily by users who want the capability to interconnect networks transparently from a variety of vendors without the fear that the networks will be incompatible.

The use of international standards also will allow hardware and software manufacturers to provide a consistent "look and feel" to their products. This should reduce end-user training requirements as well as confusion about the installation and use of the various components. Standards will continue to gain importance for both users and manufacturers as open systems architectures become the guiding force for implementation of data communications networks.

LINK SERVICES

Link services will continue to mature in the areas of features and speed. As new equipment is developed to squeeze more capacity out of existing transmission facilities, we will see a growth in the use of twisted-pair wiring for high-speed data transmission. New wireless data transmission capabilities using radio frequency and enhanced fiber optics will continue to evolve as manufacturing costs become lower. New transmission technologies such as SONET will be available in the near future to take advantage of fiber optics' high transmission capacity. SONET will support high-speed communications protocols capable of operating in the gigabit-per-second range.

HPPI, a high-speed network interface, also will be offered in the near future. Like SONET, HPPI will provide the communications protocols required for gigabit-per-second transmission. Both SONET and HPPI will allow full-motion video images that require very high bit rates to support 30 frames per second. When the high-speed capabilities are available at a reasonable cost, video imaging will become common in many companies.

OPEN SYSTEMS ARCHITECTURE

In the future, vendors will have to adopt an open systems approach to systems development to satisfy users who need interoperability to maximize the investments they make in hardware and software. The following paragraphs describe the benefits open systems will offer.

Application Portability. Application portability benefits both the end user and the hardware/software manufacturer. Portability allows end users to run the same applications across a broad range of equipment, regardless of manufacturer. In an open systems environment, users will be able to select the most appropriate system for each part of their data processing/data communications activities. They also will have a wider choice of applications from which to choose.

Software developers will no longer have to develop and support different versions of their applications. Software systems suppliers will be able to have a greater number of applications up and running sooner on new hardware platforms. This will be an increasingly important objective as hardware product life cycles become shorter and shorter.

An important aspect of an open systems architecture is that it is based on standards. Portable applications depend on standard interfaces. Therefore, conformance interfaces within an open systems environment must provide a substantial degree of application portability.

Interoperability. An open systems architecture will encourage independent software vendors to create newly distributed applications. In addition, users will be able to interconnect all of their systems into networks and communicate effectively within and among networks.

Flexibility. The restrictions of many older vendor-specific systems meant that meeting the remote needs of the end user was often not economical or even possible. By using an open systems approach, users will have the business benefits associated with flexibility. Individual machines will be bought as required from the supplier that offers the best deal at the time. Systems will be reconfigured to meet changing organizational needs. A distributed open systems architecture will make it possible to use large numbers of small systems in a variety of combinations to create a large communications environment. This means that special needs can be met much more cost-effectively and efficiently. Users will be able to buy the most appropriate system from an alternative supplier if the principal supplier does not have a system of that size at that particular time.

Independence from Suppliers. For the end users, a major benefit of an open systems architecture will be independence from hardware and software suppliers. Products will become more price competitive, and support and service will become key factors when users are no longer tied to a single provider.

Added Functions. With products that conform to an open systems architecture, users will be able to protect their investments in applications and data. Data is the lifeblood of many companies, retaining its value for many years. Software may also have a long life cycle. When new hardware is installed in a vendor-specific environment, both the data and the software often must be altered to operate on the new equipment. With open systems, users will be able to move from one processing/communications platform to another without converting data or applications.

Maximized Return on Investment. If users demand it, software and hardware manufacturers will have to invest heavily in open systems technologies and products to remain competitive. At the present time, most start-up companies are basing their product development on open systems specifications. There is a great deal of competition, resulting in more innovation and the introduction of more features than has been the case for some years.

An open systems architecture greatly influences the way vendors develop products. In particular, there is a marked increase in the use of standard systems and off-the-shelf components. Buying standard parts will allow system vendors to concentrate development resources on high-value product differentiations. For example, many products use chip-level implementations that can be purchased from various semiconductor companies.

CASE STUDY CONCLUSION

At this point, the Bank of Scotts Valley's network is functioning well and provides a foundation for increased business. In real life, the establishment of the data centers, the creation of branch operations, and the implementation of local area networking (all of which are requirements for a bank's automated operations) would have taken years. While IBM equipment has been used at the Bank of Scotts Valley, an automated processing environment and its supporting network can be created using many vendors' products.

An open systems approach to networking will provide a foundation on which an extensive array of banking services can be offered in the future. The bank of the future will be in a position to offer customers virtually all services that currently require a visit to a branch office. In the area of commercial business activities, future bank services will include interbanking debit cards used in place of checking accounts, as well as international customer accounts linked to partner banks. This will enable customers to access funds from other banks as if they were at a branch of the bank they normally do business with.

The key to a successful network implementation is the thorough preplanning phase, in which the required software and hardware are identified. The development of operational procedures and training to support the new systems also must be considered essential to the planning process.

APPENDIX A

Selected Standards

This appendix lists various standards referenced throughout this book. For a complete listing, contact the appropriate standards agency.

CCITT MODEM STANDARDS

The following V. recommendations are some of the more important standards that apply to modems and data transmission.

V.2	Specification of power levels for data transmission over telephone lines.	
V.5	Specification of synchronous data signaling rates over the switched network.	
V.6	Specification of synchronous data signaling rates over leased lines.	
V.7	Definition of other key terms used in the V series recommendations.	
V.10	Description of an unbalanced physical-level interchange circuit.	
V.11	Description of a balanced physical level interchange circuit.	
V.19	CCITT parallel data transmission modems.	

CCITT MODEM STANDARDS (CONTINUED)

V.21	CCITT Physical layer digital interface standard.	
V.21bis	CCITT EIA-232-compatible interface.	
V.24	Definition of the interchange circuit pins between DTE and DCE.	
V.28	Description of unbalanced interchange circuits operating below 20 Kbps.	
V.26	CCITT 2400-bps four-wire leased circuits.	
V.27	CCITT 4800-bps for switched/leased circuits.	
V.29	CCITT 9600-bps for leased circuits. (Standard also used for Group III Fax.)	
V.35	CCITT 56-Kbps/64-Kbps modems for leased circuits.	
V.42	CCITT LAP-B/MNP Level 5; error correction standard for modems.	
V.42bis	CCITT BTLZ Data compression standard for modems.	

CCITT DIGITAL STANDARDS

X.3	CCITT packet assembly/disassembly functions.	
X.20	CCITT interface between data communication equipment (DCE) and data terminal equipment (DTE) for asynchronous data transmission on public data networks.	
X.21	CCITT interface between DCE and DTE for synchronous data transmission on public data networks.	
X.25	Interface between DCE and DTE for terminals operating in a packet mode connected to a public data network.	
X.28	CCITT terminal-to-PAD communications formats.	
X.29	CCITT host-to-PAD communications formats.	
X.75	Terminal and transit call control procedures for data transfer on international circuits between packet-switched networks.	
X.95	CCITT network parameters in a public data network.	
X.121	CCITT International Addressing Standard.	
X.200	Reference model of Open Systems Interconnection for CCITT applications.	
X.400	CCITT interoffice electronic mail standards.	

Appendix A

CCITT RECOMMENDED ISDN STANDARDS (PARTIAL LIST)

I.431	Layer 1 physical specifications for primary rate DS-1 connections.
I.441/451	ISDN primary rate interface.
I.515	Parameters for ISDN internetworking.
Q.700	Signaling System Number 7 (CCS#7) specifications.
Q.921	Layer 2 (data link protocol) for D channel (Link Access Procedure-D).
Q.931	Layer 3 (network) ISDN user network interface specifications.
Q.932	Generic procedures for the control of ISDN supplementary procedures.
V.110/	B channel procedures.
V.120	B channel procedures.

EIA INTERFACE STANDARDS

EIA-232	25-pin interface between DTE and DCE.
EIA-269	Synchronous signaling rates for data transmission.
EIA-422	Electrical characteristics of balanced voltage digital interface circuits.
EIA-423	Electrical characteristics of unbalanced voltage digital interface circuits.
EIA-442	Electrical characteristics for balanced pairs.
EIA-449	37-pin general interface for DCE-to-DTE equipment.
EIA-496	Interface between DTE and the public switched telephone network.
EIA-530	High-speed interface for DTE-to-DCE equipment.

ANSI TELECOMMUNICATIONS STANDARDS

X3.1	Synchronous signaling rates for data transmission.
X3.4	American National Standard for Information Interchange (ANSII).
X3.15	ANSI ASCII code bit structure.
X3.16	Character structure and character parity sense for serial-by-bit data communications in ASCII.
X3.24	Signal quality for synchronous data transmission.

ANSI TELECOMMUNICATIONS STANDARDS (CONTINUED)

X3.25	Character structure and parity sense for ASCII parallel transmission.
X3.28	Procedures for using ASCII communications control characters.
X3.36	Synchronous data signaling rates between DTE and DCE.
X3.41	ASCII code set extension techniques.
X3.57	ASCII message header formats using communications control characters.
X3.66	ANSI standard for bit-oriented link control protocol, ADCCP.

ISO STANDARDS

ISO3309	Data communications HDLC control procedures and frame structure.
ISO7498	The seven-layer ISO/OSI reference model.
ISO8072	Transport service definition.
ISO8208	X.25 packet level protocol for data-terminating equipment.

IEEE STANDARDS

IEEE Standard 802.1	Architecture and internetworking standard; defines the layers of the architecture and the rules for interconnection of different LAN protocols.
IEEE Standard 802.2	Logical Link Control Standard; defines the equivalent of data link control as specified in the OSI reference model and is also the protocol used for data transfer.
IEEE Standard 802.3	CSMA/CD Access Method and Physical Layer Specifications; defines the carrier sense multiple access method with collision detection used for data transfer.
IEEE Standard 802.4	Token-Passing Bus Access Method and Physical Layer Specifications; defines the characteristics of the Token-Passing Bus Network Access Method used for data transfer in Token-Passing LANs.
IEEE Standard 802.5	Token-Passing Ring Access Method and Physical Layer Specifications; applies to those systems using Token-Passing Ring LANs and defines the access methods employed in data transfer.

IEEE STANDARDS (CONTINUED)

IEEE Standard 802.6	Metropolitan Network Access Method and Physical Layer Specifications.
IEEE Standard 802.7	Sets standards for the definition of a broadband cable plant design. It also establishes guidelines for LAN construction within a building or plant.
IEEE Standard 802.8 (Working Group)	Group established to assess the impact of fiber optics within the LAN environment and to recommend standards.

APPENDIX B

Answers to Review Questions

CHAPTER 1

1. Because of the tremendous demand from the data processing industry.
2. The components and equipment required for data communications.
3. Immediate access to current information, reduction in the amount of redundant data required to process data into information, and the ability to base business decisions on the latest information.
4. Analog transmission.
5. Yes.
6. Relatively high costs, requirements for additional personnel, and additional maintenance.
7. No. Additional factors that should be considered include needs assessment and justification and the use of alternatives such as public data network services.
8. To support the data processing at that location.
9. Cost, links, speed, hardware, software, and personnel.
10. The data is binary and computer generated.

CHAPTER 2.

1. Developed the telegraph system in 1856.
2. Developing the Baudot code for use with the telegraph.
3. ASCII and EBCDIC.
4. Both ASCII and EBCDIC support 256 character types.
5. The data processing industry.
6. Costs, speed, capacity, maintenance, and upgrade capability.
7. System software, application software, communications control software, and network control software.
8. Application control software manages all online applications and ensures that each has the ability to communicate and process data.
9. Public data networks, time-sharing services, and packet-switching services.
10. The provider of end-to-end links.

CHAPTER 3

1. The control, monitoring, and management of links, application programs, and communications pathways.
2. The management of the hardware resources for all programs and processes.
3. Applications software is responsible for manipulating data into meaningful information.
4. Polling, selection, error detection, and application management.
5. The process of establishing and maintaining a communications session until the user terminates the connection.
6. BTAM and VTAM are IBM access methods that provide the pathways for terminal connections.
7. Network management and internetwork communications.
8. True.
9. False.
10. Because the software is very complex and requires years to develop.

CHAPTER 4

1. Communications monitors manage terminal application processes in a conversational or transaction-based environment, whereas time-sharing monitors allocate slices of time to each user, allowing the user to control application program activity.
2. Yes, but it is a waste of resources to use time-sharing services for transaction or conversational processing because of slow response time.

3. Online programs must not modify themselves during execution and should not perform long record searches.

4. Conversational systems are used by programmers for session-based activities, and transaction-based networks are designed to process single transactions in random order.

5. Provide CPU access to users who need mainframe resources for processing.

CHAPTER 5

1. A pathway between the CPU and device controllers such as a communications processor.

2. Baseband transmission usually refers to a single transmission channel on the media.

3. True.

4. True.

5. False.

6. Subvoice, voiceband, and wideband.

7. Analog.

8. Half duplex.

9. Synchronous and asynchronous.

10. The synchronous transmission method.

CHAPTER 6

1. AT&T, MCI, and U.S. Sprint.

2. International links to and from North America.

3. Value-added network services, packet-switching services, and code set and protocol conversion.

4. Unreliable datagrams, reliable datagrams, and virtual circuit packets.

5. The public switched telephone network.

6. A dedicated telephone link.

7. C conditioning and D conditioning.

8. DDS.

9. The need to establish an all-digital, high-speed communications service to support data and voice transmission.

10. The ISDN Basic Rate.

11. The transfer of control information.

12. Three 384-Kbps video channels and one 64-Kbps control channel.

CHAPTER 7

1. Amplitude modulation, frequency modulation, and phase modulation.
2. The amplitude of the carrier remains the same while the timing and frequency is varied to represent digital information.
3. A carrier's cycle timing remains the same while the amplitude is varied to represent digital information.
4. The term "baud" refers to cycles per second, whereas bps refers to bits per second. The two may differ depending on the modulation technique.
5. A dibit is equal to two bits per cycle; a tribit is equal to three bits per cycle; and a quadbit is equal to four bits per cycle.
6. A technique whereby the phase or angle of the carrier is modified to represent groups of bits.
7. Yes, TCM is both a modulation technique and an encoding scheme.
8. Yes, the analog modulation technique is capable of emulating a digital signal.
9. Pulse code modulation (PCM) is a technique used for digitizing voice.
10. Binary and non-return to zero.

CHAPTER 8

1. Two-wire twisted pairs, four-wire twisted pairs, coaxial cable, and fiber-optic cable.
2. Higher bandwidth and better noise immunity.
3. Because bit rates are limited only by the transmission equipment at each end of the link and are not affected by noise and electromagnetic interference.
4. Yes.
5. Fiber-optic cable.
6. Reception and transmission on a satellite.
7. Telephone, local area network, and terminal connections.
8. Satellite and microwave transmission.
9. Distortion can modify the value of bits, changing one bits to zeros and zeros bits to ones.
10. True.

CHAPTER 9

1. Management of the physical communications network.
2. Line error detection and correction, physical polling and selection, and line control.
3. False.

4. True.

5. True.

6. Fiber-optic cable.

7. True.

8. True.

9. True.

10. True.

CHAPTER 10

1. The modulation of digital signals into analog signals for transmission over communications links.

2. True.

3. So that the terminal bit rate can be synchronized with the modem.

4. The auto-dial function automatically dials a telephone number provided by the communications software. The auto-answer feature automatically answers incoming calls.

5. V.32.

6. True.

7. True.

8. True.

9. True.

10. False.

11. Local analog loopback, local digital loopback, remote analog loopback, and remote digital loopback.

12. Loopback tests and frequency checks.

CHAPTER 11

1. EIA 232-D.

2. Up to two megabits per second.

3. 25.

4. RS-449.

5. EIA 232-D.

6. Distance is limited to 50 feet, and the maximum bit rate is 19.2 Kbps.

7. Link activation, data transfer, and link deactivation.

8. It allows for a higher level of noise control and supports balanced circuits.

9. Ground, timing, control, and data transfer signals.

10. A specification for a high-speed interface for dedicated links.

CHAPTER 12

1. CCITT V.24 and V.35.
2. Worldwide telecommunication standards.
3. The establishment of worldwide standards for telephony and telegraphy.
4. The definition of the 802 local area network standards.
5. Packet switching over X.25 networks.
6. The CCITT and ISO.
7. IBM and AT&T.
8. The Cobol programming standard.
9. Recommends the creation and adoption of standards.
10. To ensure worldwide hardware and software compatibility.

CHAPTER 13

1. Point to point and multipoint.
2. True.
3. Star, ring, bus, tree, mesh, and mesh of trees.
4. List polling and hub polling.
5. Polling refers to querying the terminal for activity, whereas selection involves a host sending information to a specific terminal.
6. True.
7. Yes.
8. Cost, location, support, maintenance, software, and user requirements.
9. Yes, because its geographic area is limited and because it uses different hardware.
10. Distributed processing refers to the use of computer systems at remote locations in support of the business activities at those locations.

CHAPTER 14

1. An architecture for the implementation of heterogeneous networks.
2. Systems Network Architecture, an IBM communications architecture similar to the OSI model.

3. SNA and OSI are generally incompatible, although there is limited compatibility in some areas.
4. SNA.
5. The data link control layer.
6. True.
7. Packet-switched communications.
8. The physical layer, the link layer, and the network layer.
9. Link access protocol.
10. Manufacturing Automation Protocol, a communications protocol designed for factory automation and control.

CHAPTER 15

1. A protocol specifies a handshaking technique for communication between computing devices.
2. Data framing, error control, timing control, and start and stop control.
3. The second layer.
4. Asynchronous transmission.
5. Acknowledgment and flow control.
6. End of Transmission (EOT), End of Text (ETX), and Enquiry (ENQ).
7. Indicates a negative acknowledgment when errors are encountered at the receiving device.
8. Vertical redundancy check (VRC), longitudinal redundancy check (LRC), and cyclical redundancy check (CRC).
9. Asynchronous protocols send one byte at a time, and synchronous protocols require clocking.
10. BSC and SDLC.
11. WACK.
12. The OSI architecture.
13. Simple Network Management Protocol, a network control and management protocol.

CHAPTER 16

1. Local area networks.
2. Carrier Sense Multiple Access.
3. CSMA.
4. Listen before transmitting.

5. Provides an environment in which nodes are able to transmit when they receive the three-byte token that circulates through the network.

6. Twisted-pair wiring.

7. Coaxial cable and CSMA technology.

8. Broadband refers to a transmission technology that provides multiple channels on a medium.

9. Baseband provides a single transmission channel and broadband provides multiple transmission channels.

10. Because it incorporates personal computing, communications, and mainframe processing into one technology.

CHAPTER 17

1. Software errors, hardware errors, and link errors.

2. Network documentation, network monitoring and error diagnosis, and follow-up on predefined problem resolution procedures.

3. Modems.

4. The capture of protocol frames for display and analysis.

5. The capture of protocol information on a timed bases.

6. Visibility of the modem and terminal communications signals.

7. Bit error rate tester.

8. Visibility of the analog communications circuits and reporting on a variety of conditions.

9. Network control monitors and monitoring software.

10. Because they enable network managers to detect and respond to errors and problems quickly.

CHAPTER 18

1. No.

2. Yes, because they indicate whether the network is performing within specified operational parameters.

3. In some cases, depending on the specific network control monitor.

4. Network monitoring, network reconfiguration, and error detection and correction.

5. No.

6. No, unless users require 100% uptime for the network.

Glossary

A

abort sequence. A sequence that prematurely terminates the transmission of a frame.

acoustic coupler. A device that converts electrical signals into audio signals, enabling data to be transmitted over telephone lines using a conventional telephone hand set.

ADCPM. Adaptive pulse code modulation. A modulation technique designed to carry digital and video signals.

address filtering. A bridge function for allowing addresses of other networks to pass through unchanged to the next bridge while identifying the addresses of that bridge's subnetworks.

amplifier. Similar to a bit repeater, but used for analog transmission. Amplifies both the signal and the noise.

amplitude modulation (AM). A method of modifying the amplitude of a carrier signal to transmit data signals.

analog. A representation of real-world events. Analog devices monitor real-world conditions such as sound, temperature and movement, and convert them into an output which resembles the real-world activity.

analog transmission. A transmission method that uses continuously variable signals that are modulated and demodulated to represent on and off electrical signals.

ANSI. American National Standards Institute. An organization made up of members from government and industry and formed to develop standards.

application layer. The layer of the Open Systems Interconnect (OSI) seven-layer model that governs application programs designed to function in an OSI environment.

ASCII. American Standard Code for Information Interchange. A seven- or eight-bit code set containing 128 characters and used extensively by most of the computer manufacturers in the world.

asynchronous transmission. The transmission of data or bits without regard to time. The data or bits to be transmitted are wrapped (surrounded by start and stop bits) to indicate the beginning and ending of the bit stream to be sent or received.

B

bandwidth. The range of frequencies assigned to a channel or circuit. The difference expressed in hertz (cycles per second) between the highest and lowest frequencies of the transmission band.

baseband. The base or starting frequency for the transmission of channels of information (data and bits). This also describes a type of communications network. Baseband networks are all-digital networks which have a transmission bandwidth of up to 10 megabits per second. *See* broadband.

basic rate interface. An ISDN service that provides two 64-Kbps links for the transfer of data and one 16-Kbps link for the transfer of control information.

baud. A unit of signaling speed that is equivalent to cycles per second.

bit. The smallest indicator of the presence or absence of information in a computer system. The foundation from which data and information is represented in a computer. A single digit of data expressed as a binary value in the computer.

bit-oriented protocol. A protocol that handles bits instead of characters and uses bits to indicate control activity.

bridge. A device that links similar pieces of equipment together using the same protocols and formats.

broadband. A type of transmission facility whose bandwidth (range of frequencies it will handle) is greater than that available on voice-grade facilities. Also known as *wideband*.

BSC. Binary Synchronous Protocol. An IBM protocol that defines a handshaking technique used between terminal controllers or remote communications processors and the host computer or front-end processor.

BTAM. Basic Telecommunications Access Method. An access method defined by IBM and used in pre-SNA environments to assist communications monitors or programs in accessing the terminal network.

buffer. A storage location used to compensate for differences in the rate of speed of the data being transferred between devices.

bus. A pathway within a computer or device that carries bits between operational activities at a very high rate of speed. Can also be referred to as an *internal communications channel*.

byte. A unit of information that consists of eight bits whose presence or absence represent characters or numbers within a computer or communications activity.

byte-oriented protocol. Also referred to as a character-oriented protocol. Characters consist of seven or eight bits and are used to represent data and control codes. The protocol does not handle bit streams. BSC is a byte-oriented protocol.

C

carrier. A continuous signal capable of being modulated or impressed with information.

CCITT. Consultative Committee for International Telephone and Telegraph. An agency of the United Nations chartered to establish worldwide communications standards.

central office (CO). A building belonging to the telephone company that houses switching equipment for establishing routing and managing local exchange telephones.

channel. A pathway for the transmission of a signal between two or more points.

channel service unit (CSU). A device designed to function in the same manner as a modem except that it works with digital signals rather than analog signaling.

CICS. Customer Information Control System. An IBM communications monitor.

coaxial cable. A cable used for transmission that consists of an unbalanced pair of wires made up of an inner conductor surrounded by a grounded braided or solid conductor. Also referred to as a *shielded cable.*

code. A set of rules established to ensure consistency and compatibility between manufacturers of electronic communications or computer equipment.

collision. The result of two packets being transmitted at the same time and colliding on the transmission medium.

common carrier. A company that undertakes to carry voice or data signals for the general public.

communications monitor. A system software component that operates under control of the operating system. Its function is to manage the terminal and communications resources for communications application programs.

compiler. A translation program designed to take high-level source code written by programmers and translate it into machine-level code understandable by the computer.

COM port. A communications doorway between the personal computer and a serial device such as a modem or printer.

concentrator. A communications device that provides connectivity for many low-speed devices or channels to one or more high-speed channels.

congestion. A condition that occurs on a network when more traffic is being placed on the network than the network can reasonably handle.

contention. The result of multiple users trying to access the network at the same time, which causes performance degradation of the entire network.

control token. A bit pattern captured by a station that gives it permission to transmit. Used with token-passing ring networks.

controllers. Devices that have independent processors and memory and that assist the CPU in input/output operations.

CPU. Central processing unit. The heart of a computer system, where programs perform the various data processing operations. Consists of components for memory, logic, I/O operations and control.

CRC. Cyclical redundancy checking. A procedure performed on transmitted data at the data link level and used for detecting errors.

CSMA. Carrier Sense Multiple Access. A local area network (LAN) access method designed to resolve contention when two or more terminals or workstations attempt to use the network at the same time. CSMA is the basic access method used in IEEE 802.3 LAN implementations.

CSU. See channel service unit.

D

datagram. A packet service that usually does not guarantee sequenced delivery of packets and may discard packets under certain conditions.

data link control. The second layer of both the IBM Systems Network Architecture (SNA) and the ISO Open Systems Interconnect (OSI) model. This layer defines how devices communicate in point-to-point or multipoint connections.

data link processor (DLP). A control unit similar to a device control unit used to connect multiple devices to the CPU.

Dataphone Digital Service (DDS). A high-speed digital transmission service offered by various telephone operating companies.

DCE. Data communications equipment. Equipment such as a modem used to establish, maintain and terminate a connection.

DDS. See Dataphone Digital Service.

decibels measured. A reference measurement that indicates the intensity of a carrier signal or the intensity of an output signal such as the sound level near the speakers at a rock concert.

digital service unit (DSU). The DSU operates in tandem with the CSU (incorporated into the same component) and supports digital transmission over the telephone company's digital network.

distortion. The unwanted and sometimes unavoidable change in an electronic signal during transmission.

DNA. Digital Network Architecture. An ISO-compliant communications architecture developed by Digital Equipment.

DSU. See digital service unit.

DTE. Data terminal equipment. The source or destination of the signals to or from DCE. Usually a terminal or computer system.

E

EBCDIC. Extended Binary Decimal Interchange Code. An eight-bit code set developed and used by IBM containing 256 characters.

EIA. Electronic Industries Association. A North American standards organization that concentrates on the electrical and functional characteristics of interface equipment.

emulation. The process of one machine performing the identical functions of another machine.

Ethernet. A local area network specification developed by Digital Equipment, Xerox and Intel. Based on the the IEEE 802 standards, Ethernet is used for communications between terminals or workstations in geographically restricted networks.

executable code. A program that has been converted from a source format understandable by programmers into a machine-readable format.

F

FDM. *See* frequency-division multiplexing.

FEP. *See* front-end processor.

flow control. A method of controlling the flow of data between two communicating devices.

frame. A message being sent or received that consists not only of data but also of transmission information such as terminal location, length of text message and routing information.

frequency. Vibrations or cycles per second. The frequency of a carrier is the number of electrical vibrations per second expressed in hertz.

frequency-division multiplexing ***(FDM).*** A process that divides the available transmission frequency range into narrower bands, each of which is used for a separate channel.

front-end processor ***(FEP).*** A communications computer associated with a host computer whose specialized function is to handle communications to and from terminals and nodes in the network.

full duplex ***(FDX).*** A transmission mode in which the channel operates in both directions at the same time.

G

gateway. An interface between two communications networks where conversion of protocols is required in order for each network to understand the other's data transmission.

gigabyte. One billion bytes.

guard bands. Used to separate transmission channels so that they do not interfere with each other.

H

half duplex (HDX). A transmission mode in which the channel operates in either direction but not in both directions at the same time.

HDLC. High-Level Data Link Control. A communications protocol used in X.25 packet-switching networks. HDLC is a subset of SDLC (Synchronous Data Link Control).

hertz. A frequency rating. The number of electrical vibrations per second is rated in hertz. One hertz is equal to one cycle per second.

host. A computer that is usually central to a terminal network and serves as the main controller for all activity required by each terminal or node in the network.

I

IEEE. Institute of Electrical and Electronics Engineers. The IEEE was founded to develop electrical and electronic standards.

interface. A device or scheme that allows the connection and operation of various types of equipment. An interface also can be software that allows programs to communicate with each other.

interleave. Used to describe a transmission process whereby messages to be sent on the link are inserted in some order so that each terminal has an opportunity to use the link.

Internet Protocol (IP). An ISO network-layer protocol used for data transmission between two networks.

ISO. International Standards Organization. A committee of the International Telecommunications Union (a United Nations organization) chartered to develop worldwide standards.

K

kilobyte. One thousand bytes.

L

LAN. Local area network. A type of network in which computers are connected to a single-wired medium and can share resources.

line driver. A converter and transmitter-receiver used for digital transmission across limited distances.

M

mark. The presence of a signal. In telegraph systems, the mark represents a closed or current flowing condition that is equivalent to a bit being present.

media access control (MAC) standards. A series of standards defined by the ISO that govern communications across IEEE 802 local area networks.

megabyte. One million bytes.

mesh topology. An organization of links and nodes within a communications network designed to provide backup and redundancy in the event of a link failure.

microprocessor. A semiconductor chip that contains all computer processes and is the heart of a central processing unit.

microsecond. One millionth of a second.

millisecond. One thousandth of a second.

modem. A device that converts digital signals into analog signals in order to transmit data across telephone lines. A modem is located at each end of the line and connects to a host or communications controller.

modulation. The process of varying the characteristics of a wave in accordance with another wave or signal, usually to make user equipment signals compatible with communications facilities.

multiplexer. An electronic device that combines data from several low-speed communications lines onto a single high-speed line.

multipoint line. A communications line that can be shared by several devices.

multitasking. The process of concurrently running more than one program in the CPU.

N

nanosecond. One billionth of a second.

NCP. Network Control Program. A communications program resident in the front-end processor designed to support SNA communications.

network layer. A layer of the ISO Open Systems Interconnect (OSI) architecture that controls end-to-end transmission across heterogeneous networks.

node. A computer or terminal used as a junction or connection point. An interface between user terminals and computers in a communications network.

noise. Undesirable disturbances in a communications system. Noise on a communications line can generate errors in data transmission.

nonvolatile memory. A type of memory that retains its ability to store and remember its contents after power has been turned off.

null modem. An interface that emulates a DCE-to-DTE connection and allows two DTE devices to communicate.

O

OSI. Open Systems Interconnect. A seven-layer model developed by the International Standards Organization for creating data communications networks.

P

packet. Used to identify control information and data for transmission across a public data network.

packet switching. The process of routing and relaying packet data across data communications networks.

parallel transmission. A method of data transfer in which all bits of a character or byte are transmitted simultaneously, either over separate wires or communication lines, or by different frequencies on the same communications line.

parity. A method used by a computer to aid in error detection by the addition of a bit to make the total number of bits turned on an even or odd number.

PCM. See pulse code modulation.

PDU. See protocol data unit.

phase modulation. An analog modulation technique modems use to transmit multiple bits per cycle of frequency across a communications network.

physical layer. The layer of the ISO Open Systems Interconnect (OSI) model that specifies how devices and network nodes are connected (wired or interfaced).

point-to-point connection. A connection between two pieces of equipment.

polling. The process of checking each terminal on the network to see if it has data to send.

port. Communication channel interface. A gateway for signals to and from the computer.

primary rate interface (PRI). An ISDN service that provides 24 or 30 64-Kbps links for the transfer of data and one 64-Kbps link for the transfer of control information.

protocol. A set of conventions governing the format and exchange of data and bits between two communication processes.

protocol data unit (PDU). Data and control information flowing through the OSI layers.

public switched telephone network (PSTN). A dial-up telephone network used by the general public for voice and data communications.

pulse code modulation (PCM). A type of modulation used for converting voice and video information into digital signals.

R

repeater. A digital device used to extend the length of a local area network.

response time. The amount of time required to return data to the transmitting device.

RF modem. A modem used to propagate analog-modulated signals onto a wired medium between communicating devices.

ring. A topology used to connect computers in a closed-loop circular network.

routing. The process of determining appropriate directions for the transmission of packets.

S

SDLC. Synchronous Data Link Control. A communications protocol like BSC, normally used in SNA networks.

serial transmission. A method of transmission in which each bit of information is sent one after another on the channel rather than simultaneously as in parallel transmission.

session layer. The layer of the ISO Open Systems Interconnect (OSI) model that specifies methods for recovery, restart and integrity in end-to-end communications across heterogeneous networks.

simplex. A transmission mode in which a channel operates in one direction only.

SNA. Systems Network Architecture. A seven-level architecture that supports the IBM data processing/data communications environment.

space. A telegraph term denoting the absence of a signal as compared with a mark, which denotes the presence of a signal.

spooling. A technique used to temporarily store output destined for a printer from programs, allowing the programs to continue processing.

star. A topology used to connect computers into a local area network.

statistical time-division multiplexing (STDM). A method of multiplexing whereby time slots are allocated to each sending device. If a device is inactive, the time slots are reassigned to other, active devices.

STDM. *See* statistical time-division multiplexing.

synchronous transmission. Transmission of data characters or bits at a fixed rate based on a clock synchronization between the transmitter and the receiver.

T

tap. A device used to connect workstations onto local area networks.

TCP. *See* Transmission Control Protocol.

TDM. *See* time-division multiplexing.

time-division multiplexing (TDM). A method of multiplexing whereby each device is allocated a set amount of link time and shares the link with other devices.

token passing. A local area network access method employed in ring or bus architectures.

topology. The organization of links and nodes to form a data communications network.

Transmission Control Protocol (TCP). A protocol developed by the U.S. Department of Defense for end-to-end communications within heterogeneous networks.

twinaxial. A type of coaxial cable having dual center conductors instead of a single conductor.

twisted pairs. Small, insulated low-grade wires used extensively in electronics and telephone connections.

V

virtual circuit. A service defined within the ISO Open Systems Interconnect (OSI) model that handles end-to-end sequenced guaranteed delivery of packets.

voiceband. A channel used for transmission of speech or music, usually with an audio frequency range of 300 to 3400 hertz (cycles per second). Also used for transmission of analog and digital data with data rates up to 14,400 bits per second.

volatile memory. A type of memory that loses its ability to remember once power is interrupted.

W

wave-division multiplexing (WDM). A technique used with fiber-optic transmission for multiplexing multiple data signals onto fiber cable.

Bibliography

Bridge, R. and Stern, K. "Getting the Most from Existing Twisted Pair Transmission Media." *Telecommunications* (Dec. 1986).

Bridge, S. *Low Cost Local Area Networks*. Sigma Press. London (1986) (Halsted Press).

Gelber, S. "Local Area Network Technology Concepts." *Faulkner Report on Data Communications*. Faulkner Technical Reports. (Dec. 1989).

IEEE Standards for Local Area Networks: Logical Link Control. IEEE. New York (1985).

Joshi, S. and Lyer, V. "New Standards for Local Area Networks Push Upper Limits for Lightwave Data." *Data Communications* (July 1984).

Mills, W. "What is a StarLAN?" *LAN Magazine* (May 1987).

Ross, F. "FDDI - A Tutorial" (Proposed ANSI Standard). *IEEE Communications* (May 1986).

Sherman, K. *Data Communications, A Users Guide (3rd edition)*. Prentice-Hall Inc. (1990).

Stallings, W. "The IEEE 802 Local Area Network Standards." *Telecommunications* (March 1986).

Stallings, W. *ISDN: An Introduction*. Macmillan Publishing Company. New York (1989).

Stallings, W. *Handbook of Computer Communications Standards*. Macmillan Publishing Company. New York (1987).

Stamper, D. *Business Data Communications*. The Benjamin Cummings Publishing Company. Menlo Park, CA (1986).

Strole, N. "The IBM Token Ring Network - A Functional Overview" *IEEE Network* (Jan. 1987).

Voelcker, J. "Helping Computers Communicate" (OSI Protocols). *IEEE Spectrum* (March 1986).

Suggested Reading

Data Communications Magazine. A monthly publication of McGraw-Hill. New York.

LAN Computing. A monthly publication of Professional Press Inc. Horsham, PA.

LAN Magazine. A monthly publication of Telecom Library. New York.

Network World. A weekly publication of CW Publishing Inc. Framingham, MA.

Index

A

ACF. *See* Advanced Communications Facility
Acknowledged information transfer service, 220
Acoustical coupler, 150
Adaptive pulse code modulation, 101-102
ADPCM. *See* adaptive pulse code modulation
Advanced Communications Facility, 39
ALOHANet, 250
American National Standards Institute (ANSI), 147, 176-177
Amplitude modulation, 97
Analog communications, 5
ANSI. *See* American National Standards Institute
Application
   Development, 45, 274
   Layer, 203
   Management, 32
   Portability, 276
Application program interface (API), 32
ARPANET, 198, 230
Artificial traffic generation, 268-269
ASCII, 18, 125, 135, 177, 232
Asynchronous
   Balanced mode, 218
   DLC protocols, 214
   Modems, 147
   Response mode, 218
   Transmission, 65
ATM, 39, 42, 47, 50
AT&T, 18, 63, 70-71, 77, 79, 81, 144, 174, 186, 269
Attenuation distortion, 261
Automatic failure detection, 267

B

Bandwidth concepts
   Baud, 60
   Carrier, 60
   Channel, 60
   Circuit, 59
   Modulation, 60
Baseband transmission, 62
   Local area networks, 242
Basic rate service, 87
Basic Telecommunications Access Method (BTAM), 37, 39
Baud, 60, 97
Baudot code, 16, 17, 65
Baudot, Emil, 16
Bell modem standards, 144
Binary encoding, 174
Binary Synchronous Communications Protocol, 127, 208, 213, 215
Bipolar current loop, 103
Bit-oriented protocols, 210
Bit synchronization, 66
Bits per second, 60
Breakout boxes, 261
Bridges, 138-139, 174, 273
British Telecom, 194
Broadband transmission
   Local area networks, 242
   Overview, 60-62
Broadcast, 38
Broadcast polling, 184
BSC. *See* Binary Synchronous Communications Protocol
BTAM. *See* Basic Telecommunications Access Method

Buffering, 47
Bus topology, 187
Byte-oriented protocols, 210
Byte synchronization, 66

C

C band satellite transmission, 114
C conditioning, 79
Cable access television. *See* CATV
Cable analyzers, 261
Cabling systems, 110-113, 274
Call number identification, 88
Call setup time, 87
Carrier Sense Multiple Access (CSMA)
    Collision avoidance, 251
    Collision detection, 251
    Frame structure, 251
Carrier services, 25, 75-76
Carriers, 60, 96, 192
Carriers, specialized
    McDonnell-Douglas, 71
    Southern Pacific, 70
    Western Union, 70
CATV, 62, 239
CCITT. *See* Consultative Committee for International Telephone and Telegraph
CCN, 200
Central office, 77, 79, 110
Centralized control, 245
Centralized networks, 182
Centralized star networks, 185-186
Centronics Interface, 166
Channel, 60, 64, 124
Channel bandwidth allocation, 243
Channel control program, 52
Channel service units, 153
Channel throughput monitoring, 266
Channel-to-channel interface, 63
CICS. *See* Customer Information and Control System
Circuit, 59
Cladding, 112
Clear-channel transmission, 83
Client-server workstation, 138
Cluster controller. *See* terminal controller
Coaxial cable, 111
COBOL, 50
Codex, 269
Coherent laser communications, 113
Common carriers, 70
Communications links
    Coaxial cable, 111
    Errors and impairments, 116-117
    Fiber-optic cable, 111-113
    Microwave transmission, 114
    Satellite transmission, 114
    Twisted-pair wire, 110
Communications media. *See* communications links
Communications processing
    Session-based communications, 47
    Time-sharing communications, 51
    Transaction-based communications, 47
Communications processor, 9, 23, 123-124, 128, 273
Communications service
    DDS, 81
    Dedicated lines, 78
    Dial-up switched, 76
    High-speed digital, 82
    High-speed wideband, 80
    ISDN, 84
    Providers, 26
    PSTN, 77
    Types, 25, 69
Communications signal compatability, 174
Communications software, 9, 31, 45
Composite data signal, 125
Concentrator. *See* multiplexer
Conditioning
    C-Level, 79
    D-Level, 79-80
Conference multipoint polling, 188
Conformance interfaces, 276
Consultative Committee for International Telephone and Telegraph (CCITT)
    Background, 143
    ISDN, 85
    Modem standards, 144
    PAD standards, 72, 133
    Responsibilities, 71, 93, 175
    V.35 interface, 165
    V series, 87
    X.21 interface, 164
    X.25 standard, 74, 133, 205
    X.400 electronic mail standard, 203
Consultative Committee for International Radio (CCIR), 177
Contention
    Conflicts, 111, 182, 185
    Resolution, 250
    Contention-based access, 250
    CSMA, 250
Conversational communications, 42, 51
Corporation for Open Systems (COS), 177
Cross-channel interference, 239
Crosstalk, 78, 113, 127
CSMA. *See* Carrier Sense Multiple Access
CUCN, 200
Current-loop circuits, 159
Customer Information and Control System, 37-38, 47, 201
Cyclical redundancy check (CRC), 131-132, 213

D

D conditioning, 79
D4 superframe, 82
DARPA, 222
Data communications hardware. *See* Hardware
Data compression, 127
Data format standards, 174
Data link communication codes, 211-212
Data link layer, 204-205
Data Products Interface, 166
Data termination equipment, 144
Data transfer, 198
Datagram packet service
    Reliable datagram, 74
    Unreliable datagram, 74
Dataphone Digital Service, 64, 76, 81-82
DDS. *See* Dataphone Digital Service
Deadlock, 211
Digital Equipment, 38, 51, 136, 139, 233, 240
Decentralized networks, 182
Decentralized star networks, 185
Decibel measured, 60
DECnet, 139
Dedicated line network errors
    Noise, 117
    Nonlinear distortion, 117
    Propagation delay, 117
Dedicated lines, 76, 78-79
De facto standards
    AT&T, 178
    DEC, 178
    IBM, 177
    Xerox, 178
Demand assigned multiple access (DAMA), 114
Department of Defense protocols, 230-231
Deterministic access, 246
Dial-up modem, 149
Dibit, 100
Differential encoding, 103
Digital circuit, 77
Digital service unit, 9, 24, 82, 103, 153, 274
Digital transmission
    Bipolar current loop, 103
    Compatibility, 83
    Digital signaling, 9, 102
    Digital-to-analog sampling, 101
    Non-return to zero, 103
    Repeaters, 77
    Return to zero, 103
    Service classes, 83
Digital video, 271
Direct distance dialing network, 77
Direction control, 211
Display formats, 48
Distortion, 116
Distributed Office Support System (DISOSS), 201
Domain, 201

Downlink, 114
Drop and bypass T1 service, 83
DS frame, 82
DS links, 82-83, 274
DS-1C, DS-2, DS-3, DS-4 service, 83
Dumb terminal, 136
Duplex transmission, 63, 110
Dynamic address routing, 139
Dynamic allocation, 129
Dynamic switching, 111

E

EBCDIC, 18, 125, 135, 211, 232
Echo, 116
Echo suppression, 116-117
ECMA, 176
Effective throughput rate, 252
EIA standards
    EIA-232, 129, 151, 160-161, 250
    EIA RS-422-A, EIA RS-423-A, 163
    EIA RS-449, 162
Electrical interfaces, 174
Electromagnetic interference, 113
Electronics Industries Association (EIA), 176
ENIAC, 4
Error-correcting modem, 154
Error detection
    Cyclical redundancy check, 213-214
    Error handling, 197
    Longitudinal redundancy check, 213
    Vertical redundancy check, 213
Error types
    Analysis, 256
    Hardware errors, 256
    Network link errors, 256
    Software errors, 256
Ethernet, 138, 239, 250
Excess line capacity, 73
Expedited data service, 139
Extended circuit modem, 152
External flow control, 129

F

Facsimile, 5
Fault isolation, 267
FCC. *See* Federal Communications Commission
FDDI. *See* Fiber Distributed Data Interface
FDM. *See* frequency-division multiplexing
Federal Communications Commission, 24, 72, 79, 176
FEP. *See* front-end processor
Fiber Distributed Data Interface, 111, 273-274
Fiber optics
    Fiber Data Distributed Interface, 111, 273-274
    Fiber links, 25

Fiber technology, 112-113
Fiber-optic bus, 274
Fiber-optic cable, 78, 111, 274
Fiber-optic modem, 151
Multimode graded-index fiber, 112
Multimode step-index fiber, 112
File Transfer Protocol, 226, 230
Filtering rate, 252
Flow control, 129, 198, 228
Forward error correction, 100
Fractional T1, 80, 82-83
Frame blocking, 128
Framing, 66
Frequency bandwidth, 64
Frequency-division multiplexing, 127
Frequency modulation, 97
Frequency shift keying, 127
Front-end processor, 9, 23, 123-124, 128, 273.
 See also Communications processor
FTP. *See* File Transfer Protocol
Full-motion video, 275
Fuzzy logic, 275

G

Gateway, 138-139, 174, 273
Geosynchronous satellite communications, 114
Global network, 265, 271
Grades of service
 Subvoice, 64
 Voiceband, 64
 Wideband, 64
Ground station, 114

H

Half-duplex transmission, 62
Hardware
 Bridge, 138
 Communications processor, 123
 DSU/CSU, 153
 Frequency-division multiplexer, 127
 Gateway, 138
 Modem, 143
 Multiplexer, 125
 Multiuser workstation, 138
 Network controller, 133
 Network job entry system, 137
 Packet assembly/disassembly device, 132
 Personal computer, 72, 136-137
 Private branch exchange, 85, 87
 Protocol analyzer, 260
 Remote job entry system, 137
 Repeater, 82, 113
 Statistical time-division multiplexer, 129
 Terminal controller, 134
 Terminal, 136
 Time-division multiplexer, 127-128

Wave-division multiplexer, 130
Hardware error determination, 256
Hardware error diagnostic tools, 259-262
Hardware interfaces
 IEEE-488, 166
 CCITT X.21, 164
 CCITT X.35, 165
 Centronics Interface, 167
 Data Products Interface, 168
 EIA-232 D, 160
 Functions, 160
 RS-449, 162
 Types, 160
HDLC. *See* High-Level Data Link Control
Hertz, 64
Hewlett-Packard, 38
High-level Data Link Control (HDLC)
 Addressing, 219
 Control, 218
 Data transfer modes, 218
 Frame formats, 219
 Information frame, 220
 Supervisory frame, 220
 Types of stations, 218
 Unnumbered frame, 220
High-Performance Parallel Interface (HPPI),
  274-275
High-speed wideband service, 80
Host node, 200
HPPI. *See* High-Performance Parallel Interface
Hub polling, 184
Hybrid coil, 110

I

I/O processor, 272-273
IBM, 4-5, 9, 36-39, 124, 127, 178, 269
IEEE. *See* Institute of Electrical and Electronics
  Engineers
Imaging, 271
Impedance, 116
Impulse noise, 117
In-band transmission, 88
Info Com, 70
Initial program load (IPL), 124
Institute of Electrical and Electronics Engineers
  (IEEE)
 488 interface, 166
 802 standards, 240
Integrated Services Digital Network (ISDN)
 Out of band signaling, 88
 SSN#7 signaling, 88
 Standards, 5, 24
 Control channel, 87
 Interfaces, 87
 Network termination devices, 87
 R interface, 87
 Rate adaptor, 87

S interface, 88
Terminal adaptor, 87
Terminal types, 87
U interface, 88
Intel, 240
Interactive Systems Programming Facility, 52
Interleaving, 125, 128
International Standards Organization (ISO), 72, 173, 177
International Telecommunications Union (ITU), 175, 176
Internet Control Message Protocol (ICMP), 224
Internet Protocol (IP), 204, 222-224
International Frequency Registration Board (IFRB), 175
IP. *See* Internet Protocol
ISDN. *See* Integrated Services Digital Network
ISO. *See* International Standards Organization
ISO X.200, 202
ITT World Communications, 71

K

Kermit, 214
Kevlar, 112
Krum, Howard, 16
Ku band, 114

L

Local area network
    Access methods, 246
    Baseband, 246
    Broadband, 246
    Centralized control, 245
    Channel bandwidth allocation, 243
    Contention-based access, 250
    Cost control, 241
    Decentralized control, 245
    Design, 240-242
    Integration, 242
    Media access control, 246
    Non-contention-based access, 246
    Performance, 252
    Security, 242
    Token-passing bus, 248
    Token-passing fiber, 248
    Token-passing ring, 246
    Wiring, 110
Laser, 130
Layered operations, 198
    Data transfer, 198
    Error detection, 199
    Flow control, 198
    Notification, 199
    Segmentation and reassembly, 199
    Sequencing, 199
Limited-distance modem, 150

Line
    Conditioning, 79
    Contention, 111
    Monitoring, 47
    Noise, 117
    Transients, 117
    Turnaround, 62-63, 211
Line drivers, 151
Line equalizer, 79
Link Access Protocol (LAP), 205
Link Access Protocol, D (LAP-D), 220
Link
    Backup, 194
    Control, 124
    Diagnostics, 126
    Services, 275
Load balancing, 190
Loading coil, 82
Local Access Transport Area (LATA), 82
Local analog loopback test, 153
Local loop, 77-78, 82
Logical byte, 232
Logical connection, 96
Logical link, 124
Logical unit, 200
    Logical Unit Type 6.2, 201
Longitudinal redundancy check, 213
Loopback testing, 259

M

MAC. *See* media access control
Manufacturing Automation Protocol (MAP), 206
Mask, 48
Master clock, 81
Matrix switch, 262
MCI, 63, 70-71, 77, 79
Media access control
    Deterministic access, 246
    Nondeterministic access, 246
Memorex Telex, 135
Mesh of trees topology, 191
Mesh topology, 189
Message delay monitoring, 266
Message switching, 53
Microcom
    MNP error correction, 154
Microsoft Windows, 273
Microwave transmission, 114
Midsplit channel allocation, 243
Modem
    Acoustical coupler, 150
    Asynchronous, 147
    Bell dataset, 5
    Diagnostics and testing, 153, 259
    Eliminator, 151
    Error correction, 154
    Extended circuit, 152

Fiber-optic, 151
Integrated, 150
Interfaces, 155, 156
Internals, 146
Limited-distance, 150
Line driver, 151
Operational modes, 148
Pooling, 152
Sharing, 151
Split-stream, 152
Standalone, 150
Standards, 144, 178
Synchronous, 148
Tail-circuit, 152
Types, 149
Modulation, 60, 93
   Amplitude, 97
   Definition, 60
   Derived techniques, 96, 100
   Frequency, 97
   Frequency shift keying, 127
   Multibit, 99
   Phase, 99-100
   Phase shift keying, 99
   Pulse code, 100-101
   Trellis-coded, 100
Morse code, 15-16, 97
Morse, Samuel, 15
Multichannel communications, 114
Multifrequency laser, 113
Multiplexer
   Concepts, 9, 23, 125, 274
   Error control, 131
   Frequency-division, 127
   Operational characteristics, 126
   Statistical time-division, 129
   Time-division, 127
   Wave-division, 130
Multipoint bus topology, 188
Multithreading, 49

N

National Bureau of Standards, 4
NCR, 124, 232
Network
   Architectures, 197-198
   Backup, 194
   Configuration and maintenance, 32, 182
   Control software, 10
   Design, 182, 191
   Distributed, 182
   Implementation, 9
   Integrity, 193
   Link error identification, 256
   Management and control, 32, 265-266
   Peer configuration, 180
   Planning, 15, 73
   Security, 193

   Self-contained, 76
   Support software, 38
   Synchronization, 81
   Troubleshooting, 255
Network control center, 266, 268
Network control monitor, 9, 133, 261-262
Network Control Program (IBM), 39
Network job entry, 22, 137
Network layer, 204
Noise, 117, 261
Non-return to zero digital transmission, 103
Nonlinear distortion, 117
Nondeterministic access, 244
Nyquist theory, 94

O

Ones density, 82
Open Systems Interconnect (OSI)
   Application control, 203
   Data link control, 204
   Network layer, 204
   Physical control, 205
   Presentation control, 203
   Session control, 204
   Transport control, 204
Operating systems
   MVS, 52, 55
   OS/2, 273
   PC-DOS, 138
   VM, 51
   VMS, 51
OSI. *See* Open Systems Interconnect

P

Packet assembly/disassembly, 72, 132
Packet layer, 203
Packet switching
   Datagram service, 74
   Packet collision, 250
   Packets, 73, 128
   Segmentation and reassembly, 139, 199, 226
   Service, 72
PAD. *See* packet assembly/disassembly
Parallel processors, 272
PBX. *See* Private branch exchange
PC-oriented protocols, 214
PC-to-host connectivity, 137
PCM. *See* pulse code modulation
PDN. *See* Public data network
Peer network, 180
Performance monitoring, 266
Permissive connection, 155
Phase jitter, 117
Phase modulation, 99-100
Phase shift keying, 99

Physical layer, 205-206
Physical unit, 200
Polling
    Concepts, 38, 47, 124, 183, 246
    Hub polling, 184
    List polling, 184
Presentation layer, 203
Private line interface, 156
Problem
    Analysis, 257
    Determination, 258
    Identification, 255
    Resolution, 258
Programmed Airline Reservation System (PARS), 47
Propagation delay, 116, 117
Protocol data unit, 223, 230
Protocols
    Binary Synchronous Communications Protocol, 215
    File Transfer Protocol, 231
    High-Level Data Link Control, 217
    Internet Control Message Protocol, 225
    Internet Protocol, 222
    Kermit, 214
    Link Access Protocol, 220
    Simple Network Management Protocol, 233
    Synchronous Data Link Control, 216
    Telnet, 230
    Transmission Control Protocol, 227
    Transport Protocol, 229
    XMODEM, 214
PSTN. *See* Public switched telephone network
Public carrier, 69
Public data network, 72, 132, 191
Public switched telephone network, 5, 24, 76-78, 110, 194
Pulse code modulation, 100-101

Q

Quadbit, 100

R

Radio frequency spectrum, 93
RBOC. *See* Regional Bell Operating Company
RCA Global Communications, 71
Read-only memory, 31, 39, 275
Regional Bell Operating Company, 64, 70, 79
Reliable datagram, 74
Remington Rand, 4
Remote analog loopback test, 154
Remote communications, 7, 123
Remote digital loopback test, 155
Remote job entry, 22, 137
Resequencing service, 139
Return-to-zero digital transmission, 103

Ring topology, 186
RJE. *See* Remote job entry
Router. *See* Gateway
RSCS, 53

S

Satellite communications
    Demand assigned multiple access, 114
    Transmission, 70
    Transponder, 114
SDLC. *See* Synchronous Data Link Control
Security, 194, 267
Self-clocking, 103
Semiconductors, 272, 275
Session layer, 201
Session-based communications, 47
Shannon theory, 94
Signal
    Attenuation, 116
    Loss, 259
    Repeaters, 111
Signal-to-noise ratio, 117
Signaling System Number Seven (SSN#7)
Simple Network Management Protocol (SNMP), 231
Simplex transmission, 62
Sine wave, 60
Single-mode fiber, 112
Slave clocking, 81
SNA. *See* Systems Network Architecture
SNA Distribution Services (SNADS), 201
SNMP. *See* Simple Network Management Protocol
Software
    Application control software, 24
    Application development software, 274
    Application software, 10, 39
    Communications control software, 10, 275
    Communications management software, 38
    Communication systems software, 36
    Error determination, 256
    Diagnostic tools, 259
    Handshaking, 209
    Memory management, 49
    Network and performance monitoring software, 25
    Network control software, 10
    System software, 33
SONET. *See* Synchronous Optical Network
Southern Pacific Communications, 70
Speedfax, 70
Sprint, 70
SSCP. *See* System Services Control Point
SSN#7. *See* Signaling System Number Seven
Standards organizations
    ANSI, 176
    CCITT, 175
    COS, 177

ECMA, 176
EIA, 176
FCC, 176
IEEE, 176
ISO, 174, 175
NBS, 176
Star topology, 185
StarLAN, 184
Start/stop communications, 65, 209
Statistical time-division multiplexer, 129
Status activity monitor, 261
STDM. *See* statistical time-division multiplexer
Store-and-forward messaging, 70, 72
Subchannel, 64
Subsplit channel allocation, 243
Subvoice service, 64
Steady-state noise, 117
STS-1, 131
Sun Microsystems, 38
Superconducting, 271
Switched-circuit service, 76
Switched-network errors, 116
Synchronization, 103
Synchronous Data Link Control (SDLC), 126, 202, 210
Synchronous Optical Network (SONET), 131, 271, 274-275
Synchronous transmission, 66
Systems Network Architecture (SNA)
    Cluster controller node, 200
    Control unit communications node, 200
    Document Content Architecture, 201
    Domain, 201
    Gateway, 201
    Host node, 200
    Layers, 201
    Logical unit, 199, 200-201
    Physical unit, 200
    System Services Control Point, 200
    Terminal node, 200

T

TCP. *See* Transmission Control Protocol
TDM. *See* time-division multiplexer
Telegraph, 64-65
Telex, 64, 70
Telnet protocol, 226, 230
Terminal
    Controller, 63, 134
    Dumb, 136
    Emulation, 137
    Mapping, 48
    Network software, 25
    Node, 200
    Page-mode, 136
    Scroll-mode, 136
    Smart, 136

T1
    Drop and bypass T1 service, 83
    Fractional T1, 80, 82-83
    Links, 80
    Service, 80
Time-out control, 211
Time-division multiplexer, 82, 127, 129
Time-sharing communications, 51, 72
Time-Sharing Option (TSO), 52
Token-passing fiber, 248
Token-passing ring, 247, 273
Topology
    Bus, 187
    Mesh, 190
    Mesh of trees, 191
    Multipoint bus, 188
    Ring, 186
    Star, 185
    Tree, 189
TP. *See* Transport Protocol
TPF. *See* Transaction Processing Facility
Transaction Processing Facility, 47
Transaction-based communications, 42, 47
Transmission
    Digital, 102
    Encoding schemes, 96
    Errors and impairments, 114-116
    Links, 24
    Overhead, 65
    Services, 73
Transmission Control Protocol (TCP)
    Connection establishment, 227
    Error control, 228
    Flow control, 228
    Segmentation and reassembly, 228
Transmission media
    Coaxial cable, 111
    Fiber-optic cable, 111
    Microwave, 114
    Satellite, 114
    Twisted-pair wire, 110
    Type 3002 line, 79
Transmission methods
    Asynchronous, 65
    Synchronous, 65-66
Transmission modes
    Duplex, 63
    Half duplex, 62
    Simplex, 62
Transparency, 211
Transponder, 114
Transport layer, 204, 226
Transport Protocol (TP)
    Classes, 229
    Formats, 230
Transport protocol data unit, 227-228
Tree topology, 189
Tribit, 100
Trellis-coded modulation, 100

Twisted-pair wiring, 78, 110
TWX service, 70
Tymnet, 71, 194

U

Unbalanced circuit, 110
UNIX, 138, 174, 178
Unreliable datagram, 74
Unshielded twisted-pair wire, 110, 272
Uplink, 114

V

V series, 87, 144-145
Value-added carrier, 71
Value-added terminal controller, 135
Video bandwidth, 62
Video frame, 271
Videotext, 74
Vertical redundancy check, 213
Virtual circuit service, 74
Virtual circuit, 227
Virtual Telecommunications Access Method (VTAM), 37, 39
Virtual terminal, 37, 230
VM
    CMS, 51
    RSCS, 53
    XEDIT, 53
VMS, 51
Voiceband service, 64
VTAM. *See* Virtual Telecommunications Access Method

W

Wave-division multiplexer, 130
WDM. *See* wave-division multiplexer
Western Union, 70
Wideband communications, 64, 94

X

X-on/x-off, 129-130
X.25
    Data link control, 204
    Network, 132, 220
    Packet layer, 205
    Physical control, 205
    Xerox, 222, 240
XMODEM, 214

Z

Zero-bit stuffing, 217